PORTABLE MODERNISMS

Edinburgh Critical Studies in Modernist Culture
Series Editors: Tim Armstrong and Rebecca Beasley

Available

Modernism and Magic: Experiments with Spiritualism, Theosophy and the Occult
Leigh Wilson

Sonic Modernity: Representing Sound in Literature, Culture and the Arts
Sam Halliday

Modernism and the Frankfurt School
Tyrus Miller

Lesbian Modernism: Censorship, Sexuality and Genre Fiction
Elizabeth English

Modern Print Artefacts: Textual Materiality and Literary Value in British Print Culture, 1890–1930s
Patrick Collier

Cheap Modernism: Expanding Markets, Publishers' Series and the Avant-Garde
Lise Jaillant

Portable Modernisms: The Art of Travelling Light
Emily Ridge

Forthcoming

Modernism, Space and the City
Andrew Thacker

Slow Modernism
Laura Salisbury

Primordial Modernism: Animals, Ideas, Transition (1927–1938)
Cathryn Setz

Modernism and the Idea of Everyday Life
Leena Kore-Schröder

Modernism Edited: Marianne Moore and The Dial *Magazine*
Victoria Bazin

Modernism and Mathematics: Modernist Interrelations in Fiction
Nina Engelhardt

Hieroglyphic Modernisms: Writing and New Media in the Twentieth Century
Jesse Schotter

Visit our website at: edinburghuniversitypress.com/series-edinburgh-critical-studies-in-modernist-culture.html

PORTABLE MODERNISMS

The Art of Travelling Light

Emily Ridge

EDINBURGH
University Press

Edinburgh University Press is one of the leading university presses in the UK. We publish academic books and journals in our selected subject areas across the humanities and social sciences, combining cutting-edge scholarship with high editorial and production values to produce academic works of lasting importance. For more information visit our website: edinburghuniversitypress.com

Edinburgh University Press Ltd
The Tun – Holyrood Road
12(2f) Jackson's Entry
Edinburgh EH8 8PJ

Typeset in 10/12.5 Sabon by
Servis Filmsetting Ltd, Stockport, Cheshire,
and printed and bound in Great Britain by
CPI Group (UK) Ltd, Croydon CR0 4YY

A CIP record for this book is available from the British Library

ISBN 978 1 4744 1959 8 (hardback)
ISBN 978 1 4744 1960 4 (webready PDF)
ISBN 978 1 4744 1961 1 (epub)

CONTENTS

ILLUSTRATIONS

ACKNOWLEDGEMENTS

An earlier version of Chapter 2 was first published as 'The Problem of the Woman's Bag from the New Woman to Modernism' in *Modernism/Modernity* 21.3, September 2014, pp. 757–80. This has been reprinted in a revised form with the permission of Johns Hopkins University Press. Copyright © 2014 Johns Hopkins University Press. A section of Chapter 3 was first published in an earlier form, as 'Elizabeth Bowen, *Howards End* and the Luggage of Modernity', in *Textual Practice*, 27.1, 2013, pp. 109–26. Thanks to Taylor & Francis (www.tandfonline.com) for allowing me to revisit that work here. I would like to express my gratitude to the Provost and Scholars of King's College, Cambridge and The Society of Authors as the E. M. Forster Estate for allowing me to use a quotation from E. M. Forster's work as an epigraph.

My further thanks go to the Hope Mirrlees Estate for allowing me to cite from 'Paris: A Poem' and to the Master and Fellows of Trinity College Cambridge for permission to use material from the Rose Macaulay archive. I would equally like to extend my appreciation to Random House and Curtis Brown for permission to quote from the following W. H. Auden poems: 'The Composer' from *W. H. Auden Collected Poems* by W. H. Auden, copyright © 1976 by Edward Mendelson, William Meredith and Monroe K. Spears, Executors of the Estate of W. H. Auden; 'Gare du Midi', copyright © 1940 and renewed 1968 by W. H. Auden, from *W. H. Auden Collected Poems* by W. H. Auden; 'Sonnets from China', copyright © 1945 by W. H. Auden, renewed 1973 by The Estate of W. H. Auden, from *W. H. Auden Collected*

Poems by W. H. Auden. All three poems are used by permission of Random House, an imprint and division of Penguin Random House LLC. They are also reprinted by permission of Curtis Brown, Ltd. All rights reserved.

I am indebted to the Arts and Humanities Research Council and the Department of English Studies at Durham University for the generous scholarships that allowed me to initiate the doctoral research out of which this book has developed, as well as for granting several travel awards to fund archival visits. The Department of Literature and Cultural Studies at the Education University of Hong Kong has provided a warm and stimulating environment in which to undertake the transition from thesis to book. I would particularly like to thank my departmental colleagues in the area of English literature: Bidisha Banerjee, Hawk Chang, Jeff Clapp, Matthew DeCoursey, Nicholas Wong and Eric Yu.

John Nash, at Durham University, has followed this project from its earliest inception over a decade ago as a scribbled word – 'suitcase' – on a list of possible modernist objects for study. This book would not exist today without his longstanding guidance and unstinting encouragement, for which I will always be grateful. I would like to take this opportunity to convey my heartfelt gratitude to series editors, Rebecca Beasley and Tim Armstrong, for their enthusiastic engagement with and astute commentary on the manuscript as it evolved. The reports of the two anonymous external readers were also enormously helpful. The manuscript has been in excellent hands at Edinburgh University Press and my sincere thanks go to Jackie Jones, Adela Rauchova, Rebecca Mackenzie, James Dale and Sarah M. Hall, whose attentiveness has been exemplary at every stage. I would further like to thank Rachel Bowlby, Evelyn Chan, Jeff Clapp, Simon J. James, Kendall Johnson, Douglas Kerr, Pamela Knights and Patricia Waugh for their thoughtful feedback on my work at various junctures in the project process. Countless others have alerted me to pertinent texts and examples, many of which came to feature in the study, and I gratefully acknowledge their collective contribution to this project.

Without the foundational support and amusing interventions of friends and family, I would have faltered long ago. Special thanks are due to Roberta Bassi, Clara Dawson, Ann-Marie Einhaus, Maebh Long, Jahnavi Misra, Debbie Tang and Jessica Valdez, as well as members of my extended family on the Ridge and Ryan sides. My parents Deirdre and Martin Ridge, my brother Barry and my sister Sarah have been my biggest and most steadfast cheerleaders. This book is dedicated to them *le grá agus le meas mór*. Finally, in the spirit of a study of portable objects, it would be remiss of me not to pay tribute to my Penguin coffee mug, which I have retained throughout the project. It has given me something to hold on to in moments of anxiety as much as reflection, and I certainly would not have made it through without the coffee it routinely delivered.

SERIES EDITORS' PREFACE

This series of monographs on selected topics in modernism is designed to reflect and extend the range of new work in modernist studies. The studies in the series aim for a breadth of scope and for an expanded sense of the canon of modernism, rather than focusing on individual authors. Literary texts will be considered in terms of contexts, including recent cultural histories (modernism and magic; sonic modernity; media studies) and topics of theoretical interest (the everyday; postmodernism; the Frankfurt School); but the series will also re-consider more familiar routes into modernism (modernism and gender; sexuality; politics). The works published will be attentive to the various cultural, intellectual and historical contexts of British, American and European modernisms, and to inter-disciplinary possibilities within modernism, including performance and the visual and plastic arts.

Tim Armstrong and Rebecca Beasley

But literature is the most exceptional and untidy affair that it has ever entered the heart of man to create. You have never done with it. It is always popping out when you think you have boxed it, and the more confident your generalities, the more certain you may be that the exceptions are dancing in beauty upon a thousand hills.

E. M. Forster, *The Feminine Note in Literature*

INTRODUCTION

In some of the outlying boulevards recently we have seen trunks piled up in grim heaps like the walls of a fortress (which they were intended to imitate) with here and there an opera-glass case projecting or a tightly-rolled hold-all, to resemble a cannon. The idea is ingenious and martial – but not successful. The window is too much transformed. You forget what you are looking at. You only see the backs of the trunks. And as a witty German said the other day, 'Trunks and portmanteaus ought not to be piled up in the shape of a fortress of defence. For they are the very things we use when we run away'.[1]

The above passage, describing a display of luggage in a German shop window, comes from a 1909 edition of the rather cumbersomely titled *The Bag, Portmanteau and Umbrella Trader and Fancy Leather Goods and Athletic Trades Review*, a trade journal targeted at businesses affiliated to the leather and travelling goods industries, with a focus, as the title acknowledges, on the luggage trade. Trade journals exist to provide specialised information and news for the benefit of specific industries in a very practical vein, but they also aim to keep abreast of any current social or cultural trends which might well impact on consumer habits. The particular article from which the passage is drawn was written by a continental correspondent, tasked with surveying the luggage scene in other parts of Europe – Germany, in this case – in order to feed back to interested parties in Britain. According to the same journal,

Germany was the innovative centre of the leather goods industry during this period, so this was a scene to be scouted with some attention. The correspondent is directly concerned here with the solutions devised by trunk-makers for the problem of how to reduce the monotony of the usual and obvious trunk-pile window display. The shop window was becoming a vital aspect of a 'new commercial aesthetic', which foregrounded the persuasive power of the visual.[2] We can see the formation of such an aesthetic in this passage in the question of how best to use a window, but we can also see the formation of a new portable aesthetic in the question of how best to present travelling goods to the public.

The writer astutely picks up on the distinctive appeal of luggage, its suggestion of an alternative ontological experience beyond the secure parameters of a built structure. To promote luggage along defensive lines is to miss the point of the experience associated with and made available by trunks and portmanteaux. They are offensive in initiative rather than defensive in stance, as Max Beerbohm discerned in his 1900 essay, 'Ichabod', which celebrates luggage and the nomadic mode: 'I have never crossed a frontier without feeling some of the pride of conquest.'[3] But conquest and all the negative connotations that go with it aside, luggage most notably promises escape: 'For they are the very things we use when we run away.' And what do we run away from but the constraints of the fortress or, more mundanely, the home. The special correspondent intuits here the devaluation of security as a selling point in line with a new drive towards facility of motion in all aspects of modern life. This is a shift that Zygmunt Bauman has famously characterised in terms of the progress from 'solid' through 'fluid' to 'liquid' phases of modernity.[4] For Bauman, the new emphasis on mobility is intimately linked to a fast-altering economic landscape – liquid modernity represents the apotheosis of a capitalist system in line with what he saw as a progressive 'disembodiment of labour' – and he spotlights 'portable or disposable belongings' as the 'prime cultural tokens of an era of instantaneity'.[5]

In the early twentieth century, during what might be characterised as the 'fluid' phase of modernity in Bauman's scheme, luggage advertisers were beginning to learn to engage with a growing desire for ease of movement, for 'travelling light'. The year after the above article from 'Our Special Correspondent', we come across the following cautionary note in *The Bag, Portmanteau and Umbrella Trader* from the pen of a columnist, known rather fittingly as 'Peripatetus':

> Reference to the travelling goods trade recalls a somewhat unorthodox and undesirable method of advertising the various lines which are so much in demand just now. We refer especially to the phrase 'Latest Impedimenta', which is employed by some tradesmen, in advertising their travelling goods. Although literally correct, the word has a double

meaning, which is likely to attract the attention of buyers of a hyper-critical turn of mind, as the term may be construed into a sense which is scarcely complimentary to the goods exhibited. The trade vocabulary is extensive, and tradesmen would do well to avoid the use of phrases which suggest that the goods offered are a hindrance and obstruction to the traveller.[6]

Clearly, this 'double meaning' has only recently come to assume an importance for advertisers. The impediments inherent in the act of travel, taken for granted of old, have no place in the commercially constructed fantasy of modern escape. In this dawning era of fluidity, mobility cannot now seem to be obstructed. Fixed property was, of course, seen to be the biggest impediment of all and a stationary construct could certainly have no place in the promotion of travelling goods except in the form of a suggestion of what has been left behind.

MODERNISM AND PORTABILITY

Such trade articles delineate an evolving culture of portability in the early twentieth century that, as this book documents, also came to inform English literary developments. The book gives a comprehensive account of the fears and fantasies surrounding this portable turn, examining conflicting tendencies towards mobility and ownership in modernist writing as reflected in ambivalent representations of portable property. It goes on to interpret the emergence of a portable outlook more pointedly in relation to the struggle for the extension of female spheres of activity and interest beyond the restrictive boundaries of the home from the late nineteenth century. It then reassesses the phenomenon in the light of the widespread dislocations arising from wartime conflict and escalating interwar tensions from the First to the Second World War, during which period portability frequently becomes associated with precarity rather than with escapism. Finally, it investigates the extent to which this move towards portability influences character conception from modernism to late modernism.

We generally ascribe the term 'portable' to objects that can be mobilised or detached from a state of fixity, objects with the capacity to move between contexts. But portability is more than simple mobilisation; the word 'portable' itself, of Anglo-Norman and French origin, suggests the act of carriage, thus conjoining subject with object. A portable object is, at root, one that can be carried by a subject. Most commonly, then, portable forms serve to destabilise the necessities associated with a domestic environment, offering the opportunity for a subject to move while retaining a functional and/or sentimental hold on a familiar material world. Portable objects thus enable portable subjects. On the basis that concrete attachments cumulatively inhibit movement, to be portable, as a subject, is to aspire to an immateriality that allows complete freedom of movement while continuing a partial embrace of material forms. Portability, in other words, gives the illusion of detachment by mobilising, in effect, a subject's attachments. It is this approximate nature of the portable state that is so fascinating; in carrying things on the move, one approximates the contrasting experiences of absolute freedom and a more rooted form of material stability at one and the same time. As such, the phrase 'travelling light' is used in the book's subtitle not just because it captures a developing aspiration towards portability during this era but because it is a phrase which aptly integrates these ideas of mobility and materiality.[7] While the phrase as a whole articulates a restless impulse to move unencumbered, the word 'light' brings the very idea of encumbrance to the fore in the process of dismissing it. Crucially, to be light is to be of little weight, rather than to be completely weightless. The phrase acknowledges that one must carry something, however small. Without any other attached paraphernalia, the body might even be viewed as a freighted vessel and thus as a burden in and of itself, so that a truly weightless freedom becomes a virtual impossibility. What 'travelling light' promises, rather, is greater leverage in negotiating between material/physical need and freedom of movement. It becomes something of a maxim for the increasingly footloose subjects of modernity, while offering a fresh and engaging ethos for writers and artists to creatively explore.

As a device for the carriage of objects and thus *the* signifier of portability and portable culture *par excellence,* luggage offers an important focal point around which the discussion to follow turns. The book identifies an increased visibility of luggage in literature from the late nineteenth century – whether as a signifying detail in descriptive terms, as a material object with an implied symbolic function, as an abstract metaphor without a direct material referent or as an analogic model for literary form – registering a new engagement with the practice and implications of carriage. Luggage is further posited as an overlooked element in the stock sketch of the itinerant modernist artist or writer from the valise-fashioned desks of both James Joyce and Vladimir Nabokov to the art/manuscript-laden cases of Ernest Hemingway, Jean Rhys, Walter Benjamin and Marcel Duchamp, among many others. Indeed, while the trope of modernist exile has long been spotlighted, little attention has been given to the material meaning of this condition to date. What things and objects do modernism's nomadic subjects carry with them? How far do representations of the material dimensions of mobility illuminate a modernist preoccupation with legacy and continuity as much as with iconoclastic forms of innovation? How does the act of carriage enter into the modernist picture more broadly?

Modernism, in fact, coincides with one of the more interesting periods in luggage design, a period marking a radical shift from the production of heavy travelling goods to an assortment of lightweight models. This shift can be interpreted as a response to technological innovations leading to new modes of transportation, from the motorcar to the airplane, and necessitating sleeker modes of carriage. Both suitcase and cabin trunk, for example, were designed with flat lids to be easily and quickly stacked or to slide under a railway seat or onto a luggage rack. Helenka Gulshan notes:

> As early as the Edwardian age, cumbersome trunks and portmanteaux, which were designed primarily for strength and durability and would literally be 'lugged' to the hold of a ship by minions employed for the purpose, were beginning to evolve towards a more portable alternative.[8]

Changing modes of transportation also opened up travelling possibilities to larger segments of the population, allowing the 'minions' themselves to lead more portable lives, rather than simply enabling the portability of others. It is a shift which can equally be interpreted as a response to what Paul Fussell calls the 'revolution in dress' that took place in the early part of the twentieth century, reducing the need for an extensive collection of appropriate attire on the move and contributing to the standardisation of travelling goods later in the century.[9] In his words, '[i]f the emblem of the traveler used to be the trunk, or at least the valise, the Gladstone, the tin box, and the hat box, it is now the backpack'.[10] But this line is telling in more ways than one. At this moment of transition towards a 'more portable alternative' in the early twentieth century, luggage had reached a high point of nuanced and multifaceted signification, only to be reduced very quickly to the utterly homogenous forms of backpack or suitcase. In other words, at this developmental stage, it was at its most tantalisingly legible and, given that more people were moving than ever before, at its most variable in terms of product type.[11] This was also the era of luggage labels, produced by hotels, ships and railway lines so that an itinerary, narrative or trumped-up personal statement might be recorded or even fabricated on a bag's surface, as a 1926 *Punch* cartoon entitled 'The Vanity Bag' (Figure 1) aptly illustrates. If, in earlier periods, portability signalled either vagrancy or affluence (in that you either carried very little of any worth at all or you had servants to carry your valuables for you), it was becoming increasingly difficult to exactly place the modern man or woman on the move through their paraphernalia, yet the material for interpretation was at its most richly detailed and diverse. From a single item of luggage, a person's class, gender, wealth, past and future trajectories, temporary or permanent lodgings, mode of transportation, age, profession, even personality might be reasonably estimated.[12] It is perhaps for these reasons that vintage luggage from this period has proven so popular in recent years, demonstrable in the widespread employment of such pieces as objects of display in shops or as decorative items in the home. The appeal of such objects has everything to do with their connection to the dawn of a new era of travel, the expanding possibilities of which stimulated

THE VANITY BAG.

Figure 1 Bert Thomas, 'The Vanity Bag', cartoon, *Punch*, 171, 18 August 1926, p. 179. Reproduced with permission of Punch Ltd, www.punch.co.uk.

increasingly sophisticated and creative approaches to luggage design.[13] But the allure of a vintage case also has much to do with its suggestion of an embedded narrative, its embodiment of the ghostly outline of a past life, thus harking back to a historical moment when the incentive to mobilise the material accoutrements of a life story was beginning to detract from the more commonplace expression of selfhood within stable domestic parameters.

Luggage was serviceable indeed to the modernist writer because it was akin to a complexly encoded material and visual language just on the verge of being scaled down (as, paradoxically, possibilities for travel were beginning to be more roundly embraced), but this accounts for only a small part of its pertinence. Above all, it could be seen to represent a break from the structural forms of nineteenth-century realism, frequently emblematised in the idea of the house. In the words of Jeremy Tambling, '[t]he house, the city and the nation in the realist novel are architectural visions, and important for the stabilising of nineteenth-century English ideology'.[14] The symbolic value of the house – that abiding structural model throughout the nineteenth century – was put to the test by modernism's 'exiles and émigrés', to apply Terry Eagleton's well-known designation, those mythologised figures of alienation and denationalisation who had rejected more rooted places in their 'domestic' societies.[15] Eagleton's account can be expanded upon, or rather sharpened, to emphasise accounts of women exiles from the home sphere, and this book works from the assumption that this form of exile has as significant a role to play in the shaping of modernism.[16] Whether invoked in relation to the figure of the denationalised artist or emancipated woman, modernist luggage, with its outward prerogative of mobility and adventurousness, as well as its implied detachment from a single stable landmark, can often be found to stand for exploratory and independent initiative, as well as the quest for a new paradigm. In this guise, it can be viewed as a peculiarly fitting symbolic form for modernism, which can be characterised as 'less a style than a search for a style in a highly individualistic sense'.[17]

Yet the critical focus on cultural and aesthetic alienation and exile as a keystone of modernist writing is, by now, both a truism *and* a point of contention. Modernist criticism has traditionally paid homage to the figure of the disconnected artist or subject. Malcolm Bradbury writes:

> Much Modernist art has taken its stance from, gained its perspectives out of, a certain kind of distance, an exiled posture – a distance from local origins, class allegiances, the specific obligations and duties of those with an assigned role in a cohesive culture.[18]

Similarly, Fussell upholds a diasporic impulse as 'one of the signals of literary modernism, as we can infer from virtually no modern writer's remaining where he's "supposed" to be except perhaps Proust'.[19] In these quintessential descriptions of modernism in terms of the formation of an 'exiled posture' or diasporic perspective, we find a vindication of a nomadic/detached over and above a static/rooted outlook as conducive to artistry. Since the 1990s, certain critics have disputed these claims of nomadic precedence and aesthetic detachment. Caren Kaplan, for example, offers a critique of the mythology which has developed around the figure of the exiled modernist writer and argues that the 'modernist trope of exile works to remove itself from any political or historically specific instances in order to generate aesthetic categories and ahistorical values'.[20] In an analogous vein, a number of studies have emerged in recent years in the 'conservative modernity' line, espoused by critics such as Alison Light, to reappraise the domestic sphere as an equally experimental locus for modernist writing, as well as to assert that the struggle to move away from traditional narrative form was 'as much characterised by continuities as by dislocation'.[21]

This book moves between these divergent interpretations of modernism and the modernist trope of exile in two ways. In the first place, it argues that modernist writers themselves became increasingly attuned to the mythologisation of exile, and this awareness is frequently manifested through more consciously fraught portrayals of portable subjects and objects; the second half of this book, for example, deals with the collision of an aesthetics and politics of portability in the context of mass displacements across Europe, instigated by the First World War and aggravated in the years to follow. Such a collision is exemplified in one promotional feature on Selfridges' stock of travelling goods in *The Times* in 1923, where we come across the following rather odd claim:

> The ladies' big Black trunk, the Saratoga, the Wardrobe, the Cabin trunk, the Kit-bag, the Gladstone bag, the Hold-all, the Hat-box, all of them have a graceful line and all of them tell their tale of holiday-making and of new lands to be seen . . . And curiously their faces never have anything of the unhappy in them, they never suggest a journey of flight from trouble or to a death-bed.[22]

The effort to sever negative associations here only serves to draw attention to them. The 'very things we use when we run away', as spotlighted in those earlier trade articles, are suddenly marked, in this postwar era, by a visceral sense of the alternative conditions that compel escape beyond the parameters of 'holiday-making' and the creative exploration of 'new lands'. A similar effect is produced in a number of interwar texts, where the 'faces' of portable forms are rendered increasingly ill-at-ease, registering a modernist mythology of exile in the process of coming undone. Additionally, where the conservative strain in modernist writing is concerned, the book shows that, alongside an exploratory initiative, modernist luggage can just as often be found to paradoxically express a continuing connection to a kind of material rootedness or homeliness which can be mobilised, at best, but never entirely eliminated. In other words, luggage effectively conveyed the contradictory imperatives expressed in many classic accounts of modernism, what Marshall Berman describes as the 'desire to be rooted in a stable and coherent personal and social past', on the one hand and, on the other, the 'insatiable desire for growth . . . that destroys both the physical and social landscapes of our past, and our emotional links with those lost worlds'.[23] As such, luggage became significant for a wide range of modernist writers precisely because it captured the complex process of negotiating the continuities *and* dislocations of modernity at one and the same time, while also enacting a clash between a portable aesthetics and politics.

The book thus extends enquiry into modernist exile beyond the usual critical parameters. In this endeavour, it also seeks to expand upon and complicate recent discussions of modernist mobility, principally by suggesting that where modernist subjects moved, they usually also carried. The concept of mobility has received considerable attention in modernist studies in recent years, building on work in the social sciences on the 'new mobilities paradigm', a concept which foregrounds a neglected mobile dimension in discussions of what constitutes modernity.[24] Giving an instructive historical overview of mobility, as well as conflicting perceptions of mobile subjects, from feudal and early modern periods to contemporary culture, Tim Cresswell demonstrates the prevalence of the 'sedentarist' point of view through history.[25] But he also charts the emergence, in relation to the evolution of western modernity, of 'nomadic' ways of thinking, ways of thinking associated with subaltern forms of power and with the process of 'becoming' as opposed to a fully consummated form of 'being'.[26] This is a shift in balance corroborated by Bauman: 'the era of unconditional superiority of sedentarism over nomadism and the domination of the settled over the mobile is on the whole grinding fast to a halt'.[27] On a corresponding literary critical level, Andrew Thacker's *Moving Through Modernity* is representative of recent modernist criticism on this subject in arguing that '[i]n the new *topoi* of the early twentieth century, transportation emphasised a sense of movement that came to be a crucial figure for the experience of modernity itself'.[28] This book substantiates the assertion that mobility assumed an unprecedented importance in terms of characterising the modern experience. However, too often, the emphasis on a pervasive sense of modern/modernist instability and dislocation tends to blot out the more tangible actualities and practicalities of movement, not least the carriage of objects in transit.[29] Portability overtakes mobility in my account because it is a concept that acknowledges a material aspect of mobile experience, what we might call the *solid* within the fluid, conceived in terms of objects moving with subjects and rendered through the iconography and imagery of luggage.

Recent modernist scholarship in the area of material culture has already done much to recuperate a fascination with the solid in works by modernist writers. Indeed, one key strand of material culture studies, as it has been invoked in the service of modernist criticism, has involved considering objects on their own terms, apart from subjects. Taking up Arjun Appadurai's call to 'follow the things themselves' as a 'corrective to the tendency to excessively sociologize transactions in things', Bill Brown, in formulating what he calls 'thing theory', has paved the way for a new 'discursive visibility' of 'things' in textual forms beyond the more usual subject–object focus.[30] Similarly, Douglas

Mao has elevated the concrete object for discussion in modernist writing, demonstrating a preoccupation with the materiality of the object – a sense of its 'impermeability to mind' or subjectivity – over and above its potential symbolic function or marketable value.[31] While my work owes an enormous debt to Brown and Mao, not least in their establishment of this discursive visibility, I depart from them in certain ways. First, I share Deborah Wynne's observation of a critical tendency to 'overlook or elide the issue of ownership in relation to objects' in material culture studies in recent years.[32] Wynne's own emphasis is on figurations of women's personal property during the Victorian period. But her observation is perhaps even more applicable to modernist literature, which, on the surface, pays less attention to themes and ideas of inheritance and possession than the Victorian novel. In general, the much-reduced (or, at least, less obvious) presence of such themes in modernist writing, in comparison to Victorian writing, has allowed more scope for the kinds of singularly thing-focused readings of Mao and Brown.[33] Yet portability brings the subject–object relationship to centre stage. Close attention, moreover, to modernist representations of the act of carriage shows that questions of inheritance, legacy and possession, so prominent in the nineteenth century, linger into the twentieth, if less obtrusively. In short, rather than following 'the things themselves' in this book, I seek to explore the phenomenon of things following subjects, whether as valued possessions or as accessories selected to achieve a certain effect.

Further, though I agree with Mao that a fixation on the impermeable solidity of the object is a 'peculiarly twentieth-century malady', questions of marketable and symbolic value cannot so easily be dismissed in discussing the more particular phenomenon of modernist portability.[34] John Plotz, in his recent study of portable property as represented in Victorian literature, argues that such property is shown to be caught between fetishism and fungibilty, much like the physical object of the novel itself.[35] Portable objects flaunt a 'commodity potential', to borrow Appadurai's phrase, over and above objects *in situ*, and a number of critical thinkers and theorists have, indeed, aligned a 'travel light' compulsion directly with the rise of capitalism.[36] It has also been argued that the innovatory and tradition-eschewing imperative of modernism arises directly from a capitalist ideology.[37] Inharmonious as this coupling of avant-garde and capitalist concerns might appear here, the disjunctive associations of portability in modernist writing will form an important part of the discussion to follow, just as modernism itself is routinely defined by its internal contradictions. The iconographic incorporation of luggage as part of a posture of aesthetic and political detachment for the early modernist escapee or exile (however ambiguous that posture might be) must thus be coupled, in these opening statements, with a parallel projection of the portable case as a circulating product within a rising modern consumer culture in the early twentieth century. The rise of a portable culture in line with more formal endeavours to 'make it new', as well as a modern impulse towards restlessness, can be seen to owe just as much to a changing marketplace as to the modernist exilic compulsion. To begin with, modern portability goes hand in hand with the progressive shortening of the projected lifespan and planned obsolescence of given commodities; to move unencumbered was to use disposable products. Moreover, it can be affiliated with the fervour generated by a newly vitalised 'packaging' industry. Rachel Bowlby identifies the package as an 'object of intense imaginative interest between the wars' in her aptly named study of modern consumer habits, *Carried Away*.[38] This package-preoccupation certainly feeds into a more specialised luggage-preoccupation. According to Bowlby, the rise of transpaper packaging coincided with a literary and artistic interest in the idea of 'changeable' identities or 'multiple selves'.[39] The consumer who buys artfully packaged goods is encouraged to package his/her mobile identity in an artful yet adaptable form in day-to-day life. For many writers, luggage would become the equivalent of the package for the modern individual in transit, allowing for the cultivation of a 'changeable' identity while keeping the taint of the marketplace at an important ideological remove, albeit not always successfully.

This brings me to a third key line of departure from the object-oriented scrutiny of thing theorists. While the physical contours and materiality of objects are central to the discussion that follows – in that the project of travelling light enacted a compromise between the weight of material necessity and the compulsion to move – the book pays equal heed to the metaphorics of portability, its function as a conceptual paradigm. Writers were as concerned with the mobilisation of ideas as with things, or, to offer an alternative angle, with the very idea of mobilising things as with the mobilised things themselves. My major concern in this book is less with portable property *per se* than with the question of what it means to carry, and this is a question which must be addressed with as much attention to conceptual as to material dimensions. Indeed, the conceptual character of portability is almost impossible to ignore. The word 'luggage' itself indicates an age-old 'metaphor we live by' of the 'conduit' genre, to refer to George Lakoff and Mark Johnson's well-known linguistic study. As they point out, the tendency to conceive of language as the putting of 'ideas (objects) into words (containers) and send[ing] them (along a conduit) to a hearer who takes the idea/objects out of the word/containers' is so innate to our understanding of communication that we are not even always attuned to the fact that we are applying metaphorical terms at all.[40] We take the inherent portability of ideas – the fact that they can be carried between people and contexts – for granted.

A literary text in the form of a printed book seems the very embodiment of such a notion, conjoining both material and conceptual dimensions, and creating what Plotz has referred to as 'a public form of portable privacy'.[41] Although this study draws attention to various kinds of authorial engagement with portability and the act of carriage during this period, from thematic to stylistic, it places a particular emphasis on the emergence of portable analogues for literary form through luggage; the extent, in other words, to which the symbolic form of the case came to underpin the artistic visions of a number of modernist writers over and above those 'architectural visions' of the nineteenth century.[42] To put it crudely, I argue that luggage offered a key structural paradigm for modernist writers in the same way that the house had offered a key structural paradigm for Victorian writers (though such an opposition is far from being as clear-cut as it might seem.) Dorothy Richardson's structural foregrounding of Miriam's Saratoga trunk in *Pilgrimage* (1915–38), Virginia Woolf's well-known 1919 conceptualisation of her diary as a 'capacious hold-all', Henry Green's framing image of writing as a form of hasty packing on the verge of war in *Pack My Bag* (1940) and Elizabeth Bowen's vision of plot in terms of 'luggage left in the hall between two journeys as opposed to the perpetual furniture of rooms' in 1945 are just some of the many modernist examples of portable visions which represent striking departures from the synecdochic architectural structures conceived in works like Jane Austen's *Mansfield Park* (1814), among others.[43] Marking a pointed move away from a Victorian architectural mode, the more episodic, subjective luggage models which come to the fore in modernist writing stress an individualistic or fragmentary, rather than an all-embracing, narrative perspective, unpredictability rather than establishment, '*route*-dness' over and above rootedness. Yet such a distinction between a modernist metaphorics of portability and a Victorian metaphorics of architecture must first be complicated before it can be elucidated, beginning with an appraisal of portable tropes in the work of one of the most prominent literary architects of the nineteenth century, Charles Dickens.

MODERNIST LUGGAGE AND VICTORIAN ARCHITECTURE?

Late in his writing career, Dickens embarked on a collaborative writing project for the Christmas special edition of *All the Year Round* in 1862, entitled *Somebody's Luggage*. For this project, he recruited Charles Allston Collins, Arthur Locker, John Oxenford and Julia Cecilia Stretton as co-authors. The story recounts a waiter's discovery of a heap of abandoned luggage in one of the rooms of the hotel at which he is newly employed. Upon further investigation, he finds that the accumulated luggage is veritably bursting with words in the form of an 'extraordinary quantity of writing paper, and all written on!'[44] The waiter goes on to explain:

> And he had crumpled up this writing of his, everywhere, in every part and parcel of his luggage. There was writing in his dressing case, writing

in his boots, writing among his shaving tackle, writing in his hat box, writing folded away down among the very whalebones of his umbrella.[45]

It transpires that these pieces of writing are short stories, which the waiter then brings to publication, each one named after the 'articles of luggage to which they were found attached' (for example, 'His Black Bag', 'His Dressing Case', 'His Hat Box', and so on).[46] *Somebody's Luggage,* as a composite piece, comprises the set of stories, collaboratively written by the aforementioned contributing authors and Dickens himself, who also composed the framing narrative of the waiter. It is through the waiter that the fascination of this luggage is articulated, implying a like fascination on Dickens's part: 'I don't know why – when DO we know why? – but this luggage laid heavy on my mind. I fell a wondering about Somebody, and what he had got and been up to.'[47] This luggage is placed in metonymical relation to the figure of the absent character/author here, the 'Somebody' of the title, but it is also proffered as an analogue for the form of the text itself. Where the latter is concerned, it is important to emphasise the disjointed and episodic quality of this formal vision. That is to say, the individual stories, named after the individual articles of luggage, are discontinuous.

Such a formal analogue is anomalous in the broader context of Dickens's work, marking a striking contrast to his usual architectural analogic mode. From his edited magazine, *Household Words* (1850–9) to that seminal Victorian monument of fiction, *Bleak House* (1852–3), domestic architecture looms as an unavoidable structuring principle in his writing, as in the writings of many of his contemporaries.[48] What *Somebody's Luggage* shows is that Dickens was also peripherally drawn to more portable forms and analogues, which he associates with an episodic compulsion, and, even more intriguingly, this peripheral appeal is also implicit in those of his works which are overtly shaped by an overarching domestic framework. As Kevin McLaughlin notes, much of the 'critical debate about novels like *Bleak House* can be seen in terms of th[e] conflict between the domestic analogy that organizes the novel and the various figures of displacement that continue to guide important novel criticism'.[49] For W. J. Harvey, this conflict, as it plays out in *Bleak House,* is a facet of the relationship between narrative whole and episodic part. If such a relation is habitually shown to be more fraught than harmonious, this tautness is part of the novel's overall effect, as he observes:

> one of the reasons for its greatness is the extreme tension set up between the centrifugal vigour of its parts and the centripetal demands of the whole. It is a tension between the impulse to intensify each local detail or particular episode and the impulse to subordinate, arrange and discipline.[50]

In other words, the episodic part threatens, at all times, to breach the synecdochic bond, to expand beyond its assigned dimensions, to disconnect from the overarching structure. In *Bleak House*, a novel in which all parts ostensibly connect together (unlike the discontinuous components of *Somebody's Luggage*) to form the larger architectural conception, episodic threat is manifested through a preoccupation with luggage as a repository for unsanctioned and private documents which find no place in the narrative house. The most prominent instance of this is Captain Hawdon's 'ragged old portmanteau', which contains written evidence of Esther Summerson's episodic origins.[51] While the domestic analogue still predominates in *Bleak House*, the prevalence and importance of luggage bears witness to a centrifugal impulse – an impulse towards portability over and above domesticity – which comes to markedly shape later conceptions of literary form, as *Somebody's Luggage* itself confirms within Dickens's *oeuvre* alone.

In positing portable forms in contradistinction to the domestic frames of reference that are so conspicuous in Victorian literature, it is not my intention to suggest a clear-cut opposition between a domesticated form of nineteenth-century realism and a portable modernism, an opposition complicated by the example of Dickens. It is also an opposition that has been interrogated in recent criticism. Some critics have highlighted the fallibility of the domestic model in the Victorian period.[52] Others have taken issue with the commonplace assertion of modernism as a 'vocabulary of anti-home'.[53] Indeed, the house is far from being an unquestioned paragon of Victorian stability, while portable objects can be found to manifest a certain allure, as the studies of Wynne and Plotz attest. By the same token, the value of the house is not completely diminished in modernist literature, nor does portability always fulfil everything it appears to promise as an alternative fictional paradigm.

This book is thus far from claiming that portable forms simply appeared to contend with architectural structures or domestic paradigms at the end of the nineteenth century. Just as Cresswell demonstrates that a 'nomadic metaphysics' has always attended and conflicted with a 'sedentarist metaphysics', so I would propose that, to a great extent, the symbolic opposition between luggage and architecture is a longstanding and prevailing one even if the balance of paradigmatic power and influence can be seen to shift.[54] Luggage, of some variety, has been around for as long as people have moved and has, as such, served as a useful and evocative literary motif and metaphor. As Fussell notes, 'both travellers and watchers have always been sensitive to its semiotic powers'.[55] When Raoul Duquette, in Katherine Mansfield's 1918 story 'Je ne parle pas français', aligns people in the modern age with restless portmanteaux, he is swift to acknowledge that it is not a 'frightfully original digression'.[56] It can be observed that the symbolic or analogic appeal of luggage to the literary imagination takes two divergent lines. In the first place, we have the fardel

imagery of the pilgrimage or puritan narrative tradition, where luggage is a burden of sin or anxiety to be carried as index to an unwanted and enforced alienation from an established structure, social and/or religious. The narrative aim is to reach a point where the burden can be shed and a re-assimilation achieved. John Bunyan's *The Pilgrim's Progress* of 1678, the archetype in this line, makes the burden of the central protagonist, Christian, carried for much of his narrative journey, of paramount allegorical importance. The pilgrimage trope has been found to inform many modernist acts of travel and twentieth-century writers such as Dorothy Richardson play upon this fardel tradition much later on.[57]

Luggage is, however, an equally visible accessory in the adventure narrative line (linked to picaresque and romance traditions), where alienation takes the form of a self-willed escape from and reaction to the fixed order of an established social structure.[58] Here, luggage signals a liberating mobility as opposed to an encumbering obstruction, and this usage, again, has a long history. One example is provided in tracing the origins of Duquette's 'not frightfully original digression' in Mansfield's 'Je ne parle pas français'. His passing remark on the unoriginality of his comparison of people with portmanteaux becomes more interesting in light of a note Mansfield made in her journal in January 1918, the same month the story was written. She quotes from a letter John Keats wrote to Fanny Brawne in August 1819: 'Better be imprudent moveables than prudent fixtures.'[59] We find an even fuller evocation of this opposition between nomadic and sedentarist perspectives in terms of an architectural/luggage opposition by appending the preceding line in Keats's original letter to Mansfield's selective quotation: 'god forbid we should what people call, *settle* – turn into a pond, a stagnant Lethe – a vile crescent, row or buildings. Better be imprudent moveables than prudent fixtures.'[60] Keats's line offers a good example of the use of luggage to convey the desire to escape and the reaction against a conventional system of values. More generally, we can characterise these two divergent luggage modes in terms of obstruction, on the one hand, and facilitation, on the other. Tim Armstrong's categories of 'negative' and 'positive' prosthesis might be productively applied to these distinct symbolic practices.[61] Armstrong defines positive prosthesis in terms of bodily empowerment through organ extension, 'in which human capacities are extrapolated', whereas negative prosthesis 'involves the replacing of a bodily part, covering a lack'.[62] Thus, in the adventure tradition, luggage can be seen as a positive prosthetic because, as home in transit and key instrument of displacement, it empowers the individual in the act of escape, while, in the fardel tradition, it is a negative prosthetic, not only because it is an encumbrance but, more importantly, because it points to the loss or 'lack' of the home left behind.

Why, then, does this book posit luggage in specific relation to modernist fiction if it has such a longstanding literary history? Far from denying such a history, the book shows that an already existing preoccupation with portability, particularly evident in the nineteenth century, intensifies during the modernist period, but with a distinct shift in emphasis. As both Wynne and Plotz describe, portable property in Victorian literature functions as a 'form of domestic retreat' away from home or as a performative substitute for the ownership of landed property.[63] An overarching architectural or domestic ideology continues to prevail here, even though the allure of a portable culture begins to unsettle its central tenets, as a closer look at Dickens's work makes clear.[64] Indeed, throughout the nineteenth century, architectural prestige is shaken by new forms of mobility. John Ruskin, in his well-known 1849 treatise on architectural design, *The Seven Lamps of Architecture*, cannot help expressing a certain fear of 'locomotion', and this fear finds expression in the form of a person-package analogy:[65]

> The whole system of railroad travelling is addressed to people who, being in a hurry, are therefore for the time being miserable. No one would travel in that manner who could help it . . . The railroad is in all its relations a matter of earnest business to be got through as soon as possible. It transmutes a man from a traveller into a living parcel. For the time, he has parted with the nobler characteristics of his humanity for the sake of a planetary power of locomotion.[66]

Dickens would himself go on to realise this very scenario in 'Mugby Junction', a collection of stories set in and around a railway station with a number of intersecting lines, published in the 1866 Christmas number of *All the Year Round*. The title of the first framing story – 'Barbox Brothers' – refers to the main character, Jackson, who is allotted this nickname from the labels on his two large black portmanteaux: 'so to call the traveler on the warranty of his luggage'.[67] What I would like to highlight here is the sense of the dehumanisation of the individual in transit between stable architectural reference points. Railroad travelling becomes threatening in its transformative effect, and such a threat is aggravated by its mobile aspect. Furthermore, if the railroad transforms people into packages, then they are packages without any agency themselves; the locomotion is not in their control. The 'nobler characteristics of humanity' are restored, for Ruskin, along with a domestic frame of reference.

With the advent of modernism, I argue, such an overarching domestic frame of reference loses its paradigmatic power to the degree that it no longer becomes the default or aspirational paradigm. A closer look at the people/ portmanteaux analogy in Mansfield's story, in contrast to Ruskin's much earlier person/'parcel' alignment, will bring this difference to light. It will also help us to understand the analogic appeal of luggage to the modernist imagination, over and above its affiliation with the fragmentary or episodic:

I don't believe in the human soul. I never have. I believe that people are like portmanteaux – packed with certain things, started going, thrown about, tossed away, dumped down, lost and found, half emptied suddenly or squeezed fatter than ever, until finally the Ultimate Porter swings them on to the Ultimate Train and away they rattle.[68]

In doing away altogether with the idea of a soul, Duquette presents us instead with a perception of the arbitrariness and negligibility of individual subjective forms in a state of modern agitation. Mansfield's use of the short-story form makes the fragmented nature of formal dislocation more acute. Yet we also find a final destination projected above. The passage can be read as a wry commentary on the relationship between character and form in modernist fiction; the sense of deliberate self-alienation from larger controlling structures and yet the enduring belief in the totalising and stabilising force of an 'Ultimate' design. For Bauman, contemporary liquid modernity can be understood in relation to 'the infinity of chances that has filled the place left empty in the wake of the disappearing act of the Supreme Office'.[69] In the fluid stage of modernity offered in Mansfield's story, the experience of an 'infinity of chances' co-exists uncomfortably with a consciousness of a 'Supreme Office', though 'Ultimate' officialdom only arrives as something of an afterthought. Where Duquette's use of the person/package analogy differs thus from Ruskin (as well as Dickens and Keats), is that it assumes a nomadic metaphysics as the dominant metaphysics, and there is just a wistful suggestion of an overarching sedentarist point of view. For Ruskin, it is only '[f]or the time' that man 'has parted with the nobler characteristics of his humanity for the sake of a planetary power of locomotion'. In Duquette's vision, the prevailing modern condition is characterised, first and foremost, by locomotion and, to loosely apply Georg Lukács's well-known idiom, a kind of 'transcendental homelessness'.[70] The stirrings of a mobile modernity are certainly in evidence in Keats, Ruskin and Dickens. As recognised by many modernist scholars, the 'potential of Modernism was long present in the development of literature'.[71] But for those earlier writers, though alert to these stirrings, the sedentarist point of view, for better or worse, still governs overall.

Modernism brings the nomadic point of view and, in conjunction, a portable ethos to the fore, establishing a new status quo. '[T]he nineteenth century, like no other century was addicted to dwelling', as Walter Benjamin put it, while '[t]he twentieth century, with its porosity and transparency, its tendency toward the well-lit and airy, has put an end to dwelling in the old sense'.[72] This development is reflected, to no small degree, in the state of architectural art from the end of the nineteenth century. A number of *fin de siècle* art magazines identify a failing confidence within the field of architecture, which is seen to have far-reaching implications. Take the following excerpt from an editorial for *The Century Guild Hobby Horse* in 1889:

> Now the present condition of the Art of this country is largely the result of the deplorable state of our architecture, and of the manner in which our Painting, Sculpture, and the Decorative arts are carried on without reference to this fundamental art, which bears the same relation to them as does the frame to the picture.[73]

It is perhaps this 'frame to the picture' mentality which is the root of the problem here. By the end of the nineteenth century, it seems that architecture has been left behind as set against advancements in other art forms, as an 1898 editorial in the *fin-de-siècle* periodical *The Dome*, a magazine with an active interest in the field of architecture, makes clear. The writer of this editorial bemoans the state of an art which 'more sorely than any other needs a fresh inspiration; for it is Architecture alone who seems to believe her last great word spoken, and the evolution of a new and yet dignified style impossible'.[74]

In the twentieth century, this fresh inspiration might be said to have arrived through the advent of rationalism and modernist architecture, foregrounding functionality, open volumes/plans and the possibilities of new materials. Yet, according to David Spurr, such innovations did not altogether align with literary innovations (for example, modernist fragmentation), at least on the surface. He argues that 'the relative harmony between architectural and literary forms of meaning characteristic of the neoclassical period later broke down in such a way as to constitute diverse if not formally opposed responses to the modern condition'.[75] Divergent as these responses might have seemed, both art forms were preoccupied with the question of how to inhabit a restless world. Spurr goes on to show that a key directive of modernist architecture was 'the demystification of "dwelling", that idealized conception of space that promises rootedness, permanence, and a womblike removal from the experience of modernity'.[76] In effect, new forms of architecture attempted an embrace of modern mobility. This is particularly true of the work of Le Corbusier, who, as Spurr notes, associated traditional architecture with a kind of 'paralysis'.[77] A broader demystification of dwelling is also perceptible in the rising popularity of flats and apartments as temporary urban footholds for those who preferred to travel light. E. M. Forster and Evelyn Waugh make much of this trend in *Howards End* (1910) and *A Handful of Dust* (1934), for instance. Cresswell points to the formation of a 'nomadic architecture' in the late twentieth century, epitomised in the work of Bernard Tschumi, but this trend is visible much earlier.[78] Helen Ashton's *Bricks and Mortar*, a novel published in 1932, concerns the life of an architect by the name of Martin Lovell from the 1890s to the 1930s, and, through his eyes, we witness the changing world of architecture during the modernist period. Most fascinating, in the context of this discussion, are the repeated descriptions of modern buildings in the novel, often the designs of Lovell's young protogé Oliver Barford, in terms of packing cases. These modern buildings have 'packing-case outlines', or look like a 'cross between a packing-case and gasometer', or, in more sizeable examples, 'like heaps of packing cases'.[79] Such structures are viewed with distaste by Lovell (who takes a rather more traditional stance on structural design), but he is eventually forced to cede to the inevitable succession of a younger generation of architects with a more modern sense of the need to somehow incorporate the concepts of movement and portability within architectural form.

Spurr acknowledges that a survey of modernist literature reveals little overt interest in the kinds of demystified dwelling places being constructed by architects such as Frank Lloyd Wright and Le Corbusier, even if 'a more fundamental correspondence of certain [architectural] principles as formal and thematic features of literary modernism' is evident.[80] By contrast, the period from the 1880s to the 1920s witnessed the enormous transformation and enlargement of the travelling goods industry, particularly the luggage trade, and, as this book establishes, such portable frameworks are spot-lighted in modernist literature at every turn. From 1860 to 1880 alone, the total value of trunks produced on an annual basis in the United States had nearly tripled and the number of workers active in that line had more than doubled.[81] This is no less true of Europe. 'The phenomenal growth of the Travelling Requisites, Fancy Leather Goods and Sports Trades during the past ten years' is cited as the primary reason for the launch of the aforemen-tioned *Bag, Portmanteau and Umbrella Trader* in 1907, a journal which was transformed, due to its 'phenomenal success', from a monthly to a weekly publication in April 1909.[82] The rapid growth of this industry was indica-tive of the needs of an increasingly mobile, but also increasingly moneyed, middle class, hungry to consume new products and experiences. The modern traveller was also a modern consumer; mobility and desire were integral to both activities. If old money was static and invested in property, then new money was moving and, more often than not, invested in movables, whether disposable products or portable goods, a shift pointedly expressed in the very expansion of the luggage trade at this time. The enlargement of this industry represents the demystification of dwelling in action as well as the ascendency of what the narrator of Forster's *Howards End* refers to as the 'nomadic civi-lisation which is altering human nature so profoundly'.[83] This book seeks to explore the similarly profound impact this new mode of dwelling-in-motion had on literary conceptions.

Mapping Portability

'How to begin to map the intersecting itineraries of mobility and materiality?' opens an article by Paul Basu and Simon Coleman on migrant worlds and material culture.[84] This question might be rephrased more precisely for my purposes here: how to begin to map the intersecting itineraries of mobility and materiality in the literature of the modern period? The book is divided into four chapters, each subdivided into three shorter sections. Chapter 1 charts the emerging influence of a portable outlook from the Edwardian period to modernism. The chapter begins by tracing the genesis of that now-prolific phrase 'house of fiction' to Henry James's belated 1908 Preface to *The Portrait of a Lady* (1881) and argues that, contrary to popular usage, the 'house of fiction' originally referred to an amorphous structure on the point of abandonment. It pays particular attention to the transitional status of the house in Edwardian writing at a time when it was visibly beginning to lose its lustre. It then looks at two conflicting responses to the parallel rise of what E. M. Forster would refer to as the 'civilisation of luggage' in *Howards End* in 1910.[85] Drawing on Max Beerbohm's homage to a beloved and well-travelled hat-box as a paragon of self-creation and prospective self-renewal in his essay 'Ichabod' (1900), it discusses the implications of this luggage civilisation on the architectural model in Forster's text. The first chapter finishes by turning to early modernist delineations of a portable culture which has become well-established by the late 1910s. '[I]t is quite obvious that the lighter articles are what the public wants', reports *The Bag, Portmanteau and Umbrella Trader* in 1919.[86] While Ellen Eve Frank, like other critics and philosophers of the architectural mode, hones in on concepts of 'building' and 'dwelling' as literary architectural keynotes, I probe the impact of acts of packing, moving and dwelling in motion upon the craft of writing at this time.[87] In particular, I discuss the perceptible move away from domestic or architectural frames of reference in imagining modernist textual forms, whether to impart a certain formal looseness or to inscribe a mobile dimension through a conduit mode.

Chapter 2 is concerned with the pride of place – or, to be more precise, pride of placelessness – assumed by the figure of the modern woman within the new 'civilisation of luggage' and the corresponding imaginative emphasis on her hand-held bag as indicative of her proprietorial autonomy as opposed to her dependence and insubstantiality.[88] From the late nineteenth century, the woman's bag emerged as a subversive emblem for female self-sufficiency as a portable framework for the formation of an autonomous narrative. It was an emblem taken up by a number of New Women writers of fiction and non-fiction, from George Egerton to Nellie Bly. Giving an overview of the historical and rhetorical associations of women with baggage in the context of legal understandings of women's property rights, the chapter also looks at *fin-de-siècle* and early-twentieth-century projections (both in literary works and satirical cartoons) of the disturbance caused by the modern women to traditional chivalric and fictional conventions. It asks why women's portable property was often so pivotal in renderings of this disturbance. More specifically, it hones in on the work of one prominent modernist woman writer, Dorothy Richardson, whose use of a portable model in *Pilgrimage* goes hand in hand with her reinvention of the female subject. The chapter contends that Miriam's Saratoga trunk, which accompanies her for the bulk of her journey, forms the visual expression of Richardson's stipulated aspiration to 'produce a feminine equivalent of the current masculine realism'.[89] After Richardson, I reflect on some of the problems faced by women beyond the domestic paradigm, considering the woman's bag as an object of modernist conflict in texts by Katherine Mansfield, Virginia Woolf and D. H. Lawrence. These depictions reveal the fine line between power and powerlessness in characterisations of women on the move.

Chapter 3 traces the progressive alignment of portability with precarity from the late 1920s to the 1940s against a backdrop of political instability. The unfolding crisis of mass displacement across Europe served to reduce earlier literary fantasies of travelling light to nightmarish visions of involuntary exodus. These changing resonances are perceptible in the pointed obfuscations of tropes of tourism, adventure and dispossession in 1930s literature as well as the noticeable intrusion of the figure of the refugee on the artistic consciousness. The refugee was, of course, not simply or primarily a literary vehicle for the exploration of imposed portability; the word defines an actual experience shared by many interwar writers, and the chapter pays equal attention to the accounts of refugees and political exiles. If luggage becomes a figurative focal point in the works of displaced writers such as Yevgeny Zamyatin, Viktor Shklovsky, Vladimir Nabokov, Hermann Broch, Irène Némirovsky, Walter Benjamin and Stefan Zweig, it is not in aid of a fantasy of creative renewal, but of material, cultural and individual preservation. The chapter ends with an analysis of the fictional and non-fictional work of Elizabeth Bowen, with the inclusion of an extended close reading of *The House in Paris* as an updated version of Forster's *Howards End* in a troubled 1930s context.

The final chapter of the book directs attention to questions of identity and selfhood. If modernism witnessed the rise of a culture of portability, what did this mean for understandings of literary character, and how did such understandings alter over the course of the interwar period? Movable forms and possessions have long been viewed with intrigue as index to a personality in transit. Yet intrigue can take on an alarmist edge in a climate of socio-political insecurity. This chapter documents, as such, the development of late modernist suspicion of portable otherness as this is conveyed through interrogative appraisals of portable property. This development coincides with the sudden pervasiveness of the literary figure of the customs official from the late 1920s, cropping up in works by writers as divergent in style as Virginia Woolf, Evelyn Waugh and George Orwell, among others. This is a figure shown to share the psychoanalyst's eye for the repressed contraband: 'Have you anything to declare?' As the chapter shows, this question of self-declaration becomes a critical one in conceptions and re-conceptions of character from modernism to late modernism. The chapter culminates with a reading of Henry Green's autobiographical *Pack My Bag* (1940) in conjunction with his fictional *Party Going* (1939), both published around the outbreak of the Second World War. Green's autobiographical use of the analogue of the packed bag to describe an opaque collection of memories, by turns deeply personal and coldly impersonal, articulates a form of self-declaration which resists the extreme demands of the moment.

Following this structural overview, it seems right to mention one road not taken in this book, yet of interest nonetheless. Though I have focused on women, war and identity in these chapters, I might well have chosen other angles. An approach to this topic from the point of view of colonialism would alike have been constructive. The decline of the British Empire in the early twentieth century would certainly have played a large part in the declining relevance of architectural forms in English fiction, and there are several lines of enquiry that might be taken with this in mind. Novels like Austen's *Mansfield Park* and Forster's *Howards End*, to cite a couple of examples, hint that the continuing stability, influence and dominance of the fictional house in each case partly relies upon foreign exploits, and this requires a venturing out, an impulse towards conquest which might be said to be inscribed in the very idea of luggage. Indeed, certain luggage designs evolved through the eighteenth and nineteenth centuries to cater for this impulse. We find, for example, popular types of trunk labelled the 'Imperial' and the 'Globe Trotter', the former a general style of trunk and the latter produced and patented by A. Garstin and Co. As Kaplan has pointed out, 'the emergence of terms of travel and displacement (as well as their oppositional counterparts, home and location) in contemporary criticism must be linked to the histories of the production of colonial discourses'.[90] Such colonial discourses are at the heart of Plotz's account of Victorian portable property which pays considerable attention to '[p]ortability's efficacy as a mechanism of imperial expansion' during the nineteenth century in allowing for the small-scale reconstruction of home abroad.[91] By the same token, if the rising importance of a modernist portable ethos can be linked to the subversive power of new forms of female mobility, we might also look to the subversive implications of migratory movements of colonised subjects to the imperial domestic hearth, whether this is viewed as destructive or regenerative. I have not taken this line here, though I recognise its bearing on the subject of the present discussion. My intention is to establish portability as a vital concept through which to explore modernist concerns, contradictions and initiatives. Yet modernism is, of course, an incredibly complex phenomenon. If my attentiveness to certain aspects of this phenomenon has been to the exclusion of others, this is an inevitable outcome of addressing a topic which provides material for research well beyond the parameters of a single book.[92]

At the same time, even within set limits, work on the rising appeal and pervasiveness of a particular idea, ethos or experience at a particular period in literary history demands a broad approach, and this presents certain challenges of its own. From the outset, I made the decision to map portability through a wide range of texts from the late nineteenth through to the early twentieth century. This is a case that can only be made through demonstrating a kind of epidemiological diffusion. Yet it also demands careful – qualitative, if you like – analysis. The book pauses periodically to pay close attention to certain more pertinent engagements with portability and portable forms in the works of key writers (Forster, Richardson, Bowen and Green). That the texts I look at are not always decisively modernist either is part of the point. We learn as much about this kind of phenomenon from its invocation in more conventional narratives as in the most experimental, and this book is as much about reflections on the experience of modernity at this time as it is about modernism *per se*. Though the overarching emphasis of the book is on prose fiction, it dwells, often briefly and occasionally at some length, on portable figurations in works of drama, poetry, art and advertising in order to support, exemplify, colour or add scope to certain points. Relatedly, though it is chiefly concerned with British/Anglo-Irish fiction, it offers regular examples of works originating elsewhere – whether other European countries or the United States – and often in translation. In some instances, these works have been included in order to cast facets of English works in a new light. In other instances, I have treated them as significant in and of themselves. Recent modernist scholarship has encouraged a more global, pluralistic and transnational perspective, and this book incorporates that approach within certain limits. As Thacker has remarked, 'modernist writing can be located only within the movements between and across multiple sorts of space'.[93] Likewise, the transgressive implications of a portable ethos – in its advocacy of movement between and across multiple sorts of space – would be lost if a confined cultural approach were taken. Of course, one must always be sensitive to contextual difference, not to mention the differently signifying varieties of movement and of travelling goods in circulation at this time. The conflation of distinctive forms of portability is something I have taken pains to avoid. Mapping portability between and across multiple sorts of spaces and cultures, while taking account of spatial and cultural specificities, has meant treading a delicate line between the general and the particular. But the negotiation of the general and the particular is, in itself, part and parcel of the development of a particular concept at a distinct point in time; that is to say, the bespoke adaptation of a prototype or prototypical idea to serve a defined purpose. It is such a development that I seek, above all, to illuminate. In this, the book might be understood as an addition to the formation of what Franco Moretti has called a '"rhetorical" historiography' or, alternatively, a 'sociology of symbolic forms'.[94] If the history of literature might be understood in terms of the historical development of rhetorical forms, discourses or concepts, then this attempt to map modernist portability is proffered as one contribution to that undertaking.

NOTES

1. 'Continental Notes: Contrasts with the English Trade by Our Special Correspondent', *The Bag Portmanteau and Umbrella Trader and Fancy Leather Goods and Athletic Trades Review*, 2.21, February 1909, p. 18.
2. Rachel Bowlby, *Carried Away: The Invention of Modern Shopping* (London: Faber, 2000), p. 47.
3. Max Beerbohm, 'Ichabod' (1900), in *Yet Again* (1909; London: Heinemann, 1928), p. 123.
4. He describes his three key phases as follows: '"Solid" modernity was an era of mutual engagement. "Fluid" modernity is the epoch of disengagement, elusiveness, facile escape and hopeless chase. In "liquid" modernity, it is the most elusive, those free to move without notice, who rule.' Zygmunt Bauman, *Liquid Modernity* (Cambridge: Polity, 2012), p. 120.
5. Ibid., pp. 121, 128.
6. Peripatetus, 'London Letter', *The Bag, Portmanteau and Umbrella Trader and Fancy Leather Goods and Athletic Trades Review*, 4.89, July 1910, p. 8.
7. The developing aspiration towards portability is evident, not least, in the near exponential growth in the popularity of the phrase itself in a range of different textual contexts from fiction to advertising. Google Ngram Viewer, for example, shows a steep incline in the usage of the phrase 'travelling light' (lower case, in the British form) from about 1800, reaching a peak in the 1920s and maintaining a high frequency level until the mid-1950s, before a moderate fall in usage once again through the remainder of the century. Some discrepancies appear through changing capitalisation, spelling and grammatical form ('Travel Light', 'Travels light', 'traveled light', and so on), though the pattern is reasonably similar across the board. Granting the limitations of Ngram data, it does usefully illustrate an undeniable rise in the general employment of this term through the modernist period, implying an increased preoccupation with portability.
8. Helenka Gulshan, *Vintage Luggage* (London: Phillip Wilson, 1998), p. 9.
9. Paul Fussell, 'Bourgeois Travel: Techniques and Artifacts', in *Bon Voyage: Designs for Travel*, ed. Nancy Aakre (New York: Cooper-Hewitt Museum and The Smithsonian Institution's National Museum of Design, 1986), p. 69.
10. Ibid., p. 76.
11. Alongside the trunk, the valise, the Gladstone, the tin box and the hat-box, numerous other recognisable models were in regular circulation (and regularly referenced in the fiction of the period): for example, the dressing-case, the dress-basket, the hold-all, the carpet-bag, the blouse-case, the wardrobe trunk, the Saratoga, the attaché case, the brief bag, the kit bag, the cabin bag, the dispatch case, the portmanteau, the Revelation expanding suitcase, the trunk designed for the motorcar, the case designed for air travel, and so on. Specified materials in use at this time ranged from leather to faux leather, from crocodile or alligator skin to vellum, from wicker to canvas, from compressed cane to compressed fibre.
12. Indeed, in 1911, a certain Alphonse Ledoux of the Hotel des Américains revealed to an American magazine the existence of a prevalently employed and universally understood system of coded marks strategically placed, by porters and hotel baggage handlers, on items of luggage in order to covertly communicate a guest's general predisposition and the extent of his/her generosity when it came to tipping. See Pierre Léonforte, '100 Legendary Trunks', in *Louis Vuitton: 100 Legendary*

Trunks, by Pierre Léonforte, Éric Pujalet-Plaà with the collaboration of Florence Lesché and Marie Wurry, trans. Bruce Waille (New York: Abrams, 2010), pp. 157–65.

13. This is a kind of sophistication which cannot be found to the same degree today, as leading vintage luggage dealers document. See Gulshan, *Vintage Luggage*, pp. 26–8.

14. Jeremy Tambling, '*Martin Chuzzlewit*: Dickens and Architecture', *English*, 48.192, Autumn 1999, p. 147.

15. The Terry Eagleton phrase comes from the title of his *Exiles and Émigrés* (London: Chatto and Windus, 1970).

16. In fact, the exclusion of women writers from the modernist canon has itself been viewed as a form of exile. See Mary Lynn Broe and Angela Ingram (eds), *Women's Writing in Exile* (Chapel Hill: University of North Carolina Press, 1989). Essays of particular interest in this collection are Shari Benstock's 'Expatriate Modernism: Writing on the Cultural Rim' (pp. 19–40) and Celeste M. Schenck's 'Exiled by Genre: Modernism, Canonicity, and the Politics of Exclusion' (pp. 225–50).

17. Malcolm Bradbury and James McFarlane, 'The Name and Nature of Modernism', in *Modernism: A Guide to European Literature 1890–1930*, ed. Malcolm Bradbury and James McFarlane (1976; Harmondsworth: Penguin, 1991), p. 29.

18. Bradbury, 'The Cities of Modernism', in *Modernism*, p. 100.

19. Paul Fussell, *Abroad: British Literary Traveling Between the Wars* (New York: Oxford University Press, 1980), p. 11. For further examples in this line, see Harry Levin's 'Literature and Exile' (1966), in *Refractions: Essays in Comparative Literature* (New York: Oxford University Press, 1966), pp. 62–81, and Malcolm Cowley, *Exile's Return: A Literary Odyssey of the 1920s* (1934; New York: Viking, 1956).

20. Caren Kaplan, *Questions of Travel: Postmodern Discourses of Displacement* (Durham, NC: Duke University Press, 1996), p. 28. Seminal works on the theme of modernist displacement from Eagleton's *Exiles and Émigrés* and Fussell's *Abroad* to Harry Levin's 'Literature and Exile' essay, among others, are subject to some justifiably astringent words in this account. Eagleton's version of exile is implied as élitist (p. 4) as is Fussell's, whose work is also criticised for its blatant 'imperialist nostalgia' (p. 53). Harry Levin is used to provide an 'instructive example of modernist critical promotion of exile as aesthetic gain' (p. 37), a promotional exercise which serves to obscure historical distinctions between different kinds of exile, for a start, but which must equally be seen to perpetuate an ideological construction of the modernist writer rather than to describe a historical reality.

21. Alison Light, *England: Femininity, Literature and Conservatism Between the Wars* (London: Routledge, 1991), p. 10; Lynne Hapgood, 'Transforming the Victorian', in *Outside Modernism: In Pursuit of the English Novel 1900–1930*, ed. Lynne Hapgood and Nancy Paxton (Basingstoke: Macmillan, 2000), p. 22. See also Chiara Briganti and Kathy Mezei's *Domestic Modernism, the Interwar Novel and E. H. Young* (Aldershot, Hampshire: Ashgate, 2006). An earlier groundbreaking study in this line is Nancy Armstrong's *Desire and Domestic Fiction: A Political History of the Novel* (1987; Oxford: Oxford University Press, 1989).

22. Callisthenes, 'The Impedimenta of Travel', *The Times*, 29 December 1923, p. 6.

23. Marshall Berman, *All That Is Solid Melts into Air: The Experience of Modernity* (New York: Simon and Schuster, 1982), p. 35.

24. In 2006, Kevin Hannam, Mimi Sheller and John Urry launched a new journal, entitled *Mobilities*, devoted to further exploring the '"mobility turn" noticeably

spreading into and transforming the social sciences'. See Hannam, Sheller and Urry, 'Editorial: Mobilities, Immobilities and Moorings', *Mobilities*, 1.1, 2006, p. 1. See also Mimi Sheller and John Urry, 'The New Mobilities Paradigm', *Environment and Planning A* 38.2, February 2006, pp. 207–26.

25. Tim Cresswell, *On the Move: Mobility in the Modern Western World* (New York: Routledge, 2006), pp. 26–43.

26. Ibid., pp. 12–20. In brief, Cresswell shows that mobility was a marginal activity in feudal times, reserved for '[w]andering minstrels, troubadours, crusaders, pilgrims, and some peripatetic monks' (p. 11). The freedom of movement of vagabonds within this pre-modern order was perceived as unpredictable and dangerous. By the sixteenth century, possibilities for mobility in Europe had greatly increased, along with the rise of mercantile capitalism, and the decline of the feudal system and mobility was newly associated with liberty and freedom. At the same time, associations of threat endured, and new forms of social surveillance evolved to control the greater facility of circulation. For Cresswell, the word *modern* 'suggests a way of thinking in terms of mobility – a metaphysics of mobility that is distinct from what came before it' (pp. 15–16), though he is equally sensitive to the fact that this advocacy of mobility exists in ambiguous tension with a 'spatialized ordering principle seen by many to be central to modernity' (p. 16).

27. Bauman, *Liquid Modernity*, p. 13.

28. Andrew Thacker, *Moving Through Modernity: Space and Geography in Modernism* (Manchester: Manchester University Press, 2003), p. 8. See also Wendy Parkins, *Mobility and Modernity in Women's Novels, 1850s–1930s: Women Moving Dangerously* (Basingstoke and New York: Palgrave Macmillan, 2009) and Alexandra Peat, *Travel and Modernist Literature: Sacred and Ethical Journeys* (New York: Routledge, 2011).

29. Bridget T. Chalk is one critic who has recently discussed the practicalities of modernist movement on an administrative level in *Modernism and Mobility: The Passport and Cosmopolitan Experience* (New York: Palgrave Macmillan, 2014). I will come back to her work later in the book.

30. Arjun Appadurai, 'Introduction: Commodities and the Politics of Value', in *The Social Life of Things: Commodities in Cultural Perspective*, ed. Arjun Appadurai (1996; Cambridge: Cambridge University Press, 2011), p. 5; Bill Brown, 'Thing Theory', *Critical Inquiry*, 28.1, Autumn 2001, pp. 1–22; Bill Brown, 'The Secret Life of Things (Virginia Woolf and the Matter of Modernism)', *Modernism/Modernity*, 6.2, April 1999, p. 2.

31. Douglas Mao, *Solid Objects: Modernism and the Test of Production* (Princeton: Princeton University Press, 1998), pp. 8–9.

32. Deborah Wynne, *Women and Personal Property in the Victorian Novel* (Farnham, Surrey: Ashgate, 2010), p. 2.

33. Elaine Freedgood's object-oriented, metonymical approach in '[t]aking fictional things literally' in Victorian novels and following them 'beyond the covers of the text' is one notable exception in Victorian studies here. See Elaine Freedgood, *The Ideas in Things: Fugitive Meaning in the Victorian Novel* (Chicago: University of Chicago Press, 2006), p. 5.

34. Mao, *Solid Objects*, p. 4.

35. John Plotz, *Portable Property: Victorian Culture on the Move* (Princeton and Oxford: Princeton University Press, 2008), p. xv.

36. Appadurai, 'Commodities and the Politics of Value', p. 13. As Wynne notes, the 'growth of industrialism conferred a greater importance on movable wealth' over and above landed estate, and, for Bauman, the very capacity of capital to 'travel light' forms the key to its influence whereas '[b]ulkiness and size are turning from

assets into liabilities'. See Wynne, *Women and Personal Property*, p. 35; Bauman, *Liquid Modernity*, p. 121.

37. For an argument in this vein, see John Xiros Cooper's *Modernism and the Culture of Market Society* (Cambridge: Cambridge University Press, 2004).
38. Bowlby, *Carried Away*, p. 83.
39. Ibid., pp. 108–9.
40. George Lakoff and Mark Johnson, *Metaphors We Live By* (Chicago: University of Chicago Press, 1980), p. 10. Michael J. Reddy has estimated that 'of the entire metalingual apparatus of the English language, at least seventy per cent is directly, visibly, and graphically based on the conduit metaphor'. Michael J. Reddy, 'The Conduit Metaphor', in *Metaphor and Thought*, ed. Andrew Ortony (1979; Cambridge: Cambridge University Press, 1998), p. 177.
41. Plotz, *Portable Property*, p. 11.
42. Tambling, 'Dickens and Architecture', p. 147.
43. Virginia Woolf, *The Diary of Virginia Woolf*, vol. 1, ed. Anne Olivier Bell (London: Hogarth Press, 1977), p. 169; Elizabeth Bowen, 'Notes on Writing a Novel' (1945), in *Pictures and Conversations* (London: Allen Lane, 1975), p. 169.
44. Charles Dickens, 'His Leaving It Till Called For', in Charles Dickens et al., *Somebody's Luggage*, ed. Melissa Valiska Gregory and Melisa Klimaszewski (1862; London: Hesperus, 2006), p. 14.
45. Ibid., p. 14.
46. Ibid., p. 16.
47. Ibid., p. 11.
48. The title *Household Words* underlines the powerful appeal of the domestic and architectural analogue for Dickens. The magazine's lofty aim, not simply of representing but of cultivating a collective household, is boldly outlined in the 'Preliminary Word' of the very first number:

    We aspire to live in the Household affections, and to be numbered among the Household thoughts, of our readers ... We know the great responsibility of such a privilege; its vast reward; the pictures that it conjures up, in hours of solitary labour, of a multitude moved by one sympathy. (Charles Dickens, 'A Preliminary Word', *Household Words*, 1, 30 March 1850, p. 1)

49. Kevin McLaughlin, 'Losing One's Place: Displacement and Domesticity in Dickens's *Bleak House*', *MLN*, 108.5, December 1993, p. 875.
50. W. J. Harvey, '*Bleak House*: The Double Narrative', in *Dickens: Bleak House – A Casebook*, ed. A. E. Dyson (Basingstoke: Macmillan, 1977), p. 225.
51. Chares Dickens, *Bleak House* (1852–3; London: Vintage-Random, 2008), p. 136. Apart from Hawdon's portmanteau, there are numerous instances of packed documentation in this novel: for example, the 'two black leathern cases' belonging to Grandfather Smallweed (p. 296) in which he keeps his financial papers. There are Miss Flite's 'documents', carried, throughout the novel, in her 'reticule' (pp. 3, 54, 56, 495–6, 638, 818–19). There are Richard's legal contributions to 'Jarndyce and Jarndyce' in 'several blue bags hastily stuffed out of all regularity of form, as the larger sort of serpents are in their first gorged state' (p. 549). These are contributions which feed, of course, into the larger bureaucratic digestive tract of the Chancery suit itself which takes shape in a 'battery of blue bags ... loaded with heavy charges of papers' (p. 7), later evolving into 'great heaps, and piles, and bags and bags full of papers' (p. 345).
52. Jeff Nunokawa has, for instance, argued that the 'novel's celebration of domesticity as a sanctuary from the vicissitudes of the cash nexus is everywhere spoiled' in

Victorian fiction. See Jeff Nunokawa, *The Afterlife of Property: Domestic Security and the Victorian Novel* (Princeton: Princeton University Press, 1994), p. 4.

53. Briganti and Mezei, *Domestic Modernism*, p. 33. They borrow this phrase directly from Rita Felski. See also Victoria Rosner, *Modernism and the Architecture of Private Life* (New York: Columbia University Press, 2005).

54. Cresswell, *On the Move*, p. 26.

55. Fussell, 'Bourgeois Travel', p. 65.

56. Katherine Mansfield, 'Je ne parle pas français' (1918), in *Collected Stories of Katherine Mansfield* (1945; London: Constable, 1980), p. 61.

57. For an account of the importance of the pilgrimage trope to modernist writers, see Peat, *Travel and Modernist Literature*, pp. 1–20.

58. Patrick Parrinder has, among others, attempted to dig back beyond the conventional account of the rise of the novel from the eighteenth century, and he finds earlier prose writing in the fifteenth and sixteenth centuries to revolve around 'cavaliers', 'puritans' and 'rogues', all figures of demonstrable mobility. He further notes: '[w]hat gradually overshadowed the prominence of individual eccentricity in the novel was not, however, an awareness of war and political revolutions but rather the growing consciousness of society as a monolithic institution or organization containing and dwarfing the individual'. We might see the growing eminence of the symbolic value of the house over the course of the eighteenth and nineteenth centuries in relation to this growing consciousness of monolithic social organisation. Correspondingly, portable modernist forms might be seen to wistfully hark back to an eccentricity embedded in the history of English prose fiction before that established symbolic eminence. See Patrick Parrinder, *Nation and Novel: The English Novel from its Origins to the Present* (Oxford: Oxford University Press, 2006), pp. 35–62, 27.

59. Katherine Mansfield, *The Journal of Katherine Mansfield*, ed. John Middleton Murray (1927; London: Constable, 1954), p. 127. January 1918 entry.

60. Letter (no. 180) from John Keats to Fanny Brawne, 5–6 August 1819, in John Keats, *The Letters of John Keats 1814–1821*, vol. 2, ed. Hyder Edward Rollins (Cambridge: Cambridge University Press, 1958), p. 138. Emphasis in original.

61. Tim Armstrong, *Modernism, Technology, and the Body: A Cultural Study* (Cambridge: Cambridge University Press, 1998), pp. 77–105. David Bissell uses Armstrong's ideas to draw attention to alternating associations of facility and obstruction in looking at 'geographies of everyday encumbrance' in the modern-day railway station. My invocation of Armstrong's discussion of prosthetic modernism in relation to *literary* luggage is prompted by Bissell's article. See David Bissell, 'Conceptualising Differently-Mobile Passengers: Geographies of Everyday Encumbrance in the Railway Station', *Social and Cultural Geography*, 10.2, 2009, p. 178.

62. Armstrong, *Modernism, Technology, and the Body*, p. 78.

63. Plotz, *Portable Property*, p. xv; Wynne, *Women and Personal Property*, pp. 15–52.

64. Another obvious fictional exemplar here is Jane Austen's *Mansfield Park* (1814) in which the rather more attractive figures of metropolitan mobility, Mary and Henry Crawford, are permitted a certain amount of space to parade their more worldly mores and values before being expunged both from house and house of fiction at one and the same time. For an engaging discussion of the not altogether straightforward opposition between the 'dangers of thoughtless restlessness' and the 'values of thoughtful rest' in this novel, see Tony Tanner's introduction to the 1985 Penguin edition. Tony Tanner, 'Introduction', in *Mansfield Park*, by Jane Austen (1814; Harmondsworth: Penguin, 1985), p. 34.

65. John Ruskin is credited by Ellen Eve Frank with 'illuminating the imaginative literature' of the literary architects she examines in her seminal 1979 study of the

relationship between literature and architecture. See Ellen Eve Frank, *Literary Architecture: Essays Towards a Tradition: Walter Pater, Gerard Manley Hopkins, Marcel Proust, Henry James* (Berkeley: University of California Press, 1979), p. 11. Frank herself takes the phrase 'literary architecture' from Walter Pater's essay 'Style', in *Appreciations: With an Essay on Style* (1889; London, Macmillan, 1907), p. 23.

66. John Ruskin, *The Seven Lamps of Architecture* (1849; London: George Allen, 1903), p. 159.

67. Charles Dickens, 'Barbox Brothers', in *The Christmas Stories*, ed. Ruth Glancy (London: Everyman-Dent, 1996), p. 611. 'Barbox Brothers', in fact, refers to Jackson's former place of work. Interestingly, this character, stalled indefinitely at Mugby Junction, is also alluded to as the 'Gentleman for Nowhere' in the text.

68. Mansfield, 'Je ne parle pas français', p. 60.

69. Bauman, *Liquid Modernity*, p. 61.

70. Georg Lukács, *The Theory of the Novel: A Historical-Philosophical Essay on the Forms of Great Epic Literature*, trans. Anna Bostock (1916; London: Merlin, 2006), p. 41. Lukács's essay was written between 1914 and 1916.

71. Bradbury and McFarlane, 'The Name and Nature of Modernism', p. 30. For Berman too, the feeling of modernity is far from new, and he traces the 'rich history' of modernity right back to the sixteenth century even if what he calls the 'maelstrom' comes to a head in the twentieth century. Berman, *All That Is Solid Melts into Air*, p. 16.

72. Quoted in David Spurr, *Architecture and Modern Literature* (Ann Arbor: The University of Michigan Press, 2012), p. 58.

73. 'A Preface', *The Century Guild Hobby Horse*, 3.13, January 1889, p. 5.

74. 'Under the Dome', *The Dome: An Illustrated Magazine and Review of Literature, Music, Architecture and the Graphic Arts*, December 1898, p. 94.

75. Spurr, *Architecture and Modern Literature*, p. 39.

76. Ibid., pp. 52–3.

77. Ibid., p. 59.

78. Cresswell, *On the Move*, pp. 51–2. See also Anthony Vidler on John Hejduk and 'Vagabond Architecture' in *The Architectural Uncanny: Essays in the Modern Unhomely* (Cambridge, MA: The MIT Press, 1992), pp. 207–14.

79. Helen Ashton, *Bricks and Mortar* (1932; London: Persephone, 2004), pp. 226, 276, 295.

80. Spurr, *Architecture and Modern Literature*, p. 60.

81. These statistics are taken from Linda Edelstein and Pat Morse, *Antique Trunks: Identification and Price Guide* (Iola, WI: Krause, 2003), p. 6. For a general overview of the evolution of luggage design at this time, see Gulshan's *Vintage Luggage* and Ralph Caplan, 'Design for Travel(ers)', in *Bon Voyage*, pp. 95–127.

82. 'By Way of Introduction', *The Bag, Portmanteau and Umbrella Trader and Fancy Leather Goods and Athletic Trades Review*, 1.1, June 1907, p. 3; 'Editorial', *The Bag, Portmanteau and Umbrella Trader and Fancy Leather Goods and Athletic Trades Review*, 2.24, April 1909, p. 3.

83. E. M. Forster, *Howards End* (1910; New York: Signet-Penguin, 1992), p. 206.

84. Paul Basu and Simon Coleman, 'Introduction: Migrant Worlds, Material Cultures', *Mobilities*, 3.3, 2008, p. 313.

85. Forster, *Howards End*, p. 119.

86. Peripatetus, 'Current Trade Topics', *The Bag, Portmanteau and Umbrella Trader and Fancy Leather Goods and Athletic Trades Review*, 13.511, August 1919, p. 16.

87. Apart from Frank, other significant earlier reference points in discussions of the architectural imagination include Martin Heidegger, Gaston Bachelard and the historian John Lukacs. Heidegger, in his influential essay, 'Building Dwelling Thinking' (first delivered as a lecture in 1951 and published in English as part of *Poetry, Language, Thought* in 1971), raises two key philosophical questions: 'What is it to dwell?' and 'How does building belong to dwelling?' He brings these words into etymological relation, through the root word *bauen* (meaning building in modern German, dwelling in original Old English/High German) and calls for a renewed understanding of building as dwelling, as being on the earth. Bachelard attempts to outline a 'topography of our intimate being', in *The Poetics of Space* (1958), through an evocative phenomenological exploration of the domestic space of the house, while historian Lukacs makes a case for a bourgeois age in which a new form of interiority, self-consciousness and privacy was developed in line with an emerging interest in the constitution of the interior space of the home in his essay 'The Bourgeois Interior' (1970). In his own words: '[t]he interior furniture of houses appeared together with the interior furniture of minds'. See Martin Heidegger, 'Building Dwelling Thinking' (pp. 143–59), in *Poetry, Language, Thought*, trans. Albert Hofstadter (1971; New York: Perennial-Harper, 2001), p. 143; Gaston Bachelard, *The Poetics of Space*, trans. Maria Jolas (1958; New York: Orion, 1964), p. xxxii; John Lukacs, 'The Bourgeois Interior: Why the Most Maligned Characteristic of the Modern Age May Yet Be Seen as its Most Precious Asset', *American Scholar*, 39.4, Autumn 1970, p. 623.

88. This dual development is reflected in bag design, which was moving away from the form of the 'dainty reticule' towards 'shapes that were sturdier and more substantial'. See Caroline Cox, *Bags: An Illustrated History* (London: Aurum, 2007), p. 33.

89. Dorothy Richardson, *Pilgrimage,* vol. 1 (London: Dent and Cresset, 1938), p. 9.

90. Kaplan, *Questions of Travel*, p. 2.

91. Plotz, *Portable Property*, p. 18.

92. For discussions of the ambivalent relation of modernism to imperialism as well as literary responses to the end of the British empire, see Peter Childs, *Modernism and the Post-Colonial: Literature and Empire 1885–1930* (London: Continuum, 2007), and Jed Esty, *A Shrinking Island: Modernism and National Culture in England* (Princeton: Princeton University Press, 2004).

93. Thacker, *Moving Through Modernity*, p. 8.

94. Franco Moretti, *Signs Taken for Wonders,* trans. Susan Fischer, David Forgacs and David Miller (London: Verso, 1983), pp. 17, 19.

I

'LIVING MODERNLY'S LIVING QUICKLY': TOWARDS TRAVELLING LIGHT

In a 1901 review of a new edition and translation of the *Arabian Nights*, G. K. Chesterton praises its 'bulk, bigness, magnitude' against anticipated charges of the inconvenience of its voluminous size: 'The "Arabian Nights" is a collection of extraordinarily good stories, and while the modern aesthetic critic will probably find the book too long, the person with a taste for literature will find it too short.'[1] In defending monumentality and scale in literature – what he sees as an 'element of value in architecture', among other forms and media – Chesterton draws attention to an emerging literary preference for brevity or succinctness.[2] Such a preference seems to suggest a 'modern aesthetic' move away from the bulkier forms of the previous century, and it is a trend he subjects to question: 'It is considered one of the elemental merits of a book that it should be "portable". But why?'[3] Chesterton's interrogation of this development is less interesting than the fact of his observation. Though his outward emphasis is on the size of the book in a physical sense, his criticism is more nuanced than this. In setting himself against those 'modern aesthetic critics', he uses the idea of portability to highlight a perceptible value shift in literary appreciation – and, by implication, literary production – which is as much conceptual as physical.

Chesterton hits on a critical transition here. He intuits that stable and stabilising forms, motifs and metaphors, establishing the kind of monumental quality he endorses, are beginning to lack relevance in an age of flux. Instead, a new portable ethos is coming to shape artistic vision and even the nuts and bolts of stylistic technique, anticipating the 1916 observation of Georg Lukács that the 'ultimate basis for artistic creation has become homeless'.[4] Chesterton's remarks can equally be found to reflect a growing thematic preoccupation with portability to the extent that literary narratives come to revolve less around domestic inheritance than departure and, accordingly, less around the symbolic form of the house than the case. While architectural forms, motifs and metaphors have received extensive literary critical attention, from Ellen Eve Frank's *Literary Architecture* (1979) through to David Spurr's more recent *Architecture and Modern Literature* (2012), this emphatic turn towards a portable paradigm from the late nineteenth century has largely been overlooked to date.[5] Chapter 1, in tracing this portable turn, begins by aligning its arc with the very origins of one of the presiding images in literary architectural scholarship, the 'house of fiction'.

HENRY JAMES AND THE HOUSE OF FICTION

The 'house of fiction' is an expression in common critical currency, usually employed to refer to fictional form as a built structure. It can be found to imply something solid and hermetic, often synecdochically representative of a larger social whole. However, tracing the term back to its root source in Henry James's 1908 Preface to the New York edition of *The Portrait of a Lady* (first published in 1881) serves to complicate this understanding. James was far from being the first author to explicitly conceive of writing as building or of the novel as a bricks and mortar construction, but he is credited with coining that now-habitual phrase. I would like to read the image as it appears in his Preface in several different though interrelated ways here: on its own terms; in relation to the novel to which the Preface was retrospectively attached; as expressive of a four-square and hermetic nineteenth-century structure which aspires towards the expansive mobility of modernism; and, most importantly, as an intriguing reflection upon the uncertain imaginative status of property and proprietorial culture in Edwardian England. To read the work of an American writer in an English context is justified, given James's expatriated position at the time of the composition both of the novel and the later Preface, published not long before he adopted British citizenship. *The Portrait of a Lady* was written between Florence and Venice, but, as he himself observes, the 'few preceding years' had been spent in London, and it is the novel 'where James makes the most articulate use of Englishness, in culture, ideology, but first and most memorably, in place'.[6] The Preface itself places *The Portrait of a Lady* in an English literary context, paying tribute to *Romeo and Juliet, Adam Bede, The Mill on the Floss, Middlemarch* and *Daniel Deronda* as providing antecedents for the creation of his heroine, Isabel Archer.[7] Correspondingly, it must be assumed that James's 'house of fiction' owes its significance as an image to the great English literary houses above all, and, as I will argue, James's structural model can be read, in part, as a comment upon prevailing concerns surrounding the question of property in Britain in the first decade of the twentieth century.[8]

We might start then with *The Portrait of a Lady,* the novel that instigates this well-known architectural figure. Beginning with afternoon tea at the English country house of Gardencourt ('the most characteristic object in the peculiarly English picture I have attempted to sketch', the narrator notes), it is a novel replete with architectural figures of its own.[9] These textual structures – whether metaphorical or actual, defensive or inaccessible, domestic abodes or psychic retreats, viewed from the inside or the outside – have been thoroughly documented by critics from a variety of angles.[10] Yet whatever angle is taken, the supremacy of the architectural paradigm is assumed and foregrounded. In Elizabeth Boyle Machlan's illustrative words, '[a]rchitectural metaphors underlie all elements in the text, from plot to character'.[11]

Far from providing one more account of literary architecture in James's *The Portrait of a Lady,* I mean to argue instead that it is the very relevance of a literary architectural framing mechanism which is centrally at issue from the outset, particularly when the novel is read through the backward-looking lens of his 1908 Preface. 'I don't care anything about his house', Isabel Archer comments disparagingly upon the proprietorial grounds of the conventional Victorian marriage during a conversation with Mme Merle on the subject of a possible suitor. Mme Merle responds to this assertion with the following oft-quoted piece of advice:

> 'When you have lived as long as I, you will see that every human being has his shell and that you must take the shell into account. By the shell I mean the whole envelope of circumstances. There is no such thing as an isolated man or woman; we are each of us made up of a cluster of appurtenances. What do you call one's self? Where does it begin? Where does it end? It overflows into everything that belongs to us – and then it flows back again. I know that a large part of myself is in the dresses I choose to wear. I have a great respect for *things!* One's self – for other people – is one's expression of one's self; and one's house, one's clothes, the books one reads, the company one keeps – these things are all expressive'.[12]

How far should the shell – and the house must be seen as the paradigmatic nineteenth-century shell – be taken into account? Mme Merle takes a stance on this question which, in its emphasis on the defining importance of the individual's 'cluster' of personal 'appurtenances', is typical of her time (though no doubt also incited by her own conspicuous want of the security of a domestic shell.)[13] Isabel, in turn, objects to Mme Merle's conception of self, and her oppositional stance must be seen as exceptional for the period: '"I don't agree with you . . . Nothing that belongs to me is any measure of me; on the contrary, it's a limit, a barrier, and a perfectly arbitrary one."'[14] It is a response which registers an undercurrent of resistance to the very idea of the inextricability of self and surrounding shell at the end of the nineteenth century. Isabel asserts here the material irreducibility of character; the irreducibility of Isabel Archer to a lady in a portrait or, indeed, a lady in a house.

Isabel's stance might be exceptional, but it is posited as the stance of an exceptional person and thus only singularly applicable. It is Isabel alone whose measure cannot quite be taken in the novel. '"It polishes me up a little to talk with you"', subsequent suitor Gilbert Osmond flashes an early glint of a sinister charm not yet fully unleashed, '"– not that I venture to pretend I can turn that very complicated lock I suspect your intellect of being!"'[15] Osmond does, however, later presume to attempt Isabel's lock, but gets her measure wrong, and this erroneous calculation is cited as the chief cause of their later marital strife. Isabel's lock is never successfully turned. Her cousin Ralph Touchett intuits this ultimate failure early on and in the same metaphorical terms:

> it was not exactly true that Ralph Touchett had had a key put into his hand. His cousin was a very brilliant girl, who would take, as he said, a good deal of knowing; but she needed the knowing, and his attitude with regard to her, though it was contemplative and critical was not judicial. He surveyed the edifice from the outside, and admired it greatly; he looked in at the windows, and received an impression of proportions equally fair. But he felt that he saw it only by glimpses, and that he had not yet stood under its roof. The door was fastened, and though he had keys in his pocket he had a conviction that none of them would fit.[16]

If Isabel cares nothing for the house of her early suitor, she herself is posited as a house which forms a centre of chivalrous attention but into which access is denied. Isabel is never quite unlocked as a character, yet she is herself eventually subsumed within the 'house of darkness, the house of dumbness, the house of suffocation' that is Osmond's own 'beautiful mind'.[17] Though she initially challenges the materiality of self, she cannot later escape the very material dimensions of the ultimate prison of that selfhood. Her realisation of this situation of imprisonment echoes and inverts her own original response to Mme Merle: 'She could live it over again, the incredulous terror with which she had taken the *measure* of her dwelling. Between those four walls she had lived ever since; they were to surround her for the rest of her life.'[18] This is the dwelling she is compelled, whether by force or her own perverse will, through Osmond, to occupy. Isabel is caught, however, in more than Osmond's house. Michael Levenson, in his study of modernist character, argues that

> the struggle between character and form often takes the aspect of a conflict between tradition and modernity and that one way to understand this moment of transition in the history of the novel is in terms of

nineteenth-century characters seeking to find a place in twentieth-century forms.[19]

I quote Levenson here because, to my mind, the reverse is equally true. In the case of many a late-nineteenth-century novel, and none more so than *The Portrait of a Lady*, the struggle is between certain enduring traits in narrative structure and certain innovations in literary character. In retrospect, Isabel Archer might be read as a modernist character caught in a nineteenth-century house of fiction, one that by the 1908 Preface is just beginning to make known the measure of its own vulnerability.

Critical debate on the politics of property was coming to a head in Britain around the time of James's Preface. The question of whether individual freedom is enabled or constrained by private property had become a troubling sticking point for an increasingly fractured Liberal Party around the turn of the century, a period marking a 'watershed of ideas about the relationship between property and citizenship in Britain'.[20] Tensions were arising between classical liberal advocates of a free market economy who sought to safeguard the liberating right to private property, cordoned off from state intrusion, and proponents of a new form of liberalism who called for systematic governmental intervention in favour of a more egalitarian distribution of wealth (a conviction culminating in David Lloyd George's controversial 'People's Budget' in 1909, which imposed, among other things, severe taxes on the landed gentry in order to fund welfare reform). Caught between these two opposing lines of thought, the status both of house and householder was set for drastic reappraisal from a political point of view. As Jordanna Bailkin notes, the 'driving question of property – how it was defined, owned, and exchanged – was linked to competing notions of the British government as an individualist or collectivist endeavour'.[21] This 'driving question of property' was at the forefront of public thought. If the novel titles of works by E. M. Forster and John Galsworthy alone during this period are anything to go by, it was at the very forefront of the literary imagination as well.[22] David Medalie comments upon this trend in the context of a discussion of the destabilising effects of the liberal crisis as manifested in the work of Forster:

> It is . . . far from coincidental that the country house features so prominently in much Edwardian literature: it is a retreat in both senses of the word – a place of sanctuary and of withdrawal, of dismay in the face of change.[23]

But the country house was also, crucially, positioned at the fulcrum of political, social and cultural change itself.

It would be no overstatement of the case to claim that the fate of the house as an imaginative construct was on the line during this period. 'In this house of his there was writing on every wall', Soames Forsyte acknowledges in Galsworthy's 1906 novel *The Man of Property*.[24] The novel is set in the mid-1880s and turns around the possibility of and potential repercussions resulting from the escape of Soames's beautiful wife, Irene, from his acquisitive grasp. The writing, it seems, is on the patriarchal wall in this case and, by extension, on the wall of the fictional house. Galsworthy himself registers an oblique concern as to the effect of this proprietorial crisis on the very form of the novel. In the following passage, the Forsyte 'habitat' is likened to the novel as conventionally conceived:

> All Forsytes, as is generally admitted, have shells, like that extremely useful little animal which is made into Turkish delight; in other words, they are never seen, or if seen would not be recognised, without habitats, composed of circumstance, property, acquaintances, and wives, which seem to move along with them in their passage through a world composed of thousands of other Forsytes with their habitats. Without a habitat a Forsyte is inconceivable – he would be like a novel without a plot, which is well-known to be an anomaly.[25]

It is striking how close the sentiments expressed in this passage are to the sentiments expressed by Mme Merle in *The Portrait of a Lady*, except that 'every human being' has been reduced tellingly to 'all Forsytes'. If Isabel Archer is an exceptional element in 1881, she is not quite so by 1906, just as the 'novel without a plot' would soon become something less of a complete anomaly. We might say that Galsworthy is exhibiting, in the words of David Spurr, 'a certain nostalgia for architectural and narrative meanings whose coherence derived from their reliable reflection of established order in the realms of politics, religion, economy, education'.[26] A similar kind of nostalgia is evident in Vita Sackville-West's retrospective novel *The Edwardians,* first published in 1930. At the beginning of the novel, the main character, Sebastian, is found escaping from his hosting duties 'upon the roof' of his stately family home, Chevron.[27] This is an estate which he is set to inherit and from which he is eventually tempted away, on the very last page, on an expedition with the explorer Leonard Anquetil, who sees Chevron as a 'dead thing, an anachronism, an exquisite survival'.[28] It is subsequently imagined as 'an old skeleton that has been laid to rest out of sight and whose presence everyone has conspired to ignore'.[29] Sackville-West picks up on a conspiracy to ignore the changing status of the architectural paradigm, as well as the disparity between a manifest solidity and an implicit fragility, which is a characteristic feature of the image of the house in Edwardian fiction.

In James's 'house of fiction' image, however, the 'old skeleton' is distinctly on display. Offhand uses of the phrase take little account of its origins, and the image that has largely been subsumed into literary discourse is a much simplified, even antithetical, version of James's original model.[30] A close reading of his model reveals a disfigured structure in the throes of transition:

> The house of fiction has in short not one window, but a million – a number of possible windows not to be reckoned, rather; every one of which has been pierced, or is still pierceable, in its vast front, by the need of the individual vision and by the pressure of the individual will. These apertures, of dissimilar shape and size, hang so, all together, over the human scene that we might have expected of them a greater sameness of report than we find. They are but windows at the best, mere holes in a dead wall, disconnected, perched aloft; they are not hinged doors opening straight upon life. But they have this mark of their own that at each of them stands a figure with a pair of eyes, or at least with a field-glass, which forms, again and again, for observation, a unique instrument, insuring to the person making use of it an impression distinct from every other. He and his neighbours are watching the same show, but one seeing more where the other sees less, one seeing black where the other sees white, one seeing big where the other sees small, one seeing coarse where the other sees fine. And so on, and so on; there is fortunately no saying on what, for the particular pair of eyes, the window may *not* open; 'fortunately' by reason, precisely, of this incalculability of range. The spreading field, the human scene, is the 'choice of subject'; the pierced aperture, either broad or balconied or slit-like and low-browed, is the 'literary form'; but they are, singly or together, as nothing without the posted presence of the watcher – without, in other words, the consciousness of the artist.[31]

James's rather peculiar vision has a marked post-impressionist, even incipiently cubist, dimension. It gestures to the more fragmented, reflexive modes of early-twentieth-century modernism, while simultaneously retaining the general outline of the domestic forms of nineteenth-century and Edwardian realism. The impetus to omnisciently survey and control a subject within set and precise boundaries is evident here in the very idea of representing fiction as a concrete structure of containment. As a structure, however, with 'not one window, but a million', each dissimilar in shape and size, not to mention a multitude of watchers with their multitudinous perspectives, James's 'house of fiction' might be said to correspond less to a Victorian house than a sort of proto-modernist Tower of Babel.

The 'house of fiction', as James presents it, certainly bears a resemblance to the Tower of Babel. The Babelian myth is derived from the Old Testament, where the elaborate construction stands for a potent and threatening monolingual order ultimately fractured by a force more powerful:

And the whole earth was of one language, and of one speech.

2 And it came to pass, as they journeyed from the east, that they found a plain in the land of Shinar; and they dwelt there.

3 And they said one to another, Go to, let us make brick, and burn them throughly. And they had brick for stone, and slime had they for morter.

4 And they said, Go to, let us build us a city and a tower, whose top *may reach* unto heaven; and let us make us a name, lest we be scattered abroad upon the face of the whole earth.

5 And the Lord came down to see the city and the tower, which the children of men builded.

6 And the Lord said, Behold, the people *is* one, and they have all one language; and this they begin to do: and now nothing will be restrained from them, which they have imagined to do.

7 Go to, let us go down, and there confound their language, that they may not understand one another's speech.

8 So the Lord scattered them abroad from thence upon the face of all the earth: and they left off to build the city.

9 Therefore is the name of it called Babel; because the Lord did there confound the language of all the earth; and from thence did the Lord scatter them abroad upon the face of all the earth.[32]

If we take James's 'house of fiction' to be a transitional structure, suggesting the perspectival fracturing of a Victorian literary architectural mode, then an evocation of the above narrative is certainly both pertinent and compelling, in surface as much as in substance. Even a cursory overview of artistic conceptions of the Biblical narrative, from the work of Pieter Brueghel the Elder ('The Tower of Babel' and 'The "Little" Tower of Babel', both 1563) and Alain Manesson Mallet ('The Tower of Babel', 1683) in the sixteenth and seventeenth centuries through to Gustave Doré ('The Confusion of Tongues', 1865) in the nineteenth century, confirms a many-windowed façade as a standard pictorial element. More often than not, the apertures are shown to be of 'dissimilar shape and size', as in James's image. More specifically, James's expression 'mere holes in a dead wall' might justly be said to describe the tiny slit-like holes in the imposing conical structure envisioned by Doré in his 'The Confusion of Tongues' (1865), engraved not long before the former began work on *The Portrait of a Lady.*[33] Yet the superimposition of tower upon house is suggestive in ways over and above simple appearance and implies an eventual desertion and fragmentation. If the Tower of Babel is about the confusion of tongues, then the 'house of fiction' is about a perspectival confusion of views in that the act of interpretation is pointedly splintered in the image. At the same time, the house itself yet remains, a memorial to a proprietorial and literary architectural approach to fiction on the part of the author, an approach that is with difficulty sustained in the new century. It is as if James is intuitively aware that his oddly crafted house, which, in its very name, is posited as the legacy of a nineteenth-century realist literary tradition, will ultimately be abandoned, a distorted 'old skeleton' of its former glorified self, the posted watchers having dispersed elsewhere.

His image, in its context, further reflects a false sense of Edwardian foursquare security, and its later critical appropriation as a paragon of solidity also mimics the retrospective nostalgic sense of that period as a sort of 'social Eden before the Fall, a time of order and harmony, the golden evening of Empire and the Pax Britannica'.[34] Early in *The Edwardians*, Sebastian is shown to evaluate the Chevron estate: 'All was warmth and security, leisure and continuity. An order of things which appeared unchangeable to the mind of nineteen hundred and five.'[35] It is his sister, Viola, who reveals this chimera for what it really is: '"I regard our love for Chevron as a weakness."'[36] By implication, the very monument of Chevron itself, and the tradition for which it stands, literary as well as socio-political, must equally be seen as structurally weak. That it is a woman who challenges the Edwardian sense of domestic security in Sackville-West's novel is of no small significance. Nancy Armstrong and Jeff Nunokawa, among others, have charted the creation of a domestic ideal from the late eighteenth century, at the centre of which was the woman, without whose presence the 'entire domestic framework would collapse'.[37] The domestic woman, viewed as 'safe estate' (secure from the unpredictable oscillations of the market), was the stabilising element in the structural whole.[38] Viola is shown to depart Chevron – and in that all-too-pivotal year of 1910, as somewhat teasingly highlighted by Virginia Woolf – in favour of an independent life at the conclusion of the novel. This is much to the chagrin of her mother, who appeals to 'all the standards within her range' to stop her.[39] Viola's reaction is important: '"Oh, darling mother!" she had said, "all that rubbish!" To [her mother] it was not rubbish; it was the very bricks of life.'[40] This is an exchange which articulates (and, crucially, through the voice of a young woman) the waning symbolic value of the 'bricks' of domestic ideology at this time.

Galsworthy's *The Man of Property* is of interest here as a study of the loosening of such a domestic ideology, on one level, but as a novel also caught up in it, on another. The exercise of absolute control over the figure of Irene is described in that novel as 'the greatest – the supreme act of property'.[41] The potential loss of this defining feature of the Forsyte 'habitat', around which the novel turns, must be seen as tantamount to a literary disruption of great proportions. By the same token, it is suggested that greater freedom for women would mean greater freedom for the novel and that these two matters are intimately related to the idea of property, connections that we will explore in more detail in Chapter 2. Galsworthy might implicitly criticise rigid novelistic conventions in his satirical treatment of the Forsyte habitat throughout, but he is also bound by such conventions, in the shape of the novel *with* a plot, just as James's 'house of fiction' is celebrated and undermined as a monument at one and the same time. 'The figure of Irene', Galsworthy comments in his 1922 Preface, 'never, as the reader may possibly have noticed, present except through the senses of other characters, is a concretion of disturbing Beauty impinging on a possessive world.'[42] An aesthetic 'concretion', Irene is an 'acquisition' of the author's as much as an acquisition of Soames Forsyte. Her subjectivity remains unaccounted for, even if Galsworthy manifests sympathy to the point of envisioning her ultimate departure from her husband. While, thematically speaking, he can understand and approve of the rupture caused to the established social order by the departure of the domestic woman, formally speaking, Galsworthy is himself an authorial 'man of property'. That is to say, while he is conscious of the imposed ideological aspect of domesticity in the novel, he does not have the capacity to see beyond the associated framework of the house.

James, too, presents a proprietorial struggle in his Preface to *The Portrait of a Lady*, a novel which questions literary architectural presupposition. Like Galsworthy's *The Man of Property*, his 'house of fiction' anticipates abandonment not, as in the Tower of Babel narrative, through the interference of a force more powerful, an external god-like entity (Edwardian writing might be said to be god-less), but because the subject is palpably clamouring to break away.[43] Those figures with their field glasses may well be looking into the 'house of fiction', but the subject is earnestly gazing out. The subject, as far as the Preface itself goes, is, of course, Isabel Archer. The 'house of fiction' was, first and foremost, the house of Isabel, as James saw it. Just after the delineation of the model of his 'large building' around the 'conception of a certain young woman affronting her destiny', he remarks:

> It came to be a square and spacious house – or has at least seemed so to me in this going over it again: but, such as it is, it had to be put up around my young woman while she stood there in perfect isolation.[44]

James continually speaks of his subject in proprietorial terms, to a much greater degree than Galsworthy. He recalls, for instance, taking 'complete possession' of his 'single character' as an 'acquisition'.[45] As such, whether consciously or unconsciously, James aligns himself with the character of Gilbert Osmond within the novel itself, a disconcerting affiliation identified by more than one critic.[46] 'Her mind was to be [Osmond's]', Isabel is shown to reflect in an attempt to come to terms with, or at least to better understand, her situation of containment: 'It would be a pretty piece of property for a proprietor already far-reaching.'[47] She is thus doubly contained, as character and subject, thematically and textually, in Osmond's 'house of darkness' and James's 'house of fiction'.

James, however, unlike Galsworthy, does gesture at an alternative in his Preface, and that alternative takes a mobile shape. In examining structural figurations of consciousness in James's novel, Jill M. Kress draws attention to the range of conflicting metaphors at work in his 1908 Preface; metaphors of enclosure as set against metaphors of expansion, elusive against concrete, the natural world of the garden against the civilised world of the interior, and so on.[48] She sees these tensions as evocative of the 'contest between the personal and the social world', battled out through his exploratory conceptualisations of the mind.[49] One conflict she overlooks, however, in this otherwise comprehensive account of the 'constant exchange of metaphors' in novel and Preface, is that of the contradictory representations of form in mobile and immobile terms.[50] Throughout James's Preface, the architectural metaphor is sustained and elaborated upon. His original aspiration is to construct a 'literary monument', and he goes into this process of construction in some detail: 'The bricks, for the whole counting-over – putting for bricks little touches and inventions and enhancements by the way – affect me in truth as well-nigh innumerable and as ever so scrupulously fitted together and packed-in.'[51] Yet within this sustained and detailed visualisation, we come across a striking metaphorical lapse, or, at least, an inconsistency. In outlining the function of his secondary cast of characters in *The Portrait of a Lady*, as well as in his other novels, he makes the following comment:

> Each of these persons is but wheels to the coach; neither belongs to the body of that vehicle or is for a moment accommodated with a seat inside. There the subject alone is ensconced, in the form of the 'hero and heroine', and of the privileged high officials, say, who ride with the king and queen ... Maria Gostrey and Miss Stackpole then are cases, each, of the light *ficelle*, not of the true agent; they may run beside the coach 'for all they are worth', they may cling to it till they are out of breath (as poor Miss Stackpole all so visibly does), but neither, all the while, so much as gets her foot on the step, neither ceases for a moment to tread the dusty road.[52]

Earlier in the Preface, the same 'subject' is neatly and comfortably 'ensconced' in the 'house of fiction', in the 'posted presence of the watcher ... the consciousness of the artist', a consciousness overriding in importance that of the subject inside.[53] However, in the above passage, as eccentric in its way as the 'house of fiction' passage, we might say that the watcher is left behind at his post as the subject is shown to speed away alone in an absconding coach. If James aligns himself, intentionally or unintentionally, with Gilbert Osmond in his acquisitive approach to Isabel, we might equally say that he aligns himself, intentionally or unintentionally, with Miss Stackpole in his unsuccessful attempt to keep pace with a bolting vehicle. This subversive centrifugal impulse, suggesting a conflict between mobile and immobile understandings of fiction, just apparent in James's Preface, further undercuts the overarching importance of the 'house of fiction' and, by extension, enunciates the inadequacy of literary architectural approaches to formal vision in the early twentieth century.

E. M. FORSTER'S CIVILISATION OF LUGGAGE

Underlying all of these Edwardian architectural representations, we can perceive a shift towards a nomadic metaphysics, inevitable in retrospect, and rendered with no small degree of anxiety in E. M. Forster's 1910 novel *Howards End*. However, I begin this discussion not with Forster but with Max Beerbohm, whose 1900 essay, 'Ichabod', presents a rather more sanguine interpretation of the implications of this shift. Indeed, Beerbohm's essay and Forster's novel can be read together as presenting contrasting appraisals of the seductive power of a mobilities paradigm, as well as the concomitant emergence of a portable aesthetic. 'So I have sat down to write, in the shadow of a tower which stands bleak, bare, prosaic, all the ivy of its years stripped from it', Beerbohm explains in 'Ichabod'.[54] The essay appeared in *The Cornhill Magazine* in 1900 and was reprinted in his collection *Yet Again* in 1909, the year after the publication of James's 'house of fiction' Preface. You would be forgiven for thinking Beerbohm's subject was yet another declining turn-of-the-century house. On the contrary, 'it is merely a hat-box', though a treasured hat-box, to which he refers.[55] The essay is framed as a homage to the fascination of the luggage label, prompted by the accidental obliteration of his carefully assembled hat-box collection. Each label within this lost collection had marked an achieved geographical destination. The obliteration of his labels is attributed to the trunk-makers, who took it upon themselves to clean the box in addition to their assigned commission to fix a broken lock. Having outlined the impetus behind the creation of a 'private autobiography' through this collection of labels, the pleasure derived from it and the pain caused by its loss, Beerbohm then ends the essay with an expression of positive renewal: 'I will begin all over again. There stands my hat-box! Its glory is departed, but I vow that a greater glory awaits it. Bleak, bare and prosaic it is now, but – ten years hence!'[56]

Forster's *Howards End,* published not long after Beerbohm's essay reappeared in *Yet Again*, also concludes on a note of renewal of sorts, as the Schlegel sisters find themselves installed at Howards End with the physically disempowered Henry Wilcox and the legally enfranchised, though illegitimate, son of Helen Schlegel and Leonard Bast, intended heir to the house after Margaret Schlegel: 'They were building up a new life, obscure, yet gilded with tranquillity.'[57] It is an image of rebuilding at odds, however, with a pervading hostility throughout the novel to the *un*-tranquil idea of 'bricks and mortar rising and falling with the restlessness of the water in a fountain', a restlessness epitomised by what Forster calls, with an inflection of disdain mixed with trepidation, the 'civilisation of luggage'.[58] It is fair to say that the 'ten years hence!' mark on Forster's envisioned horizon does not rouse the same kind of excitement in spite of this reconstructive outlook. Yet he manifests an awareness that his fictional house must move with the times or become redundant. My aim here is to think about the implications of the emergence of the 'civilisation of luggage' on the architectural conception in Forster's text. Does Howards End represent a final doomed retreat from the inevitability of modern cosmopolitanism, or is it shown to borrow from a rising nomadic spirit of mobile regeneration in order to retain a synecdochic legitimacy at the end of the novel? Is the novel about the strange death of the liberal house or the creation of a new model for a fictional house of 'the future as well as the past', to adopt Margaret Schlegel's own words?[59]

Beerbohm's hat-box offers a tentative sketch of the possibility of a portable literary model in embryo, as well as some insights into what a future modernist mode of dwelling in motion might mean. What is noticeable even upon a cursory reading of his essay is how often the hat-box is identified with architectural constructions. Quite apart from its 'tower'-like attributes, we are told that it 'has had many tenants' and that his lost collection of labels had the personal significance of a 'monument'.[60] On the surface, it seems as if such designations are unwittingly used to supply a necessary air of prestige to what is 'merely' a hat-box. '[I]t needs, I am well aware', he is compelled to justify early on, 'some sort of explanation to enable my reader to mourn with me'.[61] Even his concluding aspiration towards renewal is prompted by literary architecture: 'Like Carlyle, when the MS. of his masterpiece was burned by the housemaid of John Stuart Mill, he might have begun all over again and builded a still nobler monument on the tragic ashes.'[62] In certain ways, the hat-box replicates the function of the house in providing a framework for individual narrative continuity through the careful accumulation of the 'autobiographic symbols' that are the labels.[63] Yet in a number of key ways, it departs from the architectural paradigm. In marking his 'every darling escape' as opposed to his permanent establishment, it is evidently no house of fiction, in the popular sense of James's phrase.[64] To begin with, we are alerted to the potential narrative discontinuities facilitated by the hat-box, in that narrative itself is rendered open to interpretation, albeit often implicitly guided interpretation. He admits to using the hat-box as an instrument of 'bluffing' and 'pretence'.[65] Furthermore, its synecdochic scope is narrowed to the autobiographical level of the individual subject rather than the more expansive gesture of the house to society at large, a subjective synecdochic scope Beerbohm himself suggests: 'It was part and parcel of my life.'[66] In broader social terms, it must be seen as a fragmented rather than a representative unit and one that is geared towards manipulative effect. This is not to say that the house does not likewise provide an opportunity for the manipulation of self-image. We need only refer to Mme Merle's typically Victorian stance on the expressive nature of the shell in *The Portrait of a Lady*. The difference here is that Beerbohm's hat-box allows for recurrent self-transformation and a much more unstable form of suggestibility, something denied to all but the most affluent of house-owners, as Deborah Cohen has acknowledged of domestic spaces around the turn of the twentieth century: 'Only the truly wealthy could harmonise their interiors with a restless personality. For everyone else, purchases proved rather more durable than the frame of mind that had spawned them.'[67] Beerbohm might couch the representation of his hat-box in architectural terms as a stripped monument to be reconstructed or refurbished. He might uphold it from the first as an object which requires justification as a cause for commemoration, as indicated from the very first line: 'It is not cast from any obvious mould of sentiment.'[68] However, it becomes apparent that the architectural analogue is misplaced in the essay, a token indication perhaps of the lingering power of a sedentarist point of view which has already given way.

Indeed, despite his continuous reversion to an architectural frame of reference as well as his opening justificatory statement, Beerbohm goes to great lengths to convince us of the importance and relevance of this mere hat-box in and of itself and as a prospective vision of the shape a new kind of fictional experience might conceptually take. If the hat-box, with its accumulated autobiographical labels, is envisioned as a kind of narrative text, this process of conceptualisation is also speculatively inverted. In the essay, Homer's *The Odyssey* is playfully reimagined in the form of a modern, label-smothered hat-box, some time before its groundbreaking modernist reincarnation at the hands of James Joyce with *Ulysses* in 1922:

> Romance, exhilaration, self-importance, these are what my labels symbolised and recalled to me. That lost collection was a running record of all my happiest hours; a focus, a monument, a diary. It was my humble Odyssey, wrought in coloured paper on pig-skin, and the one work I never, never was weary of. If the distinguished Ithacan had travelled with a hat-box, how finely and minutely Homer would have described it – its depth and girth, its cunningly fashioned lock and fair lining withal! And in how interminable a torrent of hexameters would he have catalogued all the labels on it, including those attractive views of the Hôtel Circe, the Hôtel Calypso, and other high-class resorts. Yet no! Had such a hat-box existed and had it been preserved in his day, Homer would have seen in it a sufficient record, a better record than even he could make, of Odysseus' wanderings. We should have had nothing from him but the Iliad.[69]

Beerbohm proffers a mobile alternative fit for modernity's instinctual nomad, a 'monument' on the move, a portable form which records and narrates the 'humble' odyssey of the unfixed modern subject. He imbues, in so doing, the ordinary with an epic quality, as many modernist writers would go on to do. Though the narration of a journey is an age-old literary device, the analogue Beerbohm puts forward here is a deliberately current one.[70] Extended passages in the essay respond to a new machinery of fast-paced movement, technological advancements allowing for the possibility of dispelling 'as if by sudden magic, the old environment', and cultivating a widespread nomadic imperative, specific to the period.[71]

Most importantly, Beerbohm's account of his hat-box reflects a shift towards more dynamic understandings of literary form. That such a formal model is wanting at the beginning of the twentieth century is implied by his sense that literature has not yet caught up with the developing science of twentieth-century motion:

> I await that poet who shall worthily celebrate the iron road . . . I look for another, who shall show us the heart of the passenger, the exhilaration of travelling by day, the *exhilaration* and *romance* and *self-importance* of travelling by night.[72]

Note the repetition of the terms applied to his hat-box labels at the beginning of the indented quotation above. By implication, a portable model is anticipated as the proper framing device for the 'wanderings' of the modern Odysseus, as set against the backdrop of a progressively mobile world. The essay's concluding expression of renewal might well be derived from an architectural example, but it owes more to the regenerative appeal of luggage, which permits the modern individual to dispel, 'as if by sudden magic', the old personality.

The project of dispelling the old, whether personality or environment, is nowhere on Forster's literary agenda in *Howards End*, though he is arguably as attuned to new possibilities in this novel as any of his Edwardian or up-and-coming modernist contemporaries. He may not quite 'celebrate' the 'iron road' or the 'heart of the passenger', but he is, nonetheless, almost obsessively preoccupied with these facets of modernity and thus merits close attention as a 'poet' of twentieth-century modernisation. The question of his affiliation to modernism is contentious, to say the least, and often forms the focal point of discussion around the writer. Some critics swing to extremes in defining his work in this light.[73] Most, however, converge somewhere in an uncertain middle (and this is, in part, because it has become less viable to think of modernism itself in terms of set and secure categories). Alistair M. Duckworth and David Medalie employ the words 'awkward' and 'reluctant' respectively to account for his relationship to modernism, while Levenson claims that he 'belongs neither with the stout Edwardians . . . nor with the lean modernists'.[74] These extreme positions and centralised tensions can be mapped onto *Howards End* itself, through Forster's figuration of the confrontation and interaction between sedentarist and nomadic points of view as respectively typified in the forms of house and case.

It is a novel at once very sensitive to change as a function of a mobile 'make it new' mentality and resistant to it at the same time. The seeds of such a resistant sensitivity are noticeable in a diary entry written in reaction to an aeroplane flight in January 1908:

> It's coming quickly and if I live to be old I shall see the sky as pestilential as the roads. It really *is* a new civilisation. I have been born at the end of the age of peace and can't expect to feel anything but despair . . . The little houses that I am used to will be swept away and the fields will reek of petrol, and the airships will shatter the stars . . . such a soul as mine will be crushed out.[75]

This passage conveys nothing of the 'romance' and 'exhilaration' of a mobile modernity so ardently proclaimed in Beerbohm's essay. Forster's outright and emotional rejection of the aeroplane and the motor car, those modernist set pieces, anticipates his problematic approach to modernity and modernisation in *Howards End* a couple of years later. Here, the 'new civilisation', obliquely mentioned in the diary entry, is construed more specifically as the 'civilisation of luggage', a specification crystallising that earlier unformed perception of flux into a recognisable shape and implicating the little house – luggage's age-old opposite – as the primary emblem of resistance:

> The feudal ownership of land did bring dignity, whereas the modern ownership of movables is reducing us again to a nomadic horde. We are reverting to the civilisation of luggage, and historians of the future will note how the middle classes accreted possessions without taking root in the earth, and may find in this the secret of their imaginative poverty.[76]

Forster's narrator equates 'imaginative poverty' with an atavistic rootlessness here (a rootlessness that is, contrary to his presentiments, celebrated as an empowering factor in modernism by *literary* historians of the future). At the same time, this later novel also exhibits a more resigned acceptance of techno-logical advancements in favour of mobility as well as an interest in bringing such advanced technologies into play in realising his ambition of unifying dis-parate elements, as set out in his epigraph 'Only Connect'. Andrew Thacker, in exploring the representation of the motorcar in the novel, finds it to be an ambivalent symbol on the whole and not entirely a harbinger of petrol-fuelled pestilence, as his 1908 diary entry would have it; it certainly signifies the condi-tion of nomadic uprootedness he so loathed, but it can simultaneously be said to promote the model of connectivity he so desired.[77] Forster is not blind to the fact that connection requires movement. The challenge he takes upon himself in *Howards End* is to retain the stable reference points of the 'little houses',

while encouraging positive and meaningful, rather than primitive and pur-
poseless, movement between them. On a structural level, this objective might
be described as the formal assimilation of a now inevitable modern mobility
without the loss of the 'sanctity' and sanctifying influence of an underlying
architectural principle.[78]

This is made difficult by Forster's own unwillingness to think outside the
house as a metaphor for fiction, and an evident fear of a flux which cannot
quite be made to conform to his conception. It becomes progressively clear
that he intends, not to externally connect with the 'civilisation of luggage', but
to make this new civilisation connect with his house; to invite it in. Yet the
very idea of hospitality is shown to come under palpable strain in the novel.
(Indeed, the trouble begins with a crisis of hospitable relations arising from
Helen's brief engagement to Paul Wilcox on a visit to Howards End itself.)
Virginia Woolf perceived Forster to have a 'four-square attitude which walks
up to life as if it were a house with a front door, puts its hat on the table in
the hall, and proceeds to visit all the rooms in an orderly manner'.[79] She goes
on to demonstrate the way in which his literary works reflect this mind-set,
in the sense that he pervades his early works, *Howards End* above all, as a
'careful hostess'.[80] Woolf's astute description of Forster as a 'careful hostess'
goes some way to account for what has been perceived as his discomfiture
when it comes to modernist literary innovation. Modernity is portrayed as
a hostile and intrusive spectre at the door of his fictional house, on the one
hand, and what Thacker calls the 'flux that always seems to burst through the
containing strategies of literary form', on the other.[81] The unspoken rules of
fictional hospitality are at stake in Forster's work, not least the sovereignty of
the host.[82] For Forster, the dreaded prospect of a cosmopolitan culture signals
the displacement of host by guest as sovereign force leading ultimately to the
dissolution of that very relationship. In the erasure of difference and spatial
belonging implied by cosmopolitanism, the words 'host' and 'guest' must lose
their meaning, a scenario which also puts the 'sanctity' of the house as sovereign framework at risk.[83] Further to this, the sovereignty of his own position
as author is far from assured in this novel. Why, we might ask, does Woolf
rather pointedly use the feminine designation 'hostess' as opposed to 'host'?
This might first be seen as a reference to his sexual orientation. As Elizabeth
Langland has documented, Forster experienced a period of particular 'sexual
confusion' during the composition of *Howards End,* resulting, she argues, in
a defensive misogyny (a misogyny Woolf also felt in her relations with the
writer), but equally a subversion of binary understandings of gender.[84] Yet the
word additionally emphasises, I believe, the ambiguity of Forster's status in a
literary architectural sense. The false sovereignty of the classic Victorian and
Edwardian figure of the 'hostess', who cannot claim actual 'ownership' and
thus any genuine authority over the house upon which her hospitality prevails,

mirrors his own status as an author with a 'four-square' supervisory attitude to his text, while, at the same time, intuiting the free textual play at work beyond his control and despite his 'careful' arrangements. By the time *A Passage to India* is written in 1924, this is a hostess, Woolf adds, 'in some disillusionment both with his guests and with his house'.[85]

Yet in 1910, the house is still Forster's bedrock against disillusionment, and if he sets out to assimilate modern mobility within the architectural paradigm on a conceptual level, he works through this on a thematic level in his treatment of the figures of Margaret and Helen Schlegel. Their provisional homelessness and how to settle it forms the problematic core of the narrative, addressed directly by Margaret midway through: '"It's really getting rather serious. We let chance after chance slip, and the end of it is we shall be bundled out bag and baggage into the street. We don't know what we *want*, that's the mischief with us."'[86] As in James's Preface, we can observe an awakening doubt about the woman's domestic place here, revolving around the question of what Helen and Margaret '*want*'. It is a word Forster himself pointedly italicises. If the Schlegel sisters don't know what they 'want', this is also because they don't know what they 'lack', and we should be alert to this play on the dual meaning of 'want' in the above quotation. Want is fuelled by want and this Schlegel 'mischief' might be better understood in the context of a new consumer culture, in which the creation of a lack had become the motive force and 'desire began to replace property' as a means of self-identification.[87] Forster's 'civilisation of luggage' must also be regarded as a new civilisation of consumer desire, shaped more specifically around the desires of the female consumer.[88] Hostile as the Schlegels outwardly are to an ethos of consumer capitalism as it intrudes upon the unseen world of inner spirituality they mean to cultivate, their own nascent sense of discontent correlates somewhat jarringly with more commercial-led forms of mobility and changeability. It is for this reason that the question of what Margaret and Helen want has larger implications, a point accentuated by Margaret herself a few lines later: '"We cannot settle even this little thing; what will it be like when we have to settle a big one?"'[89] The 'big' question, as far as this discussion goes, is how far this Schlegel hesitancy about committing to a settlement, as implicitly linked to a wider form of commercial unrest, on the one hand, and female unrest, on the other, will be permitted to impact upon the architectural form of the novel. Modern consumerism, according to Rachel Bowlby, turned merchandise into a 'spectacle', and this is a word Forster himself chooses to convey a life '[u]nder cosmopolitanism, if it comes'.[90] It is implied that the rewards of sustained engagement will be denied to the 'nomadic horde' in line with the formation of a superficial capitalist ethos of surfaces and surface values.[91] When Margaret remarks upon the Schlegel 'mischief' of uncertain desire, Helen responds as follows: '"No, we have no real ties."'[92] Forster makes a concerted effort to prove for the remainder of the text, that the modern ownership of movables is a poor substitute for ties of a more enduring sort. The novel works to bring the Schlegels, as much as the reader, around to this conclusion and back to the fictional house, albeit on new terms.

That he succeeds comes as something of a surprise. "'I didn't know myself it would turn into a permanent home"', Margaret remarks at the end of the novel, upon finding herself 'still stopped at Howards End', over a year after the death of Leonard Bast.[93] It is important to reiterate that if the Schlegels (and their Schlegel-Bast progeny) are shown to finally oversee Howards End, this is a role which sits uncomfortably with a certain free-spiritedness, on the part of the two sisters, though particularly Helen, which surfaces throughout. Preparing for the move from Wickham Place, for example, causes Margaret much anxiety, but it is plain that this has less to do with the loss of the home she shares with her siblings than with a realisation of the obstructive bulk of their belongings:

> Chairs, tables, pictures, books, that had rumbled to them through the generations, must rumble forward again like a slide of rubbish to which she longed to give the final push and send toppling into the sea . . . Round every knob and cushion in the house sentiment gathered, a sentiment that was at times personal, but more often a faint piety to the dead, a prolongation of rites that might have ended in the grave.[94]

This free indirect discourse of Margaret's seems to rise up as a resistant strain against the dominating narrative voice, a voice pointedly disapproving of 'that shallow makeshift note that is so often heard in the modern dwelling-place'.[95] Margaret's momentary longing to be rid of the responsibility attached to belongings, as well as her suspicion of the falsity of the 'sentiment' gathered around these objects, echoes Isabel Archer's sense that belongings are an arbitrary barrier rather than an accurate measure of the self. It further effects a subversive appeal to 'only disconnect' which undercuts Forster's well-known epigraph as well as the dominant narrative voice. "'Are you aware that Helen and I have walked alone over the Apennines, with our luggage on our backs?"', Margaret asks Henry during a conversation about possible honeymoon destinations.[96] This image of Helen and Margaret making their solitary way with their luggage on their backs is somehow more powerfully evocative of the wider mischievous leanings of women at large at this time than Forster's later projection of Margaret sitting in the garden of Howards End and lamenting the current 'craze for motion'.[97]

Margaret and Helen are ultimately recovered *from* the 'civilisation of luggage' *for* the house. Yet it should be emphasised here that Forster would have seen this as a progressive step with the status of women more broadly in mind. In a paper delivered to the Working Men's College Old Students'

Club in 1906, he remarks upon the fact that the early Victorian woman was 'regarded as a bundle of goods' and that the 'woman of today' is 'by no means a bundle of goods', marriage no longer being the aspirational mark on her horizon.[98] These are representative definitions we will take up in a more interrogative fashion in Chapter 2, but the point to make here is that, when it came to writing *Howards End*, Forster was doubtless intent on proving that his Schlegels were women 'of today' in this manner; not bundles of goods, in other words. It should also be emphasised that their very establishment in Howards End is in the interests of domestic reform, an attempt to contain the current craze for commercial/cosmopolitan spectacle and motion through channelling its energy. We must not forget that the disruptive guest at the house at the beginning of the novel becomes, in effect, the mother of the future host at the end. This is a radical coup pointing to a complete overhaul of the house and, significantly, a mobilisation of household and hospitable relations, on the level of the woman's place as well as class (two of the bugbears of the troubled Liberal Party at this time). Crucially, it is a coup that does not affect the legitimacy of the underlying architectural order.[99] Levenson argues that Forster's work affords an insight into 'what the development of the novel might have been if at the turn of our century it had endured an evolutionary, rather than a revolutionary, change'.[100] I agree with Levenson to the extent that Forster works within and maintains a fidelity to an old form even if he purports to develop it, but we ought not to lose sight of the revolutionary aspect of these developments from the inside. Far from representing one more attempt to ignore an old skeleton, *Howards End* represents, on the contrary, an attempt to update the house of fiction in order to establish its continued relevance in a new era of perpetual motion. The problem is that the house has already become outdated as a model, and Forster's efforts smack of resuscitation rather than renewal or refurbishment. Though internal mobility is manifested within Howards End, the house itself remains static and so it does not work as a formal vision for a new age. Its sticking point is that it is stuck. Forster creates a 'new life' for the 'nomadic horde' in a reformed but still-standing monument.[101] This does present a solution if a short-term and somewhat contrived one. Consequently, in spite of the moving and shaking of a mobile modernity, *Howards End* – both house of brick and 'house of words' – remains standing though it is unable to hide the strain of its resistance to the pressures of modern flux, encapsulated by the idea of a 'civilisation of luggage'.[102] Beerbohm, on the other hand, intuits that luggage gives form to flux. He endows his hat-box with the semblance of a monument, but this does not detract from its motive force and thus its pertinence as a modern framing device, even if this is yet a fleeting daydream.

MODERNIST DWELLING AND WRITING IN MOTION

'*Hasty Packing*: what excitement that phrase can still engender', Paul Fussell cannot refrain from uttering in parenthesis in response to an advertisement for the Travellers' Library, a series of pocket-sized travel books published by Jonathan Cape from 1926.[103] 'Hasty Packing' would indeed have made an apt chapter title amid the array of rather eccentrically titled chapters in his well-known interwar study, *Abroad: British Literary Traveling Between the Wars*, slotted, for instance, between Chapter 3's 'I Hate It Here' and Chapter 4's 'The Passport Nuisance'. It encapsulates the restless impulse to escape an artistically compromising situation, the disruption of stable notions of the individual (where hasty packing corresponds, as it repeatedly does in modernist writing, to the hasty packing of a new identity) and the disengagement from a distasteful political reality in the interests of a 'holiday taste for the incognito', to use Elizabeth Bowen's words from her 1927 novel *The Hotel*.[104] In the years following Beerbohm's fleeting 1900 daydream, the hastily packed bag becomes an increasingly prominent literary feature, often engendering the kind of excitement referred to by Fussell. But it is in the immediate aftermath of the First World War, which prompts a more urgent need to uproot, that Foster's larger vision of a 'civilisation of luggage' comes to full fruition. In Fussell's words, the 'fantasies of flight and freedom which animate the imaginations of the 20s and 30s and generate its pervasive images of travel can be said to begin in the trenches'.[105] Later in this book, I will lay bare the fragility of such fantasies through addressing the impact of both wars on evolving understandings of portability, but, for the remainder of this chapter, the discussion will focus on the promises embedded in the figuration of the packed bag as an experimental locus for a new mode of dwelling in motion and, correspondingly, writing in motion.

The particular interwar fantasy of dwelling in motion formed part of a wider drive to operate at greater and greater speeds. 'Travelling at high speed through space was the first recreation of the age', Robert Graves and Alan Hodge note in their social history of the period, *The Long Week-End*.[106] Throughout the 1920s, *Punch* publishes cartoon after cartoon in response to the emerging popularity of the fleeting weekend getaway and motoring holiday, repeatedly caricaturing the 'speed-fiends' of the moment.[107] It is in this context that the very idea of travelling light becomes something to aspire to. Whereas in the past, such a practice had been either the luxury or the burden of the few, now it was the primary social call of the many. Even *The Times* devoted an extended editorial to the subject of 'Travelling Light' in 1922:

> He who travels light is in a fair way to travel happily. But the happy state is not compassed without effort. There must first be wisdom in selecting

the absolutely necessary, determination in discarding all else, and skill in the bestowal of the essential minimum. The principle is applicable not to train journeys alone. It is no less valid for the greater journey which is life ... Greatest encumbrance of all is fear of the journey's end.[108]

Travelling light came, as such, to be seen not just as a practical approach to facilitating movement but as an all-encompassing ethos requiring rigour and resolve, an ethos neatly articulated by Lucy Tantamount in Aldous Huxley's *Point Counter Point* (1928): 'Living modernly's living quickly. You can't cart a wagonload of ideas and romanticisms around with you these days.'[109]

Forster's fears were clearly coming to pass, and, accordingly, the palpable sense of modern lives moving quickly was perceived to be having a noticeable effect on the shape of fiction between the wars. 'It is seldom that a story is static', Watkin Haslam writes in a 1930 article entitled 'Transport in the English Novel' for *LMS Magazine,* the official organ of the eponymous railway company.[110] In considering the fictional role played by transport throughout literary history, he concludes in the present with the motorcar:

> our novelist of to-day has his characters motoring all over the world, and always in the most classic model cars, which flash them hither and thither, and give to the action of his plot that breathless speed which seems now to be essential.[111]

In such a context, packing was, understandably, on the modernist authorial brain, a fixation which tapped into the broader cultural consciousness of the time. Even speed fiends required things in transit. Prompted to recount some of her dreams during a psychoanalytic session in Rose Macaulay's 1921 novel *Dangerous Ages,* the elderly and troubled Mrs Hilary is shown to respond: '"Oh, the usual things, I suppose. Packing; missing trains; meeting people; and just nonsense that means nothing. All the usual things that everyone dreams about."'[112] Everyone at a particular historical moment, we might add. Though Macaulay is primarily concerned with sending up the psychoanalytic process in this passage as a whole (Mrs Hilary is not meant to be taken too seriously and ultimately gains very little from her analysis), her playful rendering of the subconscious preoccupations of 'everyone' in the wake of the war is telling. The compulsion to pack, the lure of the train and the fear of the train not taken as well as the intrigue of the stranger (more often than not, a stranger with a bag within a train carriage) are the very stuff of fiction at this time. These are elements Woolf uses to good effect in representing the changing approach to conveying character in fiction in 'Mr Bennett and Mrs Brown' (1924), written shortly after Macaulay's novel. By the 1930s, these modernist leitmotifs are almost taken for granted. When an anonymous 1931 *Punch* spoof of the authorial techniques and concerns of three contemporary literary figures – Ernest Hemingway, Aldous Huxley and J. B. Priestley – reimagines the same scene three times in their respective writing styles, the scene in question involves a couple waiting with their luggage on a train station platform.[113]

Subconscious preoccupations, leitmotifs and spoofs aside, packing became integrally related to the writing process in a very hands-on way for many displaced writers. Such writers were not just living but writing out of suitcases and carried their developing manuscripts with them on the move. Most famous among these mobile modernist manuscripts were those of Ernest Hemingway, comprising a large number of story drafts. These manuscripts were lost as they were carried in a valise by his wife Hadley on route from Paris to Lausanne, as recounted in *A Moveable Feast* (1964).[114] The notes for the latter work were themselves also lost for a period. Hemingway, seeking perhaps a more secure mode of transportation, had commissioned Louis Vuitton to create a custom-made library trunk in 1927 for the specific carriage of his books, notes and stationery.[115] This same trunk would go on to contain the notebooks which became the basis for *A Moveable Feast* and was later abandoned and forgotten in the basement of the Paris Ritz in the 1930s, only to be fortuitously rediscovered by Hemingway in 1956.[116] Much of Hemingway's writing can be defined, as such, by its *move*ability and thus its capacity both to evade and return to its author. As Paul Smith has observed, his various manuscript-filled trunks and valises might be seen as 'metaphors for his life', an observation which can be extended to other modernist figures.[117] Katherine Mansfield's writing life, for example, began and remained in a state of perpetual instability which meant that her works were often doubly in progress, both physically and conceptually, as a 1909 journal entry illustrates:

> In this room. Almost before this is written I shall read it from another room, and such is life. Packed again, I leave for London. Shall I ever be a happy woman again? Je ne pense pas, je ne veux pas. Oh, to be in New York! Hear me! I can't rest. That's the agonising part.[118]

When Duquette, also notably an author, envisages people as peripatetic portmanteaux in her later wartime story, 'Je ne parle pas français', he might well have been commenting on Mansfield's own authorial mode.

Luggage served, likewise, as a private authorial archive in transit for Jean Rhys, blurring the boundary between individual and narrative trajectories. In describing her beginnings as a writer in *Smile Please: An Unfinished Autobiography* (1979), Rhys recounted a frenzied burst of creativity involving a composition expanding to three-and-a-half exercise books, written over the course of a couple of days: 'I put the exercise books at the bottom of my suitcase and piled my underclothes on them. After that whenever I moved I took the exercise books but I never looked at them again for many years.'[119] Lodged underneath her underclothes, Rhys's notebooks assume a position in a mobile archive which conjoins the intimate with the professional, the body with the text, the life with the work. In fact, these notebooks, describing a dark episode of abandonment and depression in Rhys's own life, later laid the groundwork for her favourite of her novels, *Voyage in the Dark* (1934). The novel takes a dislocated female protagonist (Anna Morgan) as its subject and, not incidentally, marks the degree of that protagonist's vulnerability through her underclothing: 'And your hideous underclothes. You look at your hideous underclothes and you think, "All right, I'll do anything for good clothes. Anything – anything for clothes."'[120] 'Anything' amounts to an ill-fated affair with a wealthy businessman, a liaison which ultimately only intensifies her marginalisation, leading to prostitution as a way of making ends meet, an outcome inspired by Rhys's own experience. Rhys enacts the perfect synthesis of modernist dwelling and writing in motion, her notebooks describing a displacement they also undergo. Later on, in recounting a move from London to Paris, she even goes so far as to suggest that this very act of carriage was of providential significance in her authorial development:

> I had only my suitcase with me, with some underclothes, some blouses and the exercise books. Why I clung to those as I did is something that completely puzzles me. I never looked at them, and the idea of showing them to anyone else never entered my head, yet wherever I went, I took them. This is one of the reasons why I believe in Fate.[121]

Rhys, Hemingway and Mansfield represent just a sample of the many modernist writers who conspicuously lacked the security of traditional offices and bureaus. Such writers cultivated, whether deliberately or unwillingly, a portable work ethic, one that both threatened and sustained their writing practice.

Indeed, there is evidence to suggest that unstable, transitory and, occasionally chaotic working conditions were productive in more ways than one. James Joyce's writings were similarly packed and transported in ways that imbued them with the threat of loss while also influencing their composition. He is known to have written parts of *Ulysses* (1922) and *Finnegans Wake* (1939) on an upturned piece of luggage, which functioned as an improvised and transportable desk. As he himself wrote to Harriet Weaver in 1923, capturing something of the unruliness of his surroundings during this period, '[t]he wild hunt still continues in the Paris jungle, stampede of omnibuses and trumpets of taxi-elephants etc and in this caravanserei peopled by American loudspeakers I compose ridiculous prose writing on a green suitcase which I bought in Bognor'.[122] His faintly exasperated tone is misleading here. As Valérie Bénéjam establishes, in describing his rejection of the silence offered by Valéry Larbaud's soundproof study, Joyce's habitual portability and inhabitation of transitional spaces, in fact, fostered his creativity:

Joyce's perpetual movement and travelling abroad, as far as it seems particularly associated with his writing, is indeed in complete contradiction with the traditional image of the writer's necessary silence and isolation, from which an original voice could arise. Joyce's most original writing arose from bustle and agitation instead, from the sound of lifts and hotel luggage, from the movement going on around him.[123]

Comparable claims can be made about Mansfield. A close reading of her journal suggests that her 'agonising' restlessness was also crucial to her working practice. It infiltrates her work on every level, from thematic to stylistic, in line with an increasing awareness, as her health declined, of her writing as a race against time, her own portable lifestyle thus mirroring a compositional haste. 'I wrote as fast as possible for fear of dying before the story was sent', she remarked in 1922 of her experience of writing 'The Daughters of the Late Colonel'.[124] Like Joyce, some of her best stories were composed in a state of intense upheaval, not least among them 'Je ne parle pas français', which was written 'on a variety of sheets of paper, on the trains, in the hotel, in a flurry of frantic creativity'.[125] Her lifestyle undoubtedly contributed to her perception of her writing process as 'a kind of race to get in as much as one can before it *disappears*', producing an urgency which was a motive force for her authorial exertions.[126]

Yet portability equally induced a kind of authorial pragmatism in certain writers. Hemingway's experience of the precariousness of carriage in losing his papers could be said to have provided a *raison d'être* for, or, at the least, confirmed the value of his pared-down, minimalist aesthetic. When he sought guidance from Ezra Pound on dealing with his lost manuscript on the move, Pound responded (to Hemingway's gratification): 'If the middle i.e. *FORM* of a story is right one ought to be able to reassemble it from memory . . . If the thing wobbles and won't reform then it . . . never wd. have been right.'[127] To put this simply, Hemingway's loss should force the essential elements of his work into relief, filtering out the superfluous. One way of interpreting Pound's response, then, is as an extreme expression of the necessity for judiciousness on the part of the writer in transit, whether applied to words or things, a judiciousness that can be enabling as often as inhibiting.[128] In other words, in dealing with the absence or reduction of tangible resources, memory and selectivity become vital assets to the portable writer (in line with the sentiments of that 1922 *Times* editorial on travelling light). Mansfield's own experience of intense portability served to cultivate a scrupulousness to the extent that what she sought to retain was, in its entirety, her intended authorial legacy. This approach is elucidated in a rather prophetic 1922 journal entry, written the year before her death:

Tidied all my papers. Tore up and ruthlessly destroyed much. This is always a great satisfaction. Whenever I prepare for a journey I prepare as though for death. Should I never return, all is in order. This is what life has taught me.[129]

Portable working practices and attendant hazards came to have a marked impact on the creative visions of such writers, as well as the kinds of protagonists they conceived. Joyce is exemplary in this respect. Stephen Dedalus is shown to sit on an 'upended valise' in the Martello Tower in the opening pages of *Ulysses*, as if to confirm his conspicuous homelessness, his lack of a proper domestic affiliation, from the start.[130] This opening image also sets the scene for the novel's broader relegation of conventional domestic structures to the background, in favour of the ever-changeable flux of an urban exterior scape, on the one hand, or, on the other, alternative interiors, whether tavern or brothel, tower or shelter. In spite of its great scale, this is a work shaped more by the dynamics and complexity of circulatory flows than ideas of monolithic, architectonic construction. Portability accompanies movement at every point in the text, largely through Joyce's preoccupation with pockets (Leopold Bloom's above all) as portable repositories in which 'all sorts of everyday objects are hoarded, relinquished, exchanged, and transferred'.[131] Peter Sims has suggested that the 'pocket might be viewed as Joyce's Homeric parallel for the hold of Odysseus' ship, the place where provisions for the voyage are stored after being taken on board'.[132] From this point of view, it becomes a form of small-scale luggage for the quotidian adventurer. If Beerbohm, in 'Ichabod', saw his hat-box as 'a sufficient record, a better record than even he could make, of Odysseus' wanderings',[133] the pocket is Joyce's equivalent in the form of a portable repository of odds and ends, from the arbitrary (the kidney, chalk, bottles of rum)[134] to the everyday/functional (money, watches, soap, handkerchiefs, cough mixture, dental floss),[135] the sacred (Bloom's mysterious potato, tokens of endearment, photos of loved ones),[136] to the profane (snippets of underwear, pornographic books, illicit letters, knives).[137] In this, it gestures at *Ulysses*'s own capacity as a container of textual odds and ends. Indeed, it is particularly noticeable how often pocket contents comprise documents of diverse kinds – pocketbooks, various letters, library books, newspapers, editorial typesheets, advertisement cut-outs, postcards, telegrams and so on[138] – thus conveying a sense of textual portability and variability at one at the same time. Portability and variability go hand in hand here, the pockets exhibiting, in miniature, Joyce's embrace of a range of media and forms of expression within his larger work. In Sims's words, the 'pockets that appear in the text are symbolic of the covers into which *Ulysses* is bound'.[139] Apart from reflecting the text's emphasis on routes over and above roots, this form of symbolism ties in with an anti-establishment repudiation of a more restrictive and longstanding domestic ideology, specifically associated with an English fictional tradition, enacting a zooming out from house to nation to empire. Pockets allow for the carriage and concealment, the circulation and exchange not just of the illicit but also the seemingly inconsequential, channelling a counter-cultural flow of materials beyond the house and its implied value system. I briefly highlighted such a process at work in a contained and marginal way in Dickens's *Bleak House*, but, unlike Dickens, Joyce gives overall precedence to individual trajectory over established framework, as a comparison of the titles of the two works alone indicates. But the pocket-text analogy can be pushed one step further. Joyce's pocket preoccupation can be coupled with a pickpocketing preoccupation in *Ulysses*. 'Beware of pickpockets', Bloom cautions in 'Circe', echoing the earlier words of the bigoted Citizen in 'Cyclops', which are aimed squarely at Bloom himself in his absence: 'We know those canters . . . preaching and picking your pocket.'[140] We must assume that these words are also aimed aslant at Joyce. In producing a work as self-consciously and densely allusive as *Ulysses* – 'I am quite content to go down to posterity as a scissors and paste man', he once claimed – Joyce might justly be described as literature's most prominent intertextual pickpocket.[141]

Beyond Joyce, analogies between packing and writing and, by the same token, unpacking and interpretation abound after the First World War. These analogies come in various shapes and sizes. While portability demanded a judicious and selective approach to fiction for some writers, as in the cases of Mansfield and Hemingway, others, more akin to Joyce, associated portability with freedom over and above constraint. Woolf's 1919 aspiration to produce a diary like a 'capacious hold-all', Aldous Huxley's similarly stated aim to create 'a novel in which one can put all one's ideas, a novel like a hold-all', and Pound's initial understanding of the *Cantos*, in an early draft, as a 'rag-bag to stuff all [the modern world's] thought in', provide some further examples of the latter.[142] These writers alternatively imagine an all-embracing flexibility and ampleness in their portable analogues of choice, reflecting a strain of modernist writing which aimed to incorporate all facets and phenomena of everyday life, while retaining a sense of fluidity.[143] Significantly, Edith Wharton used the same analogic mode to criticise a particular type of modern writing. She took issue, in 1934, with what she felt to be the 'over-packed' nature of 'new' works in the stream-of-consciousness vein: 'The mid-nineteenth century group selected; the new novelists profess to pour everything out of their bag.'[144] She later added that what critics were branding a 'new form of novel' was 'really only a literary hold-all'.[145] As these examples together suggest, portable analogues can be found to vary considerably in effect or intention. Woolf's journal conception would not have been altogether in keeping with her conception of the novel, setting her apart from Huxley, for example, while Wharton's employment of the analogue serves the purpose of disparagement rather than endorsement. Yet, whatever the ultimate purpose and whether the stress is on selectiveness or inclusiveness, all present formal visions which respond in multiple ways to a rising culture of portability.

As we move into the 1930s, we can begin to see the growth of an almost routine alignment between luggage and literature (both figurative and manifest) to the extent that such an alignment starts to surface in fictional representations of writer-figures: for example, expatriated literary aspirant Edgar Naylor in Cyril Connolly's *The Rock Pool* (1936) who carries the 'neatly clipped together' bundles of the manuscript of a biography in an attaché case or W. H. Auden's 1938 image of a poet 'rummaging into his living' to fetch the 'images out that hurt and connect' in 'The Composer'.[146] However, to trace the evolution of these visions of portability from the earlier conceptions of Mansfield, Joyce, Huxley et al. in the late 1910s and 1920s through to Connolly and Auden in the late 1930s is to perceive a shift in emphasis, whereby portable forms and analogues come to attain a level of interrogatory self-reflexiveness. As the Second World War begins to appear inevitable in the mid-to-late 1930s, dwelling in motion becomes the preserve of the politically displaced, while the fantasy of travelling light takes on an increasingly nightmarish hue.

NOTES

1. G. K. Chesterton, 'The Everlasting Nights', in *G. K. Chesterton at the* Daily News: *Literature, Liberalism and Revolution, 1901–1913*, ed. Julia Stapleton (London: Pickering & Chatto, 2012), p. 255. This was first published in the *Daily News* on 7 November 1901.
2. Ibid., p. 255.
3. Ibid., p. 254.
4. Georg Lukács, *The Theory of the Novel: A Historical-Philosophical Essay on the Forms of Great Epic Literature*, trans. Anna Bostock (1916; London: Merlin, 2006), p. 41.
5. It would be impossible and, indeed, inappropriate to present a comprehensive survey of literary architectural studies here. I will be referring to more specific studies, where relevant, as the book advances. For a more general overview of the breadth of work in this area, see, for example: Chiara Briganti and Kathy Mezei, 'Reading the House: A Literary Perspective', *Signs*, 27.3, Spring 2002, pp. 837–46; Charlotte Grant, 'Reading the House of Fiction: From Object to Interior 1720–1920', *Home Cultures*, 2.3, 2005, pp. 233–50; and Philippa Tristram, *Living Space in Fact and Fiction* (London: Routledge, 1989).
6. Henry James, 'Preface to *The Portrait of a Lady*' (1908), in *The Critical Muse: Selected Literary Criticism*, ed. Roger Gard (Harmondsworth: Penguin, 1987), p. 494; Nicola Bradbury, 'Henry James and Britain', in *A Companion to Henry James*, ed. Greg W. Zacharias (Chichester: Wiley-Blackwell, 2008), p. 408.
7. James, 'Preface to *The Portrait of a Lady*', p. 487.
8. Sandra K. Fischer, for one, emphasises the 'monumental effect of the English country house on James and his narrative imagination' in her phenomenological reading of the novel. Jill M. Kress, on the other hand, demonstrates the influence of American literary predecessors (specifically Nathaniel Hawthorne and Ralph Waldo Emerson) in his application of the architectural metaphor. However, it is his engagement with English literary architecture – which, I would contend, leaves the most pronounced stamp upon *The Portrait of a Lady* and his 'house of fiction' image – that interests me here. See Sandra K. Fischer, 'Isabel Archer and the Enclosed Chamber: A Phenomenological Reading', *The Henry James Review*, 7.2–3, Winter–Spring 1986,

p. 48; Jill M. Kress, *The Figure of Consciousness: William James, Henry James and Edith Wharton* (New York: Routledge, 2002), pp. 72–3.

9. Henry James, *The Portrait of a Lady* (1881; London: Penguin, 1997), p. 6.
10. Perceiving the metaphor of the house to be as important to the novel as to the Preface, Elizabeth Jean Sabiston characterises it ultimately as an 'ambiguous symbol', signalling both creative possibility and inhibiting containment for the heroine, a conflict also identified by Elizabeth Boyle Machlan, though her own overarching focus is on the distinctive generic expectations associated with each of the built structures in the novel. For R. W. Stallman, houses point beyond themselves to the 'accumulated refinement and corruption of civilisation, our tragic history echoing throughout the House of Experience'. See Elizabeth Jean Sabiston, *The Prison of Womanhood: Four Provincial Heroines in Nineteenth-Century Fiction* (Basingstoke: Macmillan, 1987), p. 129; Elizabeth Boyle Machlan, '"There are plenty of houses": Architecture and Genre in *The Portrait of a Lady*', *Studies in the Novel*, 37.4, Winter 2005, pp. 394–411; R. W. Stallman, 'The Houses that James Built – *The Portrait of a Lady*', *The Texas Quarterly*, Winter 1958, p. 189.
11. Machlan, '"There are plenty of houses"', p. 402.
12. James, *The Portrait of a Lady*, pp. 186–7.
13. The nineteenth-century fascination with personal appurtenances is generally seen as an outcome of the industrial revolution and the increasing affluence and influence of a middle class that was beginning to look to objects in order to assert distinction and individuality. For a discussion of the 'Victorian preoccupation with possessions' from a specifically British point of view (but one which certainly also sheds some light on the remarks of the American expatriate Mme Merle), see Deborah Cohen, *Household Gods: The British and Their Possessions* (New Haven, CT: Yale University Press, 2006), p. xi.
14. James, *The Portrait of a Lady*, p. 187.
15. Ibid., p. 239.
16. Ibid., p. 59.
17. Ibid., pp. 395, 396.
18. Ibid., p. 395. Emphasis added.
19. Michael Levenson, *Modernism and the Fate of Individuality: Character and Novelistic Form from Conrad to Woolf* (Cambridge: Cambridge University Press, 1991), p. xii.
20. Jordanna Bailkin, *The Culture of Property: The Crisis of Liberalism in Modern Britain* (Chicago: University of Chicago Press, 2004), p. 11.
21. Ibid., p. 11.
22. Consider, for example, Forster's *A Room With a View* (1908) and *Howards End* (1910) as well as Galsworthy's *The Man of Property* (1906) and *The Country House* (1907).
23. David Medalie, *E. M. Forster's Modernism* (Basingstoke: Palgrave-Macmillan, 2002), p. 11.
24. John Galsworthy, *The Man of Property* (1906; London: Heinemann, 1953), p. 70. This is a Biblical reference to the *Old Testament* 'Book of Daniel'. The writing on the wall of King Belshazzar's palace forecasts the fall of the Babylonian empire. 'The Book of Daniel', 5: 1–31, in The Bible: Authorized King James Version, ed. Robert Carroll and Stephen Prickett (1611; Oxford: Oxford University Press, 1998), pp. 975–7.
25. Galsworthy, *The Man of Property*, p. 94.
26. David Spurr, *Architecture and Modern Literature* (Ann Arbor: The University of Michigan Press, 2012), p. 27.

27. Vita Sackville-West, *The Edwardians* (1930; Leipzig: Tauchnitz, 1931), p. 8.
28. Ibid., p. 60.
29. Ibid., p. 70.
30. Ellen Eve Frank is one of the few critics who has remarked upon its eccentricity: 'The house James raises curiously suggests no building we have ever seen; and if we were to see it, it would be "ugly" by even Victorian standards.' Ellen Eve Frank, *Literary Architecture: Essays Towards a Tradition: Walter Pater, Gerard Manley Hopkins, Marcel Proust, Henry James* (Berkeley: University of California Press, 1979), p. 182.
31. James, 'Preface to *The Portrait of a Lady*', p. 485.
32. 'Genesis', 11:1–9, in The Bible, pp. 11–12. Emphasis in original.
33. The two, in fact, were acquainted, as evidenced by a letter James wrote to his father in April 1876. Henry James, *The Letters of Henry James*, vol. 2, ed. Leon Edel (Cambridge, MA: Belknap-Harvard University Press, 1975), p. 37.
34. Alistair M. Duckworth, *Howards End: E. M. Forster's House of Fiction* (New York: Twayne, 1992), p. 3.
35. Sackville-West, *The Edwardians*, p. 44.
36. Ibid., p. 213.
37. Nancy Armstrong, *Desire and Domestic Fiction: A Political History of the Novel* (1987; Oxford: Oxford University Press, 1989), pp. 82–3. See also Jeff Nunokawa, *The Afterlife of Property: Domestic Security and the Victorian Novel* (Princeton: Princeton University Press, 1994), pp. 6–7, 10, 12–13, 83.
38. Nunokawa, *The Afterlife of Property*, p. 10.
39. Sackville-West, *The Edwardians*, p. 271.
40. Ibid., p. 271.
41. Galsworthy, *The Man of Property*, p. 299.
42. Galsworthy, 'Preface', in *The Man of Property*, p. vi.
43. Richard Ellmann has drawn attention to the secularist bent of Edwardian writers even if the appeal of religious imagery was still strong: 'Almost to a man, Edwardian writers rejected Christianity, and having done so, they felt free to *use* it, for while they did not need religion they did need religious metaphors.' Richard Ellmann, 'Two Faces of Edward', in *A Long the Riverrun: Selected Essays* (Harmondsworth: Penguin, 1989), p. 152. Emphasis in original.
44. James, 'Preface to *The Portrait of a Lady*', p. 486.
45. Ibid., p. 485.
46. See Machlan, '"There are plenty of houses"', p. 404; Kress, *The Figure of Consciousness*, p. 82.
47. James, *The Portrait of a Lady*, p. 398.
48. Kress, *The Figure of Consciousness*, pp. 61–86.
49. Ibid., p. 62.
50. Ibid., p. 76.
51. James, 'Preface to *The Portrait of a Lady*', pp. 489, 492.
52. Ibid., p. 492. Emphasis in original.
53. Ibid., p. 485.
54. Max Beerbohm, 'Ichabod' (1900), in *Yet Again* (1909; London: Heinemann, 1928), p. 116.
55. Ibid., p. 115.
56. Ibid., pp. 131, 134.
57. E. M. Forster, *Howards End* (1910; New York: Signet-Penguin, 1992), p. 266.
58. Ibid., pp. 38, 119.
59. Ibid., p. 268.
60. Beerbohm, 'Ichabod', pp. 115, 123.

61. Ibid., p. 115.
62. Ibid., p. 134.
63. Ibid., p. 125.
64. Ibid., p. 125.
65. Ibid., pp. 128, 129.
66. Ibid., p. 117.
67. Cohen, *Household Gods*, p. 141.
68. Beerbohm, 'Ichabod', p. 115.
69. Ibid., pp. 123–4.
70. Recent literary critical work on the subject of modernist mobility has stressed the specificity of the modernist journey. Andrew Thacker notes that the 'movement through new material spaces and by means of the new machines of modernity . . . grounds a more abstract sense of flux and change that many modernist writers attempted to articulate in their texts'. Similarly, Alexandra Peat, though concerned more particularly with the invocation of the pilgrimage narrative, lays a comparable stress on contextual grounding: 'The reconfiguration of the sacred journey in modernism reflects technological, political and social changes, as well as shifts in ethical and spiritual beliefs; it responds to a world that was, in all senses of the phrase, on the move.' Andrew Thacker, *Moving Through Modernity: Space and Geography in Modernism* (Manchester: Manchester University Press, 2003), p. 8; Alexandra Peat, *Travel and Modernist Literature: Sacred and Ethical Journeys* (New York: Routledge, 2011), p. 9.
71. Beerbohm, 'Ichabod', p. 118. By 1920, the first Ministry for Transport had been established in Britain, incited by these technological advancements. It was tasked with concentrating on what the new Minister for Transport, Sir Eric Geddes, called the 'science of movement', an area which he claimed, in a speech delivered at the London School of Economics in October 1919, had been overlooked up to that point and demanded further attention, a necessity precipitated by the war. See 'Editorial', *Transport and Travel Monthly (Formerly The Railway and Travel Monthly)*, 20, April 1920, p. 215.
72. Beerbohm, 'Ichabod', p. 118. Emphasis added.
73. According to Randall Stevenson, in an essay in the *Cambridge Companion* dedicated to the writer, though Forster should be considered 'alongside modernist writing', he is himself 'scarcely a modernist', and he goes so far as to suggest that the use of modernism as a criterion of assessment might even be reductive. Jane Goldman, on the other hand, in thinking about his treatment of female characters in the same volume, contends that an 'acknowledg[ment] that Forster is a modernist writer' makes for a better understanding of his work. See Randall Stevenson, 'Forster and Modernism', in *The Cambridge Companion to E. M. Forster*, ed. David Bradshaw (Cambridge: Cambridge University Press, 2007), pp. 221, 209; Jane Goldman, 'Forster and Women', in *The Cambridge Companion to E. M. Forster*, p. 129.
74. Duckworth, *Howards End*, p. 137; Medalie, *E. M. Forster's Modernism*, p. 1; Levenson, *Modernism and the Fate of Individuality*, p. 78.
75. Cited in Duckworth, *Howards End*, p. 131. Emphasis in original.
76. Forster, *Howards End*, p. 119.
77. Thacker, *Moving Through Modernity*, pp. 46–79.
78. Forster, *Howards End*, p. 175. Again, a secular adoption of religious terminology is notable here, as with James and Galsworthy, as if the house is the last bastion of the spiritual and the sacred when the space of the church is no longer viable in a secular society.
79. Virginia Woolf, 'The Novels of E. M. Forster' (1927), in *The Essays of Virginia Woolf*, vol. 4, ed. Andrew McNeillie (London: Hogarth Press, 1994), pp. 499–500.

80. Ibid., p. 500.
81. Thacker, *Moving Through Modernity*, p. 73.
82. I borrow the term 'sovereignty' here from Jacques Derrida's well-known discussion of hospitality. See Derrida, *Of Hospitality: Anne Dufourmantelle Invites Jacques Derrida to Respond*, trans. Rachel Bowlby (Stanford: Stanford University Press, 2000), pp. 53, 55.
83. For a close analysis of Forster's running critique of cosmopolitanism in *Howards End*, see Mary Ellis Gibson, 'Illegitimate Order: Cosmopolitanism and Liberalism in Forster's *Howards End*', *English Literature in Transition*, 28.2, 1985, pp. 106–23.
84. Setting this apparent misogyny to one side, Langland makes a case, on the contrary, for a radical sexual politics in Forster's novel through his persistent undoing of hierarchical constructions. As for Woolf, we learn from an April 1919 diary entry that she perceived a certain reticence on Forster's part when it came to intellectual women: 'I was beckoned by Forster from the Library as I approached. We shook hands very cordially; and yet I always feel him shrinking sensitively from me, as a woman, a clever woman, an up to date woman.' Yet, as Langland suggests, to take this seeming misogyny at face value would be short-sighted. The comment might even be said to be more illustrative of Woolf's own uncertainty with regard to Forster. The two had a complex relationship, and, as Hermione Lee records, they 'circled warily around each other all their lives'. Indeed, Forster was, throughout, more generous in his appraisals of Woolf's writings than the other way around. Elizabeth Langland, 'Gesturing Towards an Open Space: Gender, Form and Language in *Howards End*', in *E. M. Forster*, ed. Jeremy Tambling (London: Palgrave-Macmillan, 1995), pp. 81–99; Virginia Woolf, *The Diary of Virginia Woolf*, vol. 1, ed. Anne Olivier Bell (London: Hogarth Press, 1977), p. 263 (12 April 1919 entry); Hermione Lee, *Virginia Woolf* (London: Vintage-Random, 1997), p. 273.
85. Woolf, 'The Novels of E. M. Forster', p. 500.
86. Forster, *Howards End*, p. 125. Emphasis in original.
87. David Trotter, *The English Novel in History 1895–1920* (London: Routledge, 1998), p. 13.
88. 'It was above all to women that the new commerce made its appeal', Rachel Bowlby outlines. See Bowlby, *Just Looking: Consumer Culture in Dreiser, Gissing and Zola* (New York: Methuen, 1985), p. 11.
89. Forster, *Howards End*, p. 125.
90. Bowlby, *Just Looking*, p. 6; Forster, *Howards End*, p. 206.
91. Forster, *Howards End*, p. 119.
92. Ibid., p. 125.
93. Ibid., pp. 268, 265.
94. Ibid., p. 118.
95. Ibid., p. 39.
96. Ibid., p. 141.
97. Ibid., p. 268.
98. E. M. Forster, 'Pessimism in Literature', in *Albergo Empedocle and Other Writings by E. M. Forster*, ed. George H. Thomson (New York: Liveright, 1971), p. 135.
99. This reading accords with Langland's review of the radical sexual politics in *Howards End*. Though traditional gender relations are subversively overturned in the text, Langland acknowledges that a patriarchal ideology raises its head once again at the end of the novel in Margaret's 'conquest' of Henry in the 'masculine mode'. I would add that this paradoxical state of affairs is substantiated by the

endurance of the domestic framework. See Langland, 'Gesturing Towards an Open Space', p. 91.

100. Levenson, *Modernism and the Fate of Individuality*, p. 78.

101. Forster, *Howards End*, p. 266.

102. 'If there is on earth a house with many mansions, it is the house of words', Forster wrote in 1951. See E. M. Forster, *Two Cheers for Democracy* (London: Edward Arnold, 1951), p. 90.

103. Paul Fussell, *Abroad: British Literary Traveling Between the Wars* (New York: Oxford University Press, 1980), p. 59.

104. Elizabeth Bowen, *The Hotel* (1927; Harmondsworth: Penguin, 1984), p. 34.

105. Fussell, *Abroad*, p. 4.

106. Robert Graves and Alan Hodge, *The Long Week-End: A Social History of Great Britain 1918–1939* (1940; London: Faber, 1950), p. 281.

107. The 'speed fiend' label appears in an unnamed 1926 cartoon by D. I. Ghilchik, depicting a couple driving through the countryside with the following caption: 'Passenger: "I think the country round here is extraordinarily pretty." Speed-fiend: "Is it? I must see it some day."' D. I. Ghilchik, cartoon, *Punch*, 171, 29 September 1926, p. 362. This is representative of the kinds of speed and motoring related cartoons which recur in the magazine.

108. 'Travelling Light', *The Times*, 27 December 1922, p. 11.

109. Aldous Huxley, *Point Counter Point* (1928; London: Chatto and Windus, 1934), p. 282.

110. Watkin Haslam, 'Transport in the English Novel', *LMS Railway Magazine*, 7.4, April 1930, p. 84.

111. Haslam, 'Transport in the English Novel', p. 85.

112. Rose Macaulay, *Dangerous Ages* (London: W. Collins, 1921), p. 109.

113. 'Going Home: (Three Variations on a Holiday Theme.)', *Punch*, 180, 14 January 1931, p. 52. This tableau calls to mind David Trotter's recent proposal of 'transit' over and above travel writing as more characteristic of this age. One distinguishing feature of transit is that it involves 'suspension' as much as movement. David Trotter, *Literature in the First Media Age: Britain Between the Wars* (Cambridge, MA and London: Harvard University Press, 2013), p. 265.

114. Ernest Hemingway, *A Movable Feast* (1964; New York: Scribner, 2009), p. 69.

115. See Pierre Léonforte, '100 Legendary Trunks', in *Louis Vuitton: 100 Legendary Trunks*, by Pierre Léonforte, Éric Pujalet-Plaà with the collaboration of Florence Lesché and Marie Wurry, trans. Bruce Waille (New York: Abrams, 2010), pp. 259–61.

116. A. E. Hotchner, 'Don't Touch "A Moveable Feast"', *The New York Times*, 19 July 2009, <http://www.nytimes.com/2009/07/20/opinion/20hotchner.html?_r=1> (last accessed 27 January 2016).

117. Paul Smith, '1924: Hemingway's Luggage and the Miraculous Year', in *The Cambridge Companion to Hemingway*, ed. Scott Donaldson (Cambridge: Cambridge University Press, 1999), p. 36.

118. Katherine Mansfield, *The Journal of Katherine Mansfield*, ed. John Middleton Murray (1927; London: Constable, 1954), p. 41. April 1909 entry.

119. Jean Rhys, *Smile Please: An Unfinished Autobiography* (Harmondsworth: Penguin, 1979), p. 130.

120. Jean Rhys, *Voyage in the Dark* (1934; London: Penguin, 1969), p. 22.

121. Rhys, *Smile Please*, pp. 140–1.

122. Quoted in Richard Ellmann, *James Joyce* (New York, Oxford and Toronto: Oxford University Press, 1982), p. 556

123. Valerie Bénéjam, 'Passports, Ports, and Portraits: Joyce's Harbouring of Irish

Identity', *Genetic Joyce Studies 5*, Spring 2005, <http://www.geneticjoycestudies.org/GJS5/GJS5Benejam.htm> (last accessed 28 January 2016).

124. Mansfield, *The Journal of Katherine Mansfield*, p. 287. January 1922 entry.

125. Mary Burgan, *Illness, Gender and Writing: The Case of Katherine Mansfield* (Baltimore: Johns Hopkins University Press, 1994), p. 122.

126. Mansfield, *The Journal of Katherine Mansfield*, p. 287. January 1922 entry. Emphasis in original.

127. Letter from Ezra Pound to Ernest Hemingway, 27 January 1923. Quoted in Smith, '1924', p. 41.

128. Erich Auerbach's famous remarks on the composition of *Mimesis* in Istanbul in the 1940s with limited resources also comes to mind here:

> it is quite possible that the book owes its existence to just this lack of a rich and specialized library. If it had been possible for me to acquaint myself with all the work that has been done on so many subjects, I might never have reached the point of writing.

These restrictions were, of course, the result of Auerbach's flight from Nazi persecution, and this darker side of travelling light will be considered more fully in Chapter 3. See Erich Auerbach, *Mimesis: The Representation of Reality in Western Literature*, trans. Willard R. Trask (Princeton: Princeton University Press, 2003), p. 557.

129. Mansfield, *The Journal of Katherine Mansfield*, p. 292. January 1922 entry.

130. James Joyce, *Ulysses*, ed. Jeri Johnson (Oxford: Oxford University Press, 1998), p. 12.

131. Karen Lawrence, '"Twenty pockets aren't enough for their lies": Pocketed Objects as Props for Bloom's Masculinity in *Ulysses*', in *Masculinities in Joyce: Postcolonial Constructions*, ed. Christine van Boheemen-Saaf and Colleen Lamos (Amsterdam, Netherlands and Atlanta: Rodopi, 2001), p. 165.

132. Peter Sims, 'A Pocket Guide to "Ulysses"', *James Joyce Quarterly*, 26.2, Winter 1989, p. 239.

133. Beerbohm, 'Ichabod', p. 124.

134. Joyce, *Ulysses*, pp. 58, 382, 593.

135. Ibid., pp. 58, 218, 229, 305, 326, 519, 210, 118, 175, 118, 335, 351, 434, 407, 123.

136. Ibid., pp. 175, 450, 75, 606–7.

137. Ibid., pp. 696–8, 70–4, 584.

138. Ibid., pp. 29, 606, 70, 74, 288, 63, 606, 69, 88, 138, 140, 581, 191.

139. Sims, 'A Pocket Guide to "Ulysses"', p. 257.

140. Joyce, *Ulysses*, pp. 416, 319.

141. From a 1931 letter to George Antheil. See James Joyce, *Letters of James Joyce*, vol. 1, ed. Stuart Gilbert (New York: Viking Press, 1957), p. 297.

142. Woolf, *Diary*, vol. 1, p. 266. 20 April 1919 entry. Huxley's words come from an interview conducted by Yoi Maraini, quoted in Donald Watt, 'Introduction', in *The Critical Heritage: Aldous Huxley*, ed. Donald Watt (London: Routledge, 1975), p. 2. At the beginning of an early version of 'Canto 1', published in 1917, Pound suggests that the 'modern world/needs such a rag-bag to stuff all its thought in'. Though this line was omitted in subsequent versions, such a sentiment was retained in contemporary responses to Pound's work. It was described, for example, as a 'mental grab bag' by George Santayana in a 1940 letter, and variations of this phrase recur in Pound criticism. See Ezra Pound, 'Three Cantos', in *Personae: The Shorter Poems*, ed. Lea Baechler and A. Walton Litz (New York: New Directions, 1990), p. 229. The Santayana letter is quoted

in John Tytell, *Ezra Pound: The Solitary Volcano* (New York: Anchor, 1987), p. 256.

143. Amusingly, the difference between the Hemingway and Huxley parodies in the aforementioned 1931 *Punch* sketch chimes with this discussion in that Hemingway's bag is minimalist in its description – 'The breeze was cool, but I was still sweating with the weight of those bags' – while Huxley's is overwrought:

> The bags were extremely heavy, heavy with disgust, with disappointment, with frustration. He carried them one in each hand, a martyr balanced on his knife edge; tralatitiously at every step he felt his unhappy feet being lacerated; his brain writhed under the bludgeonings of angry thought. ('Going Home', *Punch*, p. 52)

144. Edith Wharton, 'Tendencies in Modern Fiction', in *The Uncollected Critical Writings*, ed. Frederick Wegener (Princeton: Princeton University Press, 1996), p. 172.

145. Wharton, 'Permanent Values in Fiction', in *The Uncollected Critical Writings*, p. 176.

146. Cyril Connolly, *The Rock Pool* (1936; Oxford: Oxford University Press, 1981), p. 15; W. H. Auden, 'The Composer', in *Collected Poems*, ed. Edward Mendelson (1976; London: Faber, 1991), p. 181.

2

'A PURSE OF HER OWN': WOMEN AND CARRIAGE

And then Mrs Brown faced the dreadful revelation. She took her heroic decision. Early, before dawn, she packed her bag and carried it herself to the station. She would not let Smith touch it. She was wounded in her pride, unmoored from her anchorage; she came of gentlefolks who kept servants – but details could wait. The important thing was to realize her character, to steep oneself in her atmosphere. I had no time to explain why I felt it somewhat tragic, heroic, yet with a dash of the flighty, and fantastic, before the train stopped, and I watched her disappear, carrying her bag, into the vast blazing station. She looked very small, very tenacious; at once very frail and very heroic. And I have never seen her again, and I shall never know what became of her.[1]

'[D]etails could wait', Virginia Woolf interjects in the culminating image of her version of the Mrs Brown story, as recounted in her well-known 1923 essay on the subject of character in fiction. She immediately adds that 'the story ends without any point to it'.[2] However, she does pointedly draw attention to one particular detail: the fact that Mrs Brown carries her own bag. It is a fact she states twice in quick succession, though it is a detail tellingly overlooked by her imagined Edwardian literary counterparts, in the versions of Mrs Brown respectively allotted to each. Why is this detail worth repeating, while others can wait? Why does Woolf stress Mrs Brown's adamant refusal to let Mr Smith touch her bag, and what does this gesture imply? Why is it something only she purports to notice? And since this is, to all intents and purposes, a discussion of the changing approach to fictional character, and thus to fiction itself, in the early twentieth century, what does this particular detail add to that particular discussion?

This chapter contends that the woman's bag became a central symbolic point of focus and literary motif in portrayals of shifting gender relations during the modern period, dating back to the emergence of literature by and about 'New Women' at the *fin de siècle*. Chapter 1 showed that the 'Woman Question' and the thorny issue of women's desires persistently surface as key contributing factors in the declining relevance of the house in the early-twentieth-century literary imagination. If the figure of the domestic woman formed the ideological heart of the house, then her departure put the structure itself in jeopardy. This is most conspicuously felt in relation to James's 'house of fiction' and most conspicuously resisted in Forster's *Howards End*. Even James himself intuited as early as 1899, long before he wrote his Preface, that the future of the novel lay, in part, in the domestic desertion of the woman: 'we may very well yet see the female elbow itself, kept in increasing activity by the play of the pen, smash with final resonance the window all this time kept most superstitiously closed'.[3] It is a woman's ability to move freely in conjunction with a freedom of expression that is at issue here. The concept of mobility has, indeed, figured prominently in re-evaluative efforts to bring matters of gender, as well as the centrality of women's writing and experience, to the forefront of studies of modernism, in defiance of traditionally male-dominated modernist canons.[4] As Marianne Dekoven appositely remarks, at the beginning of one seminal essay on this subject, '[m]odernism is an ideal literary territory for the feminist critic to rechart'.[5] A range of critics have initiated this reappraisal by *charting*, in effect, the represented movements of women themselves through classic modernist terrains. Critics such as Griselda Pollock, Rachel Bowlby and, more recently, Wendy Parkins, have further asserted the distinctiveness of women's mobility as set against the mobility of men in allowing for alternative trajectories, both scholarly and literary.[6] In Bowlby's words,

> The woman in the street is not the equivalent of the man in the street, that figure of normal representativeness; and her sexually dubious associations give to her stepping out a quality of automatic transgressiveness that is also the chance of her going somewhere different.[7]

Such women were, however, rarely shown to be entirely unencumbered; in fact, the act of carrying belongings on the move can frequently be found to override straight mobility in portrayals of the footloose female subject. As this chapter will show, the woman's bag points to a markedly feminine version of modernist portability, highlighting a longstanding historical and cultural link between women and portable property. The bag was, as such, not just an object poised in metonymical relation to those transgressive and restless women of the street; it also drew attention to the troubling issue of women's proprietorial rights, pivotal in so many contemporary feminist debates. Even more compellingly, it functioned as a powerful symbolic form for a number of women writers who were attempting to conceive of a narrative approach beyond typically masculine tropes of architectural construction. This is not to suggest that this object tells a single, representative story about modernism's bag-carrying women or that portability itself offered a necessary and foolproof feminine counterpoint to a man-made house of fiction, not least because such an opposition presupposes a straightforward understanding of femininity. Like Rita Felski, I believe we should avoid the temptation of 'constructing a counter-myth of emblematic femininity' in favour of an approach which 'aims to unravel the complexities of modernity's relationship to femininity through an analysis of its varied and competing representations'.[8] It is precisely these various and competing representations of modernity's relationship to feminin- ity which a close survey of the motif of the woman's bag illuminates above all.[9]

PROPERTY, MOBILITY AND THE MODERN WOMAN

From the emergence of the figure of the New Woman, women's bags, in all shapes and sizes, became a singular area of semiotic attention, often evoca- tive of a female interiority to be newly explored. The disclosure of what was perceived to be a withheld female essence (or, indeed, a paradoxical plethora of conflicting female essences) was assumed, in many quarters, to be critical to future literary developments, particularly in the novel form. Much scholarly work has since been done to establish that the 'emancipation of women and the emancipation of the English novel', from the end of the nineteenth century, went hand in hand.[10] This concurrent and connected development is directly inscribed in portraits of emancipated women, during this period, through the image of the woman's bag, representing a break away both from house and house of fiction at one and the same time. The opposition generated between bag and house in the texts to be analysed in this chapter might be fruitfully compared to Susan Stewart's differentiation between the 'miniature' and the 'gigantic'. She conceives of the miniature as a 'metaphor for the interior space and time of the bourgeois subject', while the gigantic is a 'metaphor for the abstract authority of the state and the collective, public life'.[11] Stewart's terms are useful here because, as she describes, there is a degree of exaggeration and abstraction involved in perceptions of the miniature and the gigantic, distortions of scale which will enter into this account in various ways.[12] Moreover, these terms point to the relation of self with world through the negotiation of ideas of interiority and exteriority. I am suggesting that the bag operated as a metaphor for the interior space and time of the bourgeois female subject as set against the 'abstract', external authority of an established public order, encapsulated in the image of the house as representative of a larger social structure.[13] In generating this metaphorical opposition, certain women writers, working in what Cicely Hamilton was later to call the 'experimental stage', saw the house as an imposed framework for a kind of domestic privacy and 'feminine' interiority that was publicly sanctioned and collectively monitored.[14] The bag, by contrast, in its miniature and, therefore, mobile form, offered a framework for self-reinvention, one that could be carried and controlled, though not always without hindrance.

The 'woman who did' then was also a woman with a bag, and this was a bag that she emphatically carried herself.[15] This gesture signalled, first and foremost, a dynamic domestic abandonment but, further, an assertion of autonomous self-control and desire for adventure. As early as 1853, the pioneering American women's rights campaigner, Susan B. Anthony, known by her red alligator-skin handbag in which she carried her speeches, added a note in her journal that anticipates, with fascinating prescience, the title of Woolf's famous feminist manifesto of 1929:

> Woman must have a *purse* of her own, & how can this be, so long as the wife is denied the right to her individual and joint earnings. Reflections like these caused me to see and really feel that there was no true freedom for woman without the possession of all her property rights.[16]

Anthony's statement is integral to an understanding of the pertinence of the woman's bag as a political expression for the right of a woman to financial independence. But to put political significations momentarily to one side, I would like to contend that the expressive potency of the woman's bag for the *fin-de-siècle* artistic imagination must be seen to derive, in large part, from Henrik Ibsen, whose 'subversive female character roles were . . . immensely influential in the formation of the identity of the New Woman in 1890s London'.[17] Nora, in *A Doll's House* (1879), is the most obvious case for consideration here, though the progressive Hilda Wengal, first identified with a rucksack on her back, in *The Master Builder* (1892) should be factored in peripherally too. The '*small travelling bag*' Nora carries away from the family home at the end of *A Doll's House* forms the material manifestation of her 'duty' to herself over and above her domestic duty as a wife and mother.[18] This travelling bag was *the* pivotal symbol in Ibsen's play. Its significance can be gleaned from the fact that in his alternative conciliatory ending to *A Doll's House,* written to appease a disgruntled German theatre in 1880, Nora '*lets her travelling bag fall*' at the moment she reverses her decision to leave her husband.[19] One Norwegian pastor, in responding to the furore caused by Ibsen's work, predicted (not inaccurately) the extension of the symbolic impact of Nora's gesture far beyond the play itself: 'The emancipated woman has taken her place at the door, always ready to depart, with her suitcase in her hand. The suitcase – and not as before, the ring of fidelity – will be the symbol of her role in marriage.'[20]

In order to understand why Nora's single small travelling bag might have assumed such a reverberating importance for late-nineteenth- and early-twentieth-century writers in English, we need to think about the complex significations and codes of conduct surrounding women's baggage – and underpinning, by extension, the relationship of women to property – from a historical as well as a linguistic point of view. To start with, Nora's gesture most vividly highlighted the changing status of married women in relation to property in the late nineteenth century. Traditionally, a woman (in Norway as in most Western countries) resigned her own property to her husband upon marriage, under the legal doctrine of 'coverture', as it was known in English-speaking countries.[21] However, the rights of married women to own and control their own property were significantly extended through a range of Married Women's Property Acts, passed in a number of European countries and across the United States from the mid-nineteenth century.[22] These Acts reduced the financial hold of a husband over his wife and thus made it easier for her to leave him if she so wished. In determinedly taking only what belongs to her, Nora anticipates the possibilities opened up by such legislative reform while, simultaneously, illuminating the proprietorial and political disenfranchisement of most married women in Western societies during the nineteenth century. In other words, Nora might escape the house, but she escapes with little of her own. (Technically, she is likely to have owned nothing at all from a legal perspective, though 'paraphernalia' proved to be a grey area within the wider practice of coverture.)[23] That her act of carrying her own bag out of the family home is essentially a symbolic gesture is made clear by the fact that she is shown to arrange for her friend, Kristine, to collect the remainder of her few belongings the following morning. This allowed Ibsen to make the small travelling bag a closing object of visual focus in the play. What I would like to suggest here is that its symbolic centrality in A Doll's House, as well as in later re-conceptualisations of gender relations in English fiction, was due to the fact that the woman's bag had, in effect, long been imaginatively central to women's proprietary suppression.

An elucidatory detour in the way of English rhetorical tradition is useful in this context, tangentially so where Ibsen is concerned but directly relevant when it comes to writers in English to follow. The very word 'baggage' had been derogatively deployed, since the seventeenth century, in relation to loose women of questionable morals and social standing. This expression goes some way, on its own, to explain sensitivities relating to the question of women's luggage. The tag was, in fact, originally applied to men as well as women of disrepute, but the male-specific usage quickly slipped out of currency. This marked feminine bias, on a linguistic level, corroborates Jordanna Bailkin's assertion that women have 'traditionally been identified with mobile property, highlighting a perceived division between masculine worth and feminine insubstantiality'.[24] According to the range of early examples offered by the *OED,* it was an expression used as much to refer to a woman bound as an impediment to a man as a woman too free in her ways. As such, the most salient point about the idea of the 'baggage' is the proprietorial assumption in the word; it automatically raises the question of *whose baggage?* The idiomatic label must be seen to describe the relationship of a particular woman to a man or to society rather than to describe the woman in her own right. Its application points to a perception of that woman as a social and/or sexual liability, as unwanted property or, what is more likely, as *any* man's property for the taking (and – naturally – for the leaving too). Even financially independent, unmarried women who lawfully owned property were represented in impedimental terms at this time (by Victorian feminists as much as social conservatives); such women figured in property debates 'not as active independent agents but as either "redundant" women, devalued by over-supply, or as socially wealthy spinsters and widows: paradigms of the woman who must find something useful to do in a society that overlooks her existence'.[25] Whether *femes sole* or *femes covert,* women were thus conceived as social baggage. Furthermore, though most often used as a derogatory word for a certain kind of woman, 'baggage' was employed concurrently as a playful term of endearment for *any* woman. Respectable or not, all women were 'identified with mobile property', to reiterate Bailkin's words, from the worthless 'common baggage' to the aristocratic bride with her opulent trousseau.

This is exactly the point that Nora makes in walking out with her single travelling bag. In other words, stripped of the accoutrements of class, no respectably married woman was, in the eyes of the law, much better off than the 'common baggage'; in fact, they were 'regarded legally as merely appendages of their husbands'.[26] Nora's gesture foregrounds an unsettling correlation between women of all classes on this level, illustrating the dual playful/derogatory connotations of the word 'baggage' in the English language. Middle-to-upper-class women were, however, afforded the means of concealing the accompanying perception of 'feminine insubstantiality' to greater or lesser degrees. A respectable lady, in Europe as much as in the United States, would never have travelled with a single handheld bag. A lady of good social standing, on the contrary, travelled with a lot of baggage, signalling a financial means to travel but, equally, access to the help required to carry all those possessions in transit, in the form of protector, maid or chaperone. Only a woman without means or protection and of a lower social standing would have been seen to carry her own bag, usually for short distances and rarely for leisure.[27] The beginning of Ibsen's later *Hedda Gabler* (1890) forms a very deliberate counterpoint to the ending of *A Doll's House* in drawing the audience's attention to Hedda's 'great many cases' on her return from her honeymoon, even before she herself takes to the stage.[28] This abundance of luggage is underlined in order to communicate Hedda's newly attained status as a married woman of the bourgeois classes under the protection and patronage of her husband, and Hedda is herself figured as part of this baggage as newly acquired wife.[29] In contrast, Nora's act of carrying her own bag asserts self-ownership and, through this, a repudiation of class-based distinctions where the question of a woman's proprietary status in society is concerned. In assuming control of herself outside of a proprietorial relationship, Nora must become a woman without means and without bourgeois patriarchal protection. Most vitally, the elevation of the woman's bag as the focal point of this gesture stands for a reclamation of power through the invocation of that old figurative expression of a woman's dependence. Deborah Wynne has shown that Victorian women, in the absence of real property rights and the social value property ownership conferred, found, in 'less substantial property', a means of vicariously performing a proprietorial identity beyond strictly legal sanction.[30] Portable property had thus long formed a basis of resistance for women. Yet, while in the past, such property had been substitutive for a larger proprietorial stake in society, in that 'women *made do* with securing their identity on [. . .] personal, portable things', by the end of the century, such 'personal, portable things' had become important in and of themselves.[31] If baggage had formed the metaphorical locus of a woman's subjugation, it was transformed into the subversive locus of her emancipation.

At the crux of these proprietorial questions was the troubling issue of female mobility. No longer posited as a poor substitute for the rightful ownership of a dwelling place, the bag became instrumental in developing and enacting a new mode of dwelling in motion. The most public female figure to command a travelling bag in order to assert her mobility during the 1890s was, unquestionably, the American journalist, Nellie Bly. Her written account of her travel experiences sheds light on some of the luggage-related issues which would come into play in English fiction after Ibsen. In response to a claim made by Phileas Fogg, in Jules Verne's *Around the World in Eighty Days* (1873), that 'an Englishman like him could make a round-the-world tour with just one bag to hand' but 'a woman couldn't undertake a similar voyage under these conditions', she proceeded to break his record by travelling around the world in just seventy-two days and without her own 'Passepartout', producing a book with a corresponding title in 1890.[32] The trip was sponsored by the *New York World*. One aspect of Bly's act of daring and defiance that captivated the public was her solitary handheld bag. It became an integral feature of her popular image. Her disregard for convention on this score is marked, and an early conversation with her business manager, in which she broaches the idea of the trip, gives us an insight into the issues at stake:

'It is impossible for you to do it', was the terrible verdict. 'In the first place you are a woman and would need a protector and even if it were possible for you to travel alone you would need to carry so much baggage that it would detain you in making rapid changes. Besides you speak nothing but English, so there is no use talking about it; no one but a man can do this'.

'Very well', I said angrily, 'Start the man, and I'll start the same day for some other newspaper and beat him'.[33]

The terms in which the 'terrible verdict' of her business manager is couched, echoing Fogg's dictum, indicate that this is a social judgement over and above a judgement of an individual kind. The exchange discloses the deep-seated ideological implications of Bly's rejection of extensive baggage for the purpose of greater speed. Up until the late nineteenth century, 'adventure' was seen to be the prerogative of men, something exposed by the lack of an equivalent term to match the designation of 'adventurer', as Alexandra Lapierre makes clear: 'Whereas the term adventurer suggests a passion for new frontiers, the term adventuress suggests neither departure, nor travel, nor great distance; rather, it connotes ambitiousness, intrigue, mercenary sex.'[34] The idea of a woman's travelling light was translated thus from a literal sense of physical mobility to a metaphorical sense of moral questionability. Building on Lapierre's point, I would add that it was also, paradoxically, through figuring women in terms of mobile property that a more mobile form of female adventurousness was strictly curtailed; baggage, after all, requires external agency to enable movement, and man had long acted as that agent. In enumerating the advantages of ladies travelling alone in 1857, travel writer Emily Lowe comes to an oblique realisation, long before Bly, of the debilitating effects of such an implicit conflation of women with luggage. She finds that the only justifiable response to such a conflation is to rewrite the terms of feminine portability through removing the supposed object of chaperonage: 'The only use of a gentleman in travelling is to look after the luggage, and we take care to have no luggage. "The Unprotected" should never go beyond one portable carpet-bag.'[35] Lowe and Bly, in line with Nora, proved that the figure of the adventuress could be reinvented, as independently mobile rather than sexually licentious, but only if she was shown to stand alone and outside of any kind of relationship of proprietorial protection.

Yet as the response of Bly's business manager might suggest, such acts of reinvention did not meet with unqualified enthusiasm in all quarters. The more troubling depictions of 'unprotected' women that emerged during this period throw underlying proprietorial issues into even sharper relief. The woman who carried her own bag was figured as a woman who revelled in not knowing her place and, in this way, wilfully disrupted preconceived notions of what that place might be. She thus unsettled the status quo, textual as much as sociopolitical. Her disruptive impact is particularly palpable in the popular press. Most critical studies of the New Woman acknowledge the role played by periodicals, particularly *Punch,* in promulgating various comic stereotypes of the figure, caricatures which worked to level anti-establishment threats through forms of parody. What has not yet been documented, however, is the recurrent appearance of the woman's bag in these cartoons, often serving as the focal point of comic disturbance. In an 1889 cartoon entitled 'The Lady Guide and the Tory Tourist' in the comic Victorian magazine, *Fun,* we find, for example, a woman in gender-ambiguous dress (a skirt/trouser amalgamation with a military-style jacket on top) holding forth on the issue of suffrage.[36] She has a cigarette in one hand, and strapped around her is a bag with the words 'Vote Woman Suffrage' boldly emblazoned on the front.[37] Her bag – besides the skirt, the only unmistakeably feminine element in the costume as a whole – carries her feminist message here. Even more interestingly, in an 1895 issue of *Punch*, we find a mock front cover of that most notorious of decadent *fin-de-siècle* journals, *The Yellow Book,* which features a stooped and sinister-looking woman with flowing hair, drawn in the style of Aubrey Beardsley, clutching a handbag inscribed 'Destination Inconnue?' (Figure 2). In this example, the sense of mobility and unpredictability associated with the New Woman is invoked through the object of her bag with its unknown destination loudly proclaimed. Whatever the destination, a sexually transgressive route is implied, a route away from home and family. By the mid-1890s, the object of the bag, in and of itself, had become synonymous with a form of radical activism which challenged the proprietorial basis of social and family relations. When Oscar Wilde famously spotlights a handbag as the disruptive dramatic element in *The Importance of Being Earnest,* it is the bag's usurpation of the house as an ideological structure which forms the mock-horrific crisis around which the play turns. 'To be born, or at any rate bred, in a hand-bag, whether it had handles or not', Lady Bracknell remarks dismissively of the purported beginnings of her daughter's suitor, 'seems to me to display a contempt for the ordinary decencies of family life that reminds one of the worst excesses of the French Revolution.'[38]

Many such figurations can be found to enact a distortion of traditional chivalric codes, whereby questions of property become embroiled with questions of propriety. An 1894 cartoon entitled 'What It Will Soon Come To' (Figure 3) which depicts a lady in the act of offering to carry the bag of a man, is particularly noteworthy where *fin-de-siècle* anxieties surrounding gender, property and propriety are concerned. For a woman to carry her own bag was one thing. For her to carry the bag of a man – and a 'smithereen' of a man at that – was another. It stood for a complete inversion of the balance of proprietorial power between the sexes, an inversion likely to turn the rational order on its head towards a more 'feminine' state of capriciousness. The extremity of this reversal is articulated in a verse which accompanied one of the most

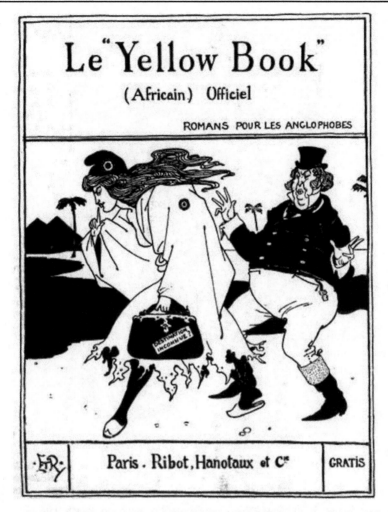

Figure 2 Edward Tennyson Reed, 'Le "Yellow Book"', cartoon, *Punch*, 108, 13 April 1895, p. 178.

widely recognised *Punch* caricatures of the New Woman, 'Donna Quixote', published a couple of months later: 'The newest Chivalry brings the newest Craze.'[39] Chivalry was frequently used as a framework through which to view the 'shifting debates around sexual politics' during this era, debates in which the woman's bag recurrently featured as a metonymic object.[40] This *Punch* cartoon provocatively captures a representative moment of fraught negotiation, subjecting the 'protection' conferred by chaperonage to an uncomfortable form of scrutiny.

The 'What It Will Soon Come To' future scenario of this cartoon title was

WHAT IT WILL SOON COME TO.

Miss Sampson. "PRAY LET ME CARRY YOUR BAG, MR. SMITHEREEN!"

Figure 3 'What It Will Soon Come To', cartoon, *Punch*, 106,
24 February 1894, p. 90. Reproduced with permission of Punch Ltd,
www.punch.co.uk.

all to play for during the 1890s, and the man seemingly stood to lose as much
as the woman stood to win. Just as the woman's gain was displaced upon
the object of her bag, it followed that the man's projected loss was displaced
upon the object of his bag. This was also conceived as a textual bag, extending
those *fin-de-siècle* anxieties surrounding the ascension of the 'newest chivalry'
to the domain of authorship and textual authority. In George Gissing's 1895
short story 'The Poet's Portmanteau', written not long after *The Odd Women*
(1893), the idea of chivalric distortion is pressed disquietingly further; the

man's bag is not only carried, it is carried *away*. Gissing's story describes the theft of the portmanteau of a male poet, containing a cherished manuscript, by a mysterious figure with all the popularly ascribed traits of the New Woman. She is defined, for instance, as a '"girl who did what is supposed to be the privilege of men – sowed wild oats"'.[41] The theft of the portmanteau, with its precious cargo, envisages a threat to, if not complete seizure of, the authorial and proprietorial power of the man. This threat is reflected in the poet's patent sense of uncertainty as to how the woman should be appraised. He cannot make up his mind as to her character and is repeatedly shown to question and revise his original perceptions. In an analysis of the woman's persistent use of pseudonyms throughout this story, Robert L. Selig traces her first alias, 'Miss Rowe', to the 'common pseudonym for unknown legal defendants', a pseudonym applied in British law 'only to defendants in real estate dispossession cases'.[42] In light of this, we might say that the theft of the portmanteau is an act of proprietorial repossession, on the part of this woman, taken a step beyond those other gestures of symbolic reclamation. But the theft of this poet's portmanteau is also shown to correspond to the theft of his artistic authority, through the sudden redundancy of inherited convictions where the nature of female character as written construct is concerned. The woman is shown to be impossible for the poet to pin down from beginning to end. In this, Gissing's story corresponds to other short stories by New Woman writers of the period, which feature the intrusion upon and then abandonment of a male writer/artist figure by an unconventional woman: Sarah Grand's 'The Undefinable' (1894) and Ella D'Arcy's 'The Pleasure-Pilgrim' (1895), for example.[43] The loss of the portmanteau dramatises the loss of an old idea of woman in line with the unsettling emergence of a New Woman beyond conventional authorial control, as the poet's dream immediately following the theft reveals: '[he] dreamt that he was chasing that mysterious girl up hill and down dale amid the Devon moorland; she, always far in advance, held his fated manuscript above her head, and laughed maliciously'.[44] Going beyond the fears of that earlier Norwegian pastor, here we find the emancipated woman taking her place at the door, always ready to depart, with the man's suitcase in her hand, threatening his monopoly on adventure, whether expeditionary or authorial.

DOROTHY RICHARDSON'S SARATOGA TRUNK

Prompted by Ibsen and Bly, the solitary handbag or travelling bag in various forms was incorporated as a (not unproblematic) symbol for the New Woman as New Adventuress by writers at the *fin de siècle*. But the larger question was how to move beyond the symbol towards a more radical reconceptualisation of form, narrative as much as social. Neither legal acts nor defiant gestures could alone overhaul a structure imbued throughout with the ideology of proprietorial patriarchy, and this is an obstacle that many New Woman writers of the 1890s found difficult to overcome. Dorothy Richardson's novel sequence *Pilgrimage*, published from 1915 to 1938 (with the addition of an unfinished chapter in 1967), is one example of a work which enacts a radical move beyond the symbolic. However, before turning to this work, I would like to briefly consider George Egerton's 1894 short story 'Virgin Soil', first published in her *Discords* collection, as an interesting earlier case study.

This story opens with the image of a distressed young woman, later identified as Florence, looking ahead to her marriage night in fearful ignorance of what is before her, a circumstance the title enunciates. She is given inadequate comfort by her 'scarcely less disturbed' mother, before her new husband hastily conducts her away to the train station and into the sinisterly secluded confines of an 'engaged carriage'.[45] Five years later, she returns to her mother, prematurely aged and disillusioned, bearing a 'dressing-bag in her hand', along with the shocking news that she has walked out on her husband.[46] She additionally bears a grudge against her mother for 'delivering' her into the entrapment of a loveless marriage to an unfaithful man.[47] This entrapment is foreshadowed in the earlier image of that locked first-class train carriage. One telling observation of Bly's, relating to the distinction between enclosed English carriages and open-plan American trains, is instructive here:

> [T]he English railway carriage make[s] me understand why English girls need chaperones. It would make any American woman shudder with all her boasted self-reliance, to think of sending her daughter alone on a trip, even of a few hours' duration, where there was every possibility that during those hours she would be locked in a compartment with a stranger.[48]

In Egerton's story, the mother does send her daughter on a trip, but her protector, her chaperone, *is* the sinister stranger within the 'engaged carriage', and he is aided in claiming this woman as property – it is with a 'curious amused proprietary air' that he hands her into the carriage – by all around him.[49] Early on, there is an implied collusion between husband, station-master and porter in securing the private train carriage. More disconcertingly still, it is a collusion to which her mother is party. She has, according to her daughter, materially gained from the arrangement: '"You sold me for a home, for clothes, for food."'[50] Egerton's story, like Ibsen's *A Doll's House*, is all about the exposure of the proprietary structure of marriage as the 'structure that maintains the Structure, or system', in Tony Tanner's words.[51] However, unlike Ibsen in his dramatic work, Egerton takes the reader beyond the domestic framework to explicitly disclose the manner in which the underlying order of the private space is replicated in the underlying order of the public space, a space which can itself be privatised with an authoritative nod in the right direction. Trajectories of structural escape are here revealed as trajectories of structural enclosure. The train carriage also recalls Hedda Gabler's perception of marriage as a long train journey in Ibsen's earlier play.[52] But if Florence begins as Hedda in setting out on a claustrophobic marital train, she ends as Nora with a dressing-bag of departure.

The dressing-bag must be seen as a vital subversive element in the all-enclosing ideological apparatus which the story exposes. Florence cuts a defiant (if also cynical and disillusioned) figure. She echoes Nora's declaration of her duty to herself in emphasising the '"demands of her individual soul"' and that her '"life must be [her] own"'.[53] This idea of autonomy is manifested through the dressing-bag, which accompanies her as she returns to the train station to take 'the train in the opposite direction' in embarking on her 'long journey' at the very end of the story.[54] Before she leaves, Florence's mother, the woman who is accused of having 'sold' her daughter for a 'home' is shown to covertly slip a 'little roll of notes into the dressing-bag' while Florence sleeps.[55] Sally Ledger reads this as a sort of awakening 'insight', on the mother's part, to the plight of her daughter, which cannot be expressed in words.[56] It might be seen as an expression of her realisation of the importance of a woman's financial independence, in line with the reflections of Susan B. Anthony. As such, it becomes a symbolic reinvestment of her ill-gotten gains both in an alternative future and in the search for an alternative framework, as her state of mind just prior to her act attests: 'She feels as if scales have dropped from her eyes, as if the instincts and conventions of her life are toppling over, as if all the needs of protesting women of whom she has read with a vague displeasure have come home to her.'[57] This alternative framework can only yet be imagined. Egerton's story is primarily concerned with 'toppling' the supremacy of former 'conventions'. Ledger goes on to suggest that the promising 'open-endedness' exhibited at the close of this story – which nods beyond the emphatically slammed door at the end of *A Doll's House* – is one characteristic of Egerton's work that 'preempt[s] the modernist aesthetic which was to reach its high watermark in the early years of the twentieth century'.[58]

Short story and dramatic forms were well suited for representing the act of a woman's breaking away from a toppling structure, but what Egerton refers to prospectively as the 'long journey' required a different mode. The bag, like the journey, can only be glimpsed in that forward-looking short story 'Virgin Soil', as in *A Doll's House*. For certain experimental women writers to follow, it was elevated as an analogic model for a new kind of narrative, one focused on the trajectory of a new kind of woman. Richardson's *Pilgrimage* is exemplary in this respect, innovatively charting the extended journey of one such modern woman, Miriam Henderson. Miriam is not, strictly speaking, a bag-carrying woman in the manner outlined up to this point. She travels with a hefty Saratoga trunk, not a single handheld bag, and is even shown to require help to move it on several occasions through the sequence. Yet *Pilgrimage* is an essential inclusion here in representing the progression beyond the symbolic gesture towards a process of lived experience, evolving into a formal principle.

Pilgrimage was, indeed, perceived to pioneer 'in a completely new direction' and to epitomise, in textual terms, a peculiarly *'female* quest'.[59] This was integral to Richardson's project. In her foreword to the Dent and Cresset four-volume edition of *Pilgrimage*, issued in 1938, she describes herself as having embarked on a 'fresh pathway, an adventure', as she took up her pen to begin *Pointed Roofs* in 1913 in an effort to 'produce a feminine equivalent of the current masculine realism'.[60] The sense of a metaphorical departure from a domestic frame of reference, towards a more erratically mobile conception of form, was evident even at the time. John Cowper Powys, in considering Richardson's oeuvre on the whole, remarked that she, in contrast to James, Conrad, Hardy and Proust, offered no 'mounting up to an architectural dénouement'.[61] These are sentiments echoed in the text itself. Miriam, for example, is suddenly struck in the seventh chapter, *Revolving Lights*, by the thought that men 'hovered about the doors of freedom returning sooner or later to the hearth', implying her own difference in this respect.[62] This is not to suggest that Miriam is not also drawn to the hearth; she manifestly experiences a recurring difficulty in reconciling conflicting desires for the safety and society of the known world, on the one hand, and the insecure and necessarily solitary experience of independence, on the other.[63] However, Miriam manages to negotiate this conundrum more successfully than many modernist female protagonists. 'To remember, whatever happened, not to be afraid of being alone' she tells herself in *Interim*.[64] Although she is acutely sensitive to what she later calls the 'shadow of incompatibility' between her desires for security and freedom, it is a feminine form of freedom beyond the hearth to which *Pilgrimage* aspires.[65]

Fundamental to Richardson's artistic endeavour, then, is her emphasis on portability, as opposed to hereditary property, mobility as opposed to architectural fixity. This is something she alerts the reader to from the outset, as Miriam begins her journey in the opening section of *Pointed Roofs*: 'The train had made her sway with its movements. How still Sarah [her sister] seemed to sit, fixed in the old life.'[66] The inference is clear; movement is integral to change, and movement was to be the vital and vitalising element in this experimental stage of women's writing, as exemplified by *Pilgrimage*. Furthermore, though Miriam rejects what she calls the 'sheltered life', she finds a paradoxical form of security in transit, described in *Backwater* as the 'tranquil sense of being carried securely forward through the air away from people and problems', a sentiment reiterated in relation to a train journey in *The Tunnel*: 'She breathed deeply, safe, shut in and moving on.'[67]

In *Pointed Roofs,* Miriam's Saratoga trunk provides the initial focus, as index to the imminence of the uncertain stages of movement that her pilgrimage will entail and indefinitely prolong: 'Her new Saratoga trunk stood solid and gleaming in the firelight. To-morrow it would be taken away and she would be gone.'[68] Jean Radford reads this opening in the context of an allegorical pilgrimage fiction in line with Bunyan's *The Pilgrim's Progress* (which Miriam repeatedly invokes), her trunk thus becoming the 'symbolic burden' Miriam must bear with her until 'she finds her salvation'.[69] As Radford acknowledges, however, Richardson, in confronting those tricky ideas of ending and destination, is compelled to deviate from the concluding point assumed in this allegorical structure. Ending aside, Miriam's Saratoga primarily evokes the traditional pilgrimage narrative through registering the 'old' in conjunction with the 'new'; that is, Miriam's past as well as the textual history of *Pilgrimage* itself. One biographical incident sheds light on this function of memorialisation. Following the return of the manuscript of *Pointed Roofs* by a publisher who did not grasp its meaning in 1914, Richardson put it 'away in a trunk' and occupied herself temporarily with other kinds of writing.[70] Such an act of self-conscious stowing away is replicated in *Pointed Roofs* itself. Shortly after her arrival in Germany, Miriam puts a sheaf of old songs from home, of which she is ashamed, 'away at the bottom of her Saratoga trunk'.[71] Whether or not this scene was added on final publication of *Pointed Roofs* in 1915 is not so important as the fact of Richardson's vivid association of the trunk with past retention, as well as future possibility, the personal (even painful) souvenir, but also the arbitrary object: '[Miriam] had packed some [of her books]. She could not remember which and why.'[72] The use of the 'trunk as a store' for the personal and the random, recurs throughout the sequence and reflects her broader textual approach to memory, as evoked by Powys: 'One can only surmise that what she does is to cast a deep-sea net ... into her memory and then make a blind, almost prophetic, use of all she finds in that occult scoop.'[73] In effect, Miriam's trunk represents the materialisation of memory as an indiscriminate load, yet also as a continual archival work in progress with, I would argue, a more refined ordering principle than Powys's image would suggest.

Significantly, luggage/packing imagery was repeatedly used, by male and female writers alike, to disparage Richardson's work for what was perceived as the lack of an ordering principle. For Katherine Mansfield, most famously, *The Tunnel* was all-too-hastily and excessively packed as a text:

> Things just 'happen' one after another with incredible rapidity and at break-neck speed. There is Miss Richardson, holding out her mind, as it were, and there is Life hurling objects into it as fast as she can throw. And at the appointed time Miss Richardson dives into its recesses and reproduces a certain number of these treasures – a pair of button boots,

a night in Spring, some cycling knickers, some large, round biscuits – as many as she can pack into a book, in fact. But the pace kills.[74]

Graham Greene, in a 1951 essay on Richardson's work, entitled 'The Saratoga Trunk', referred to the 'stream of consciousness' as an 'embarrassing cargo' and asserted that Miriam's 'saratoga trunk [was becoming] progressively more worn and labelled' in line with what he felt to be the 'weariness' of *Pilgrimage* itself as an ongoing project.[75] Leon Edel's pronouncement of the 'need to become the author so as to bring some order into the great grab-bag of feminine experience offered us' in *Pilgrimage,* supplies one more illustration of such censure.[76] All of these writers objected to a deficiency in formal craftsmanship on Richardson's part, accentuated by an ostensibly indiscriminate approach to content. This was, of course, partly the intention. Stewart remarks that far from reflecting day-to-day life, realistic genres reflect its 'hierarchization of information', a system of selective classification David Trotter has referred to as a generic 'criterion of relevance'.[77] Disturbing the ideological interests of the prevailing hierarchical system of relevance was intrinsic to Richardson's work, a motive force in the production of that 'feminine equivalent of the current masculine realism'.[78] The prolonged development of this 'feminine equivalent' proved a large part of the overarching problem for her critics. They further baulk at a certain 'embarrassing' stylistic indiscretion surrounding the articulation of 'feminine experience'. But Richardson's 'bag' of feminine experience belies accusations of indiscriminate exposure upon further scrutiny. Of her aforementioned critics, only Greene pays any tribute to the specific type of bag largely conveyed by Miriam: a Saratoga trunk. This kind of trunk (predominantly employed by women) is characterised by intricate compartmentalisation, an arrangement suggesting an internal coherence and refinement at odds with the implied disorder of the 'grab-bag'.[79]

Indeed, the use of luggage imagery in the service of a criticism of stylistic indiscretion and authorial self-indulgence jars uncomfortably with the more complex application of such imagery in the service of a modernist reinvention of the female subject in *Pilgrimage* itself. It is a text which deliberately treads the line between discretion and indiscretion, flaunting an air of unforeseen and 'embarrassing' disclosure, while, at the same time, rigorously documenting and exploring an obsession with the undisclosed. Bags and trunks do not simply promise unprecedented access to the female subject within this text; they are also employed, by Richardson, to investigate perceptions of female subjectivity from the outside. For example, Miriam is shown to register an admiration for an elusive female figure, explicitly associated with luggage. This is the aloof and 'different' Ulrica Hesse, with her 'three large leather trunks'.[80] (We find a similar expression of fascination, a little later on, in response to the 'strange luggage' of Meg Wedderburn in *Backwater*.)[81] The trunks, in this instance, stand for all that is unknown, and captivating in consequence, about this woman. Contrary to those critical charges of indiscriminate revelation, this text is *as* concerned – and self-reflexively so – with the intrigue surrounding a secreted interiority, with the closed luggage container as much as with the open. By publicly lifting her own lid, Richardson might '[break] out at last a public defiance of the freemasonry of women', but that freemasonry is, in itself, the subject of the book, breached in order to be understood.[82] The call for greater openness in women's writing was being sounded in more than one literary quarter at this time. Ford Madox Ford (or Hueffer, as he was then known) condemned what he referred to as the 'woman of the novelists' in an open letter to womankind in 1911. He saw this idealised conception of womanhood in fiction as a gross distortion and a 'crime against the Arts', the propagation of which women, as much as men, were culpable. He concluded his letter by laying down the literary gauntlet: 'You have the matter a great deal in your own hands, for to such an extent is the writer of imaginative litera-ture dependent on your suffrages.'[83] While Richardson readily embraces this challenge, she is not insensitive to the cost of, or difficulties involved in, public exhibition. She acknowledges that '[f]eminine worldliness' means 'perpetual hard work and cheating and pretence at the door of a hidden garden', impart-ing to revelation the quality of transgression.[84] For all Miriam's determination to lay herself bare, she concedes, to her chagrin, that it is sometimes 'better to pretend'.[85] In other words, to adopt a posture of extreme openness is tanta-mount to prescribing oneself as socially unfit, an admission which pre-empts certain reactions to the novel sequence itself.

Discussions of honesty in women's writing stem, in part, from a wider contemporary fascination with the nature of female desire. With an eye to Miriam's foregrounded Saratoga, a brief foray into the developing field of psychoanalysis during this period is useful. Gaston Bachelard has observed, in contemplating hiding places, that an 'anthology devoted to small boxes . . . would constitute an important chapter in psychology'.[86] The figuration of female sexuality through the image of the small, *mobile* box would constitute an important section of this chapter. The first of Dora's dreams, described in Sigmund Freud's famous *Fragment of an Analysis of a Case of Hysteria* (1905), concerns, for example, a prized and threatened jewel-case:

> A house was on fire. My father was standing beside my bed and woke me up. I dressed quickly. Mother wanted to stop and save her jewel-case; but Father said: 'I refuse to let myself and my two children be burnt for the sake of your jewel-case'. We hurried downstairs, and as soon as I was outside I woke up.[87]

In presenting his interpretation of the sexual implications of this dream, Freud directly links the jewel-case to a reticule carried by Dora during analysis:

> Dora's reticule, which came apart at the top in the usual way, was nothing but a representation of the genitals, and her playing with it, her opening it and putting her finger in it, was an entirely unembarrassed yet unmistakeable pantomimic announcement of what she would like to do with them – namely, to masturbate.[88]

He earlier associated luggage interchangeably with women, sin, the female genitals, and the uterus/womb in *The Interpretation of Dreams*.[89] The word 'hysteria' itself derives from the Greek term 'hystera', meaning that which proceeds from the 'uterus'.[90] It is not surprising, as such, that receptacles would feature so centrally in Freud's account of Dora as objects well-placed to stand as metaphorical containers for a not-quite-containable female sexuality. He drew considerable attention to the jewel-case (and, by implication, the reticule) in his analysis: 'is it not, in short, admirably calculated both to betray and to conceal the sexual thoughts that lie behind the dream?'[91] Freud's lengthy and often insightful reading of the complexity of this symbol fails, however, to recognise its representational role as disputed element in a conflict of contrary interests surrounding female desire. When probed on the root source of the dream object of the jewel-case in her waking life, Dora recounts a heated argument between her parents pertaining to a piece of jewellery: 'Mother wanted to be given a particular thing – pearl drops to wear in her ears. But Father does not like that kind of thing, and he brought her a bracelet instead of the drops. She was furious.'[92] Far from Freud's assumption of Dora's envious regard of her father's attention to her mother (an assumption since vehemently disputed by critics), jewellery must first have signalled unsatisfied female desire, and also discordant views on its appropriate expression.[93] It naturally follows that Dora's dream would register this sexual contention. The jewel-case, as object of contention, is cast, in her dream, as something of elevated value for the mother figure *and* as an incomprehensible and dangerous distraction from the father's point of view. This is a conflict of interests which might equally be said to surface around the object of Dora's reticule in its exemplification of Freud's controversial 'method of "authoring" female behavior'.[94]

Such a pointed conflict of interests reflects oppositional stances pertaining to the nature of female sexuality at this time. That female sexual desire actively existed was no longer in doubt in Freud's era. At issue, instead, were the implications of exposing and thus devaluing 'men's emotional investment in woman's problematic sexuality'.[95] This investment comes under threat in Dora's dream and comes under interrogation in Richardson's *Pilgrimage*. Miriam reflects on a prevalent double standard in *The Tunnel*:

> They invent a legend to put the blame for the existence of humanity on woman and, if she wants to stop it, they talk about the wonders of civi-

lisation and the sacred responsibilities of motherhood. They can't have it both ways. They also say women are not logical.[96]

Miriam is herself shown to be intrigued by the question of unfulfilled female desire from an early stage – 'What was it women wanted that always made them so angry?' – but is also perfectly conscious of the inevitable misapprehension of her own compulsions.[97] Later on, she playfully figures herself as the confounding woman, whose complex, conflicting and (crucially) mobile desires, beyond the parameters of a heteronormative marital paradigm, threaten to cast her into the role of 'hysterical' woman:

> she was the sport of opposing forces that would never allow her to alight and settle. The movement of her life would be like a pendulum. No wonder people found her unaccountable. But being her own solitary companion would not go on for ever. It would bring in the end, somewhere about middle age, the state that people called madness. Perhaps the lunatic asylums were full of people who had refused to join up? There were happy people in them? 'Wandering' in their minds.[98]

Richardson nods to the ancient idea of the 'wandering womb' here, which posited a physically displaced uterus as the root cause of hysteria. Miriam's Saratoga becomes a kind of uterine prosthetic in this projection, its perpetual displacement pointing to a psychotic disorder. Yet Miriam ultimately refuses the age-old pathological implications of this model in favour of the open-ended pleasure of a feminine form of 'wanderyahre' which does not involve putting the uterus back in its given place.[99] If her Saratoga trunk is posited as a wandering womb in *Pilgrimage*, this is primarily in order to challenge the seemingly straight and narrow course of nineteenth-century sexuality.

Correspondingly, Miriam's Saratoga can be found to challenge the seemingly straight and narrow course of nineteenth-century narrative. In *Pointed Roofs*, the idea of an unsatisfied and inconclusive female sexual desire takes on a structural function. Indeed, I would contend that Richardson's early critics pick up on the luggage motif, not just because of its uterine connotations, but because of its subversive importance as a central and innovative structural metaphor within the novel sequence. As Rachel Blau DuPlessis remarks, '[r]esistance to conventional varieties of romance and resistance to conventional narrative are exactly congruent in Richardson'.[100] This is visible in the final pages of *Pointed Roofs* which perform the collision of two opposing dénouements:

> Hurriedly and desolately she packed her bag. She was going home empty-handed. She had achieved nothing. Fräulein had made not the slightest effort to keep her. She was just nothing again – with her Saratoga trunk

and her hand-bag. Harriett had achieved. Harriett. She was just going home with nothing to say for herself.[101]

Miriam refers here to her sister's engagement. Richardson strikingly juxtaposes her portrait of a bag-carrying, self-supporting woman with the conventional portrait of a lady who has 'achieved' her household place through the imperative of the marriage plot. A number of critics have stressed the masculine pattern of 'ejaculatory' desire inscribed in traditional love plot formulas, and the palpable sense of comparative anti-climax above is a very deliberate rejection of that pattern, a 'mockery of that expectation'.[102] Though Richardson ends *Pointed Roofs* with the deflation of Miriam's own expectations ('She was just nothing again – with her Saratoga trunk and her hand-bag'), it would be no exaggeration to say that the *raison d'être* of *Pilgrimage* as a whole is to disprove this statement of failure, reflective less of Miriam's sense of self than of her sense of how others must perceive her.

Miriam, with her Saratoga trunk and her handbag, is, on the contrary, *everything* in *Pilgrimage*. Her 'long solitary adventure', endorsing a principle of openness and circularity rather than ejaculatory culmination or redemptive linearity (in the allegorical pilgrimage line), is only beginning here, whereas her sister's adventure, according to the conventional masculine pattern, has ended.[103] The final paragraph of *Pointed Roofs* finds her alone aboard a moving train and in a 'compartment marked Damen-Coupé', shuttling towards the second section of *Pilgrimage*.[104] The question of an appropriate ending or climax remains deferred, as it does throughout the novel sequence. Desire, sexual and narrative, is unfulfilled in the anticipated way. 'If Rosa Nouchette Carey knew me', she notes of the popular domestic fiction writer in *Backwater*, 'she'd make me one of the bad characters who are turned out of the happy homes'.[105] Creating a 'feminine equivalent' involved a reappraisal of narrative conventions through a resistance to the idea of domesticated closure, as well as a redefinition of the female 'adventuress'.[106] Several critics have interpreted Richardson's stated aspiration to produce a female quest narrative in terms of her emphasis on adventurous 'being' rather than climactic 'becoming'.[107] The image of the Saratoga fittingly lent itself to the idea of an ongoing process of 'being' as set against the achievement of 'becoming', evoked in the image of the happy home. I agree with Bryony Randall that, though Richardson acknowledges the 'pleasure' of an ending within the text itself, 'overriding this pleasure is a more profound impetus, to resist ending, which is the most vital aspect both of the text, and of Richardson's life and work'.[108] The same might be said of the acknowledged pleasure she shows in houses and domestic spaces throughout *Pilgrimage*, a pleasure which is overridden by the more profound impetus of adventure, promised by her Saratoga.[109] She goes so far as to attempt to combine the two paradigms in conceiving of her boardinghouse bedroom walls in *Deadlock* as 'travellers' walls'.[110] But, over and above the walls in whatever abode she inhabits, the trunk figuratively prevails in this text, as her early critics well realised. Hers is the counter-cultural emancipatory bag, *par excellence*.

Finally, I would like to suggest that Richardson's work embodies Ursula K. Le Guin's much later vision of a portable form of feminine fiction, first proposed in 1986. Le Guin was prompted by anthropologist Elizabeth Fisher, who, in 1979, had provocatively pointed to 'women's invention of the carrier bag' as a critical point in human development.[111] For Fisher, this invention came about from the necessity to gather in the most proficient way, and was integral to human evolution in freeing the hands in the process of upright modes of gathering.[112] She further related the woman's role as gatherer with her role as mother: 'Women, then, would have been the first to devise containers: they themselves were containers of children.'[113] Integrating evolutionary and aesthetic concerns, Le Guin found in this bag–womb equation the secret of a new kind of creative empowerment. She proffered a 'Carrier Bag Theory of Fiction', noting that 'the thing to put things in, the container for the thing contained' is a 'new story' in contrast to the 'sticks and spears and swords, the things to bash and poke and hit with, the long, hard things'.[114] Le Guin's 'carrier bag' theory can be retrospectively applied to the works of a number of modernist women writers, Richardson above all. In *Pilgrimage,* the portable object of the woman's trunk is foregrounded as a powerful emblem of a woman's right to compose her own private narrative as a 'new' story, one that hasn't been told before, a story that elevates those feminine impulses to gather and receive, while interrogating perceptions of passive maternal 'lack' or, as Freud and his predecessors had it, pathological womb-like displacement.

MODERNISM AND THE 'NEWEST CHIVALRY'

'It is a perfectly true statement to make', declares the 'Pour Les Dames' columnist at *The Bag, Portmanteau and Umbrella Trader* in 1911, 'that, though the very new woman hates to be loaded up with luggage, there are still many of the old-fashioned people who prefer to keep their own intimate belongings with them'.[115] We can surmise two things from this statement; first, by 1911, the New Woman was commonly taken to travel light and, second, that not all women followed suit. Moreover, despite those earlier wild projections of the ascendancy of the 'newest chivalry' and of the adventurous 'very new woman' absconding with the authorial bag, the old chivalry was not to be rooted out so abruptly. Depictions of the struggle for the control of the woman's bag, amid competing forces of new and old forms of chivalry, became something of a set piece for modernist writers, providing a means of interrogating the ideal of 'feminine' emancipation upheld in Richardson's work, for example, and feeding into a wider modernist preoccupation with questions of freedom, property and the relation between the two. The woman's bag was, by its very nature, an object of contention in signifying obstructive hindrance as much as mobility, dependence as much as pioneering autonomy, narrative disruption as much as innovation. The main cause for dispute, however, arose from the implied lack of a fixed point of final settlement. Duquette, in comparing 'people' to 'portmanteaux' in Mansfield's 'Je ne parle pas français', allowed for the possibility of a concluding point in his depiction of human restlessness: 'finally the Ultimate Porter swings them on to the Ultimate Train and away they rattle'.[116] Richardson, in her depiction of one restless woman, did not, and this proved a source of much critical discontent, epitomised in the words of Greene: 'this novel, ignoring all signals, just ploughs on and on, the Saratoga, labelled this time for Switzerland, for Austria, shaking on the rack'.[117] The implication is that an ultimately point-less journey makes for an ultimately pointless narrative. Did the bag simply promise an escape – from domesticity, from a patriarchal and proprietorial ideology, from associated pressures of narrative expectation – that was impossible in practice? This was an issue addressed by a number of modernist writers in conceiving of the woman who struck out on her own. While there is little sense of easy resolution in such works, there is evidently a desire to get at the core of the controversy provoked by the figure of the woman who carried her own bag, rather than simply to register the effects of the phenomenon.

Before turning to specific examples from the works of Mansfield, Woolf and D. H. Lawrence, I would like to take a moment here to stress the amplification, with the advent of the twentieth century, of *fin-de-siècle* chivalry debates, in relation both to fictional developments and the question of women's mobility. The interrogation of chivalry was at the forefront of the suffragette agenda though views on the subject were not always in harmony.[118] It absorbed literary writers too. Forster, for one, was acutely sensitive to the issue. In *A Room with a View* (1908), for instance, he invokes and sends up the archaism of the old chivalric code, attempting a distinction between the 'worn-out chivalry of sex' and the 'true chivalry that all the young may show to all the old'.[119] In his paper, *The Feminine Note in Literature,* delivered both to men-only and mixed audiences in December 1910, his opening address to the latter audience included the line: 'There are . . . two things that this paper would not like to be. It would like not to be chivalrous, and it would like not to be insulting.'[120] The paper, inquiring into the relation between literary style and gender, as well as the possibility of rising above gender in writing, portrays traditional chivalry in stultifying terms: '[c]hivalry entails reaction'.[121] For Forster, chivalry prevents men and women from making meaningful connections, on one level, and inhibits the sincerity of the woman writer, on another. Yet, as my earlier discussion of *Howards End* underscores, Forster was himself torn by progressive and reactionary impulses on a formal level, and these expressions on chivalry arise from a noticeably conflicted point of view where women are concerned. It is with no small irony that Woolf, who was present in the mixed audience, later opens her essay on Forster's *Aspects of the Novel* with the following line: 'That fiction is a lady, and a lady who has somehow got herself into trouble from which many gallant gentlemen are ready to rescue her without precisely knowing how, is a thought that must have struck her admirers.'[122] Woolf suggests that fiction and approaches to fiction are so embroiled in the traditional chivalric mode that even those endeavours to 'rescue her' from chivalry, along Forster's lines, are themselves somehow compromised.

This is a running theme in *Pilgrimage*, throughout which Miriam is shown to periodically encounter the power of the 'charming, chivalrous gentleman' in navigating her own authorial bag.[123] Even when her lover Michael Shatov declares himself a feminist, his 'gentillesse' in the matter is seen to be part of the wider problem:[124]

> He was serene and open in the presence of this central bitterness. If she could summon, in words, convincing evidence of the inferiority of man, he would cheerfully accept it and go on unmaimed. But a private reconstruction of standards in agreement with one person would not bring healing. It was history, literature, the way of stating records, reports, stories, the whole method of statement of things from the beginning that was on a false foundation.[125]

Michael's 'serene' support here is tantamount, in figurative terms, to a well-intentioned, we might even say 'gallant', offer to help carry her Saratoga trunk for the duration of her journey, without thinking too deeply about what that journey or his gesture might mean. But if Miriam herself advocates a different form of chivalry in *Pilgrimage* – and there are indicative nods in this direction – it is cast as a *writing against* the whole masculine method of things rather than a gender-neutral *rewriting* of that method.[126] She thus keeps the idea of sex very much in the chivalric equation in line with her idea of creating a 'feminine equivalent' in formal and stylistic terms. I invoke Forster and Richardson here primarily to accentuate the fact that chivalry was a sensitive and controversial topic at this time, and that, moreover, fraught representations of chivalry were bound up with the question of what it meant for a woman to write. The three examples to be considered here put to the test two contrasting possibilities: that of separating a 'true chivalry' from a 'worn-out' or 'old' chivalry of sex, on the one hand, or of further cultivating an oppositional and decidedly feminine 'newest' chivalry, on the other. These are tests carried out around the question of whether the emancipatory bag of the woman represents a false escape, on a par with the 'false foundation' of the home left behind. It is a question which surfaces repeatedly in modernist writing. In 1916, Rebecca West, for example, casts doubt on the supposed achievement of the woman who has liberated herself from domestic parameters:

> One will never really believe in the alleged magnificence of the Younger Generation till one reads a book about the Daughter who Stayed at Home and the father who, in consequence, started at the sound of her voice as at the crack of a whip.[127]

In her 1915 story, 'The Little Governess', Mansfield makes the struggle for the control of a woman's bag one of the key narrative concerns. The story describes the ill-fated adventures of a young girl on her way to take up the post of governess with a family in Germany, placing her in that liminal social position alike occupied by Miriam Henderson at the beginning of *Pilgrimage*. On her journey, the girl is punished in turn by a porter and a waiter for her refusal to tip them, adequately or at all, for carrying her dress-basket. A dress-basket is a type of suitcase. Nominally speaking, it intimates something more juvenile than the dressing-cases the girl spots in the 'Ladies' Cabin' on the boat over, and in which she spies certain 'mysterious rustling little packages'.[128] The distinction between these two kinds of case suggests a distinction between an initiated and an uninitiated sexuality. The young girl's concern for her case, coupled inharmoniously with her desire for adventure, tells a tale of sexual confusion in a context of transition, tapping into those contentious contemporary debates surrounding female sexuality, as highlighted in relation to Freud's 'Dora'. The girl's refusal to pay porter and waiter ('with frigid English simplicity' in the latter case) anticipates her eventual refusal to sexually gratify a seemingly harmless old man she naïvely allows to act as her chaperone for much of the journey.[129] The punishing consequences of her withholding of payment – in the first instance, the porter removes the '*Dames Seules*' designation of her carriage, paving the way for the entrance of the old man, and, in the second, the waiter knowingly renders her suspect in the eyes of her prospective employers – serve to lay bare the idealistic simplicity of the image of the emancipated woman when the sexual and economic roots of the existing social power structure are so gnarled and entangled.[130]

Traditional chivalry is disturbingly cast in the light of sexual and monetary exchange in this story. The covertly discriminatory and commodified basis for the interaction between the sexes was proving a problematic sticking-point for the figure of the newly independent woman, as outlined by Cicely Hamilton in her 1909 *Marriage as a Trade*: 'what is commonly known as "chivalry" is not a spontaneous virtue or impulse on the part of modern man, but the form in which he pays his debt for value received from woman'.[131] This state of affairs is, in fact, unsettlingly reversed in the figure of the porter in Mansfield's story, who is shown to demand reimbursement rather than to reimburse through his actions, thus brutally exposing the remunerative expectation which underlies 'what is commonly known as chivalry', as this is subsequently illustrated in the sordid behaviour of the old man later on.[132] The little governess is warned from the outset by the 'lady at the Governess Bureau' that in order to become a '[woman] of the world', she must adopt a general attitude of distrust.[133] She maintains this attitude, manifested in her concern for the security of her bag, throughout her dealings with the porter. What is noticeable, however, is the degree to which she is, by contrast, taken in by the old man, and this is the direct result of a class-based bias, intrinsic to the practice of chivalry at its very source. One of the reasons the little governess distrusts and is, in turn, treated with such disdain by both porter and waiter is because, as a working woman herself, she is scarcely above them on a social and economic scale. By the same token, she is deceived by the old man precisely because he appears aristocratic: '"Herr Regierungsrat . . . ." He had a title! Well, it was *bound* to be all right!'[134] He treats her like a little lady rather than like a little governess. Her posture as an independent agent, a self-sufficient woman of the world, a woman who carries her own bag, is soon subdued under the protective agency of her 'titled' chaperone: 'He found her a porter, disposed of his own luggage in a few words, guided her through the bewildering crowd out of the station.'[135] The ease with which the old man disposes of his own luggage in a few co-conspiratorial words, much like the husband's engagement of the private train carriage in the earlier 'Virgin Soil', reveals a system designed to facilitate the desires of men; more specifically, men of a certain class and means.

The process by which the desires of the girl are eventually and systematically superseded over the course of the story can be measured through her increasing disregard for and loss of control over her dress-basket. It is entirely forgotten in her hotel room, while she enjoys the pleasures of Munich for the day under the dubious patronage of the old man. We are given a jolting reminder of the implications of this disregard when she returns in distress to the hotel that evening, following the revelation of the old man's prurient intentions. Upon arrival, she finds herself in a position of acute vulnerability at the hands of the waiter who has orchestrated, it is implied, her dismissal at the hands of her new employers. In the final lines, she looks on as the waiter is shown to 'pounce' on the luggage of a new arrival, just as the porter earlier 'pounced' on her own: '"That's it! that's it!" he thought. "That will show her". And . . . he swung the new arrival's box on to his shoulders – hoop! – as though he were a giant and the box a feather.'[136] This is a blatant expression of victory, not least of gigantic over miniature. The little governess's defeat here is prefigured from the beginning, through her thwarted attempt for control of her own bag in her dealings with the porter:

> 'But I don't want a porter'. What a horrible man! 'I don't want a porter.
> I want to carry it myself'. She had to run to keep up with him, and her

anger, far stronger than she, ran before her and snatched the bag out of the wretch's hand.[137]

The disembodied anger of the little governess is shown to have no real agency. Her failed assumption of self-*governance* through carrying her own bag, not to mention her punishment for resisting a system in which she is posited as both helplessly dependent and indebted, figures the emancipated woman as a disembodied phantom.

The image of the dress-basket works on many levels in this figuration. On one level, it is an appropriate prop for the dramatisation of the conflict in question, and it situates that conflict socially as well as spatially. On another level, the object of the dress-basket defines the conflict as sexual. It is not inconceivable that Mansfield was directly nodding to Freud here, whose comments on luggage, in *The Interpretation of Dreams*, were available in English from 1913. Finally, it is upheld as a binding rather than a liberating element, as set against more affirmative conceptions of bag-carrying women, where the bag is shown to represent escape from an inhibiting ideological framework envisioned in the form of the patriarchal house. In Mansfield's conception, the bag – to which the woman is tied, but over which she has no firm control – *is* this inhibiting ideological framework writ small. This story has been read as a deliberate subversion of the fairy-tale narrative, specifically 'Cinderella'.[138] I would add that, in the same gesture of subversion, the emancipated woman of the world, the woman who carries her own bag, is simultaneously dismissed as a fairy-tale figure in an unrealistic fantasy. Published in the same year as *Pointed Roofs*, the little governess is like a disempowered literary shadow of Richardson's Miriam Henderson. The old chivalry is shown to topple the 'newest' chivalry in Mansfield's story.[139]

Woolf was equally well attuned to the significance of the attempt of the woman to carry her own bag as well as the wider meaning of her failure or inability to do so. At the beginning of the third chapter of her 1922 novel *Jacob's Room*, Jacob Flanders is externally assessed by an elderly lady, Mrs Norman, on the carriage of a train. Intuiting a threat, largely arising from her conviction 'that men are dangerous', she discreetly reaches into her dressing-case to ensure that she has a means of defence to hand in the form of a 'scent bottle and a novel from Mudie's', both well set to be pitched effectively if necessary.[140] Woolf was here drawing on the popular knowledge of one mode of suffragette militancy in the 1900s and 1910s, where weapons of aggression were stowed in innocuously ladylike Dorothy handbags, or 'Dorothy bomb-bags', as a 1908 *Punch* article dubs them.[141] A later 1913 *Punch* cartoon, 'The Spread of Tango: Arrest of a Militant Suffragette', featuring a suffragette with a hammer in her handbag, explicitly illustrates this popular association.[142] So powerful did such associations become that, by 1912, *The Bag, Portmanteau and Umbrella Trader* reports on the demise of the 'vogue for hand-bags of the Dorothy type' and that 'ladies are now chary about carrying Dorothy bags nowadays lest they become a "suspect"'.[143]

Mrs Norman is certainly not presented as a hammer-wielding militant suffragette, but her agitated impulse to aggressive retaliation is deliberately situated within a broader prewar context of political dissatisfaction on the part of the woman, a context in which 'women's militancy was justified as an assertion of their own chivalry and as an exposure of the hypocrisy of the chivalry of men'.[144] A new chivalric terminology was activated at this time, to counter the belief that women needed the protection that the old chivalry purported to provide. In the new feminine chivalric order, the woman's bag became an important symbol of self-sufficiency, but, equally, of aggression, as an anonymous reporter in a 1917 article from *The Globe* suggests, with tongue firmly in cheek:

> It is obvious that there is going to be a sex war, and with devilish cunning women are preparing for it. When the ranks are locked in deadly combat, the hand-bag will be revealed in its true light – as a weapon of offence.[145]

Like Mansfield, however, Woolf shows that it is also through the bag that the old chivalry asserts itself and counters any resistive impulses. Mrs Norman's assessment of Jacob's threat by the 'infallible test of appearance' is shown to be entirely misguided.[146] Far from proving a danger to her, he comes to her assistance on arrival at the station by carrying her dressing-case onto the platform in an act of awkward chivalry, thus confounding her original perception of him as potentially dangerous. Ostensibly about the limitations of gaining any insight into character through external appearance, the same passage – more obliquely and thus subversively – tackles the subject of the appeasement of a woman's impulse towards aggressive retaliatory action through the old chivalric gesture, centred on the handling of the woman's bag.

Such a reading is elucidated further upon situating Mrs Norman's impulse to defensive aggression here within the larger outline of Woolf's writing. Mrs Norman's initial anxiety is prompted by a sense of spatial infringement. 'This is not a smoking carriage', she protests as Jacob enters.[147] However, we know from Woolf's earlier novel *The Voyage Out* (1915), that this objection, and the ensuing urge to aggression that it provokes, is also a reaction to a sexual inequality made manifest in the spatial arrangement of the train. To Terence Hewet's mind, in that novel, the allocation of train carriages exhibits a prejudicial and skewed form of sexual representation:

> '[W]e're always writing about women – abusing them, or jeering at them, or worshipping them; but it's never come from women themselves. I believe we still don't know in the least how they live, or what they feel or what they do precisely . . . It's the man's view that's represented, you see.

> Think of a railway train: fifteen carriages for men who want to smoke. Doesn't it make your blood boil? If I were a woman, I'd blow someone's brains out'.[148]

While the operation of traditional chivalry is explicitly revealed in a grotesque light in Mansfield's story, Woolf is more understated, though no less potent, in her criticism. If Mrs Norman gets Jacob's measure wrong in practice, she does not get it wrong in theory. In other words, his patently disinterested courtesy in carrying her bag proves he is not to be practically feared as a dangerous man, but that same courteous action must also be seen to form an insidious part of a larger ideological structure which allows 'fifteen carriages for men who want to smoke' and, correspondingly (not to forget), Jacob's ill-fated conscription. Mrs Norman's aggressive impulse is quelled just as the little governess's anger is rendered ineffectual in its disembodied form; the temporary loss of control of a bag is at issue in both cases. Woolf and Mansfield suggest that the old chivalry functions, on an implicit level, to conceal an inherent inequality and to contain a 'sex war', to re-invoke the amplificatory note of the *Globe* article. It follows that the woman's bag becomes a contested article, a prop around which old and new forms of chivalry compete for precedence.

D. H. Lawrence likewise depicts a sexual struggle in and around the object of a woman's bag towards the end of *Women in Love* (1920), but the emphasis is alternatively placed in this instance, striking a sort of syncopated note in juxtaposition with Mansfield and Woolf. The bag belongs to the progressive Gudrun Brangwen, and it plays a critical role within her protracted conflict with her lover, Gerald Crich. This time, the chivalric manipulation is shown to be all on the woman's side, and it is the man who is left in a position of frustration, turning the balance of power on its head. It is a passage worth quoting at some length and begins at a point where Gudrun, sensing a waning influence in her relationship with Gerald, attempts to recover a position of dominance:

> Summoning all her strength, she said, in a full resonant, nonchalant voice that was forced out with all her remaining self-control:
> 'Oh, would you mind looking in that bag behind there and giving me my –'
> Here her power fell inert. 'My what – my what – ?' she screamed in silence to herself.
> But he had started round, surprised and startled that she should ask him to look in her bag, which she always kept so *very* private to herself. She turned, now her face white, her dark eyes blazing with uncanny overwrought excitement. She saw him stooping to the bag, undoing the loosely buckled strap, inattentive.
> 'Your what?' he asked.

'Oh, a little enamel box – yellow – with a design of a cormorant pluck-ing her breast –'

She went towards him, stooping her beautiful, bare arm, and deftly turned some of her things, disclosing the box, which was exquisitely painted.

'That is it, see', she said, taking it from under his eyes.

And he was baffled now. He was left to fasten up the bag, whilst she swiftly did up her hair for the night, and sat down to unfasten her shoes. She would not turn her back to him any more.

He was baffled, frustrated, but unconscious. She had the whip hand over him now.[149]

This rather perplexing exchange defies easy interpretation, but this is part of the point. We might begin by asking how exactly Gudrun regains the 'whip hand' over Gerald? In the first place, she calls for his assistance in the tradi-tional chivalric mode by setting him a task. Yet this is not a task which falls within the scope of the traditional chivalric duty of the man. It is, in fact, a task more suited to a lady's maid and designed to emasculate him, to render him socially inferior, as well as to orchestrate his failure. In staging this failure, Gudrun not only distorts the terms of traditional chivalry, but, in line with some of the *fin-de-siècle* examples earlier studied, she also overturns them by taking charge of the situation and accomplishing the task he cannot com-plete. The 'newest chivalry' ostensibly triumphs here, and Gudrun succeeds in carrying the advantage of power where the little governess and Mrs Norman respectively *mis*carry, in effect.

This reading is complicated, however, by a simultaneous interrogation of the concept of possession, on Lawrence's part. The novel itself manifests a deep fascination with those conflicting human impulses – material and emo-tional – towards freedom and self-sufficiency, on the one hand, and possessive attachment, on the other. It provides no definite resolution to this conflict, and the passage we have been looking at presents a microcosmic depiction of the impasse. It should be noted that Gudrun's overt denial of the terms of ownership is marked. She asks for '*that* bag' and '*a* little enamel box' (emphasis added), anticipating her later profession of a desire to get away from people who 'own things'.[150] When it comes to using the possessive pronoun, she falters, and her 'power falls inert'. Regaining this power and thus the 'whip hand' over Gerald requires exercising that possessive pronoun and thus entering into a proprieto-rial relation, one in which *she* gains the balance of power but compromises, in turn, her own autonomy. It is implied that Gudrun, 'her dark eyes blazing with uncanny overwrought excitement', is *possessed* by some kind of sinister force just as she is in the act of possessing. This is a circumstance underlined by the enamel box with a design of a cormorant plucking her breast, a reworking of the traditional Eucharistic symbol of a pelican piercing her breast to feed her young with her own blood. Through the substitution of the cormorant, a bird popularly associated with the devil and reputed to have a voracious appetite, the original image of Christian self-sacrifice becomes an image of satanic self-destruction. For Lawrence, to own is to be owned. By confusing, in this sinister way, the figures of possessor and possessed, as well as the balance of power between them, he implies a disconcerting correlation. Both figures have meaning only in proprietorial relation. In other words, in assuming proprietary power over Gerald, Gudrun is herself proprietarily bound.

In presenting Gudrun as the subject of control as much as the controlling subject, Lawrence undermines her ostensible victory in this scene. How then should we read this anti-victory in the context of the other examples we have been exploring here? As an exposure of the unnatural inclinations or destructive force of what Lawrence was to refer to, in a later essay, as the 'cocksure woman'?[151] Is it a subtle reassertion of a male-oriented sexual politics in line with Kate Millett's radical attack on Lawrence in the 1970s?[152] Should we view it, on the other hand, as an illustration, through inversion, of the proprietorial submission of the man *as well as* the woman in the traditional chivalric relation? Is it a critique of the 'property instinct', as one character in *Lady Chatterley's Lover* (1929) later dubs it, over and above the chivalric impulse?[153] Or is it an account of the unsettling relation between the two? And should we read the cormorant image less as a denunciation of the 'cocksure' form of modern woman and more as a skewed vision of Christianity in a postwar context? The point is that all of these readings have some validity. Further to this, none of these interpretations is allowed to assume complete validity, that is to say, to fully *triumph* and the woman's bag is deliberately used to convey this interpretative contention. The particular struggle surrounding the woman's bag is an interpretative struggle as much as it is a sexual struggle in Lawrence's text. Anne Fernihough, in pointing to the recent critical embrace of the disorienting elements in Lawrence's work, remarks upon the '*bafflement* and the fascination of many of Lawrence's readers and . . . the difficulty in doing critical justice to his works'.[154] This interpretative 'bafflement', highlighted by Fernihough, is itself inscribed in this passage through the repetition of Gerald's own 'baffled' response to the illegibility of the '*very* private' self purportedly held by Gudrun's bag.[155] But even more importantly, the contents of that same bag are also illegible to Gudrun. Her attempted expression of the '*very* private' self within the bag falls into ellipsis – 'My what – ?' – until filled by Lawrence himself with a plethora of conflicting suggestions. Rachel Potter, with a particular eye to Lawrence as well as Ford Madox Ford, has surveyed the way in which women were shown, again and again, to 'embody the contradictions of modernity'.[156] The woman's bag here stands as a framework for such contradictory imperatives and impulses.

The struggle to control the woman's bag in each of these examples, but particularly so in Lawrence's case, must be seen as a struggle to control meaning in the context of the competing interests of new and old forms of chivalry, new and old understandings of the relations between the sexes. But above all, the very idea of escape from the proprietorial and fictional paradigm of the house is rendered problematic, and it is as such that Mrs Brown's bag assumes importance as an overlooked detail in Woolf's seminal essay, 'Mr Bennett and Mrs Brown'. Woolf offers us, as an exemplar of modern character fit for modern fiction, a portrait of an ordinary woman outside of the fictional house and on a moving train carriage, a woman 'unmoored from her anchorage', and, emphatically, a woman who carries her own bag.[157] Yet this is not quite figured as the triumphant gesture of emancipation we might suppose it to be, as set within the lineage we have been considering in this chapter as a whole. For a start, Mrs Brown is no feisty modern woman, and, if anything, her denial of Mr Smith's conventional courtesy in reaching for her bag amounts, in the imagined context, to a seemingly paltry retention of control in an otherwise desperate situation. The 'man of business', the 'respectable' Mr Smith is palpably no 'Mr Smithereen', and Mrs Brown herself is no burly 'Miss Sampson', to refer back to Figure 3.[158] The burliness is decidedly on the other side, while Mrs Brown is portrayed as 'extremely small' and visibly apprehensive.[159] There is no question of Mrs Brown's offering to carry Mr Smith's 'stout leather bag', a bag as prominently placed, in this passage, as Mrs Brown's own.[160] Indeed, this seems to me an encounter as much between two bags as two beings; it is an encounter, in other words, with proprietary implications. Woolf makes one rather telling observation in her account of Mrs Brown: 'Perhaps she was going to London to sign some documents *to make over some property*. Obviously against her will she was *in Mr Smith's hands*.'[161] Mrs Brown's seemingly paltry retention of control in denying Mr Smith's chivalric gesture acquires symbolic potency in this light. By refusing to 'make over' her portable property to 'Mr Smith's hands', she herself remains out of his hands and retains a measure of 'heroic' autonomy far beyond that achieved by the little governess, or even Gudrun.[162]

Mrs Brown's visceral attachment to her bag must, by the same token, be seen as a vehement expression of continued attachment to a proprietorial framework as opposed to a rejection of the very notion of stable property in line with previous conceptions of bag-carrying women. Her bag is presented as a touchstone of continuity at a point of instability. This is a curious paradox at the centre of an essay which sets out to undermine the materialistic bent of Edwardian fiction, the 'enormous stress upon the fabric of things' manifested in such writing.[163] It is the material fabric of Mrs Brown's world which is presumed to be under threat in her encounter with Mr Smith. Though Woolf pleads for the character of Mrs Brown to be 'rescued' by Georgian novelists 'at whatever cost of life, limb, and damage to valuable property', her own chosen sketch offers us a figure seeking to preserve herself *through* preserving her 'valuable property'.[164] Mrs Brown's bag stands for Mrs Brown's house. Correspondingly, Woolf's essay subtly holds to the idea of a house of fiction at the same time as it urges that house to be destroyed. It is no small wonder that her appeal on behalf of the woman writer several years later, in 1929, was for a metaphorical room within the canonical house and not for a seat on a non-smoking counter-cultural train carriage: 'But, you may say, we asked you to speak about women and fiction – what has that got to do with a room of one's own?'[165] Woolf's 'Mr Bennett and Mrs Brown' demonstrates that the struggle surrounding the bag was a necessary and integral stage in the struggle surrounding the room. But it further establishes that the woman's bag worked exceptionally well, in itself, as an object and symbol through which to renegotiate three key terms in relation: 'woman', 'property' and 'freedom'.

NOTES

1. Virginia Woolf, 'Mr Bennett and Mrs Brown', in *A Woman's Essays*, ed. Rachel Bowlby (Harmondsworth: Penguin, 1992), p. 74. The essay was first published in the *Nation and Athenaeum* on 1 December 1923.
2. Ibid., p. 74.
3. Henry James, 'The Future of the Novel', in *The Critical Muse: Selected Literary Criticism*, ed. Roger Gard (Harmondsworth: Penguin, 1987), p. 344.
4. For an overview, see Marianne DeKoven, 'Modernism and Gender', *The Cambridge Companion to Modernism*, ed. Michael Levenson (Cambridge: Cambridge University Press, 1999), pp. 174–93. A further important work in this area is Bonnie Kime Scott, *Refiguring Modernism*, 2 vols (Bloomington: Indiana University Press, 1995). I will refer to other relevant texts as the chapter progresses.
5. Marianne DeKoven, 'Gendered Doubleness and the "Origins" of Modernist Form', *Tulsa Studies in Women's Literature*, 8.1, Spring 1989, p. 19.
6. 'The *flâneur* is an exclusively male type', Pollock writes of that modernist icon, offsetting this characterisation against the woman's experience of movement in the late nineteenth century, as this is delineated, for example, in the journal of artist Marie Bashkirtseff. Bowlby gives a more developed account of the implications of female mobility through street walking/haunting – she defines the street walker against the figures of *flâneur* and *passante* – as positively evinced in writings by Woolf and more poignantly envisioned in the work of Jean Rhys. Parkins extends the discussion to the possibilities opened up by new technologies, asserting that '[w]omen's mobility is an important means through which the reconfigurations of the modern female subject are textually represented'. See Griselda Pollock, *Vision and Difference: Femininity, Feminism and Histories of Art* (London: Routledge, 1988), p. 67; Rachel Bowlby, *Still Crazy After All These Years: Women, Writing and Psychoanalysis* (London: Routledge, 1992); Wendy Parkins, 'Moving Dangerously: Mobility and the Modern Woman', *Tulsa Studies in Women's Literature*, 20.1, Spring 2001, p. 90. For a more sustained discussion, see also Parkins's monograph on the subject, *Mobility and Modernity in Women's Novels, 1850s–1930s: Women Moving Dangerously* (Basingstoke and New York: Palgrave Macmillan, 2009).

7. Bowlby, *Still Crazy After All These Years*, p. viii.
8. Rita Felski, *The Gender of Modernity* (Cambridge, MA: Harvard University Press, 1995), p. 7.
9. For the sake of consistency, I will be using the general term 'bag' in an overarching capacity throughout this chapter. To start with, this is a term which encompasses a range of moveable containers, from handbags to more weighty items, but it additionally intimates portability, more pronouncedly than certain alternatives, which is where my own stress in this analysis falls. This does not mean that the various specifications of moveable container, in the texts to be considered, are indistinguishable. On the contrary, precise designations must be seen to bear very particular connotations in context, and the distinctions, both obvious and subtle, between bag types call for and will receive close consideration.
10. Gail Cunningham, *The New Woman and the Victorian Novel* (London: Macmillan, 1978), p. 3. For further accounts of the importance of *fin-de-siècle* and Edwardian interrogations of gender relations in the development of early modernism, see Ann Ardis, *New Women, New Novels: Feminism and Early Modernism* (New Brunswick, NJ: Rutgers University Press, 1990), Gerd Bjorhovde, *Rebellious Structures: Women Writers and the Crisis of the Novel 1880–1900* (Oslo: Norwegian University Press, 1987), and Jane Eldridge Miller, *Rebel Women: Feminism, Modernism and the Edwardian Novel* (London: Virago, 1994).
11. Susan Stewart, *On Longing: Narratives of the Miniature, the Gigantic, the Souvenir, the Collection* (1984; Durham, NC: Duke University Press, 2003), p. xii.
12. Ibid., pp. 101–3.
13. The New Woman was, in the main, a middle-class phenomenon, and it is mostly bourgeois women I will be considering here, since it was a rejection of bourgeois domestic ideology that the bag, more often than not, flaunted. However, the bag, in certain other cases, signalled an enforced social marginality, and several of these bag-carrying women will be shown to hold manifestly uncertain positions in relation to class. It is through the unsettled status of the woman's bag – which can be interpreted, in turn, as residual bourgeois baggage and as a symbol of class-based proprietorial emancipation – that uncertainties of social standing, as well as wider feminist tensions are, indeed, frequently brought to light.
14. 'To no man alive', Hamilton stated, 'can the world be quite as wonderful as it is to the woman now alive who has fought free … The world to her is in the experimental stage.' Cicely Hamilton, *Marriage as a Trade* (1909; Detroit: Singing Tree Press. 1971), p. 30.
15. Grant Allen's *The Woman Who Did* (1895), concerning a woman who enters into a 'free union' with a man of her 'free choice' culminating in the birth of child out of wedlock, is arguably the most famous and notorious New Woman novel of the 1890s. Grant Allen, *The Woman Who Did* (1895; Oxford: Oxford University Press, 1995), pp. 60–1.
16. Quoted in Judith E. Harper, *Susan B. Anthony: A Biographical Companion* (Santa Barbara: ABC-CLIO, 1998), p. 146. Emphasis in original. Deborah Wynne alerts us to a remarkably similar recognition of women's disenfranchisement within a contemporary British context. She describes the case of the well-known feminist Millicent Garrett Fawcett, who 'only discovered that she did not legally own the purse she used' when a pickpocket was legally charged with stealing the purse in question from her husband. See Deborah Wynne, *Women and Personal Property in the Victorian Novel* (Farnham, Surrey: Ashgate, 2010), p. 9.
17. Sally Ledger, *The New Woman: Fiction and Feminism at the Fin De Siècle*

(Manchester: Manchester University Press, 1997), p. 81. This was also true of the United States. *A Doll's House* premiered both on Broadway and in London in 1889 (although a much watered-down American version of the original was produced much earlier, in 1883).

18. Henrik Ibsen, *A Doll's House* (1879), in *Four Major Plays: A Doll's House, Ghosts, Hedda Gabler, The Master Builder*, trans. James McFarlane and Jens Arup, with an introduction by James McFarlane (Oxford and New York: Oxford University Press, 1998), pp. 85, 82. Emphasis in original.

19. Ibid., p. 88. Emphasis in original.

20. M. J. Færdon's address to his congregation in 1884. Quoted in Gail Finney, 'Ibsen and Feminism', in *The Cambridge Companion to Ibsen*, ed. James McFarlane (Cambridge: Cambridge University Press, 1994), p. 91.

21. For interpretations of the development of the courtship plot and romance genre, in part, as a compensatory response to the legal disinheritance and economic disempowerment of daughter-figures, see Ruth Perry, *Novel Relations: The Transformation of Kinship in English Literature and Culture, 1748–1818* (Cambridge: Cambridge University Press, 2004), pp. 38–76, and Rachel Blau DuPlessis, *Writing Beyond the Ending: Narrative Strategies of Twentieth-Century Women Writers* (Bloomington: Indiana University Press, 1985), p. 19.

22. Acts in this line were passed in New York in 1848 and 1860 (extending from there to other American states), and in the United Kingdom in 1870 and 1882. Legislative reform with the aim of increasing women's participation in society was set in motion in Ibsen's Norway before the mid-nineteenth century, but, interestingly, a corresponding form of Married Women's Property Act was not introduced until 1888, almost ten years after the first staging of *A Doll's House*. See Karin Bruzelius Heffermehl, 'The Status of Women in Norway', *The American Journal of Comparative Law* 20.4, Autumn 1972, pp. 630–46.

23. See Wynne, *Women and Personal Property*, pp. 33–4.

24. Jordanna Bailkin, *The Culture of Property: The Crisis of Liberalism in Modern Britain* (Chicago: University of Chicago Press, 2004), p. 25.

25. Tim Dolin, *Mistress of the House: Women of Property in the Victorian Novel* (Aldershot, Hampshire: Ashgate, 1997), p. 9.

26. Lee Holcombe, *Wives and Property: Reform of the Married Women's Property Law in Nineteenth-Century England* (Toronto and Buffalo, NY: University of Toronto Press, 1983), p. 4.

27. It is no accident that George Moore later pointedly connects servant-figure Esther Waters with the carriage of her luggage at the beginning and end of *Esther Waters* in 1894. In Moore's novel, the opening description of the self-sufficient Esther with her 'oblong box painted reddish brown' in tow, is repeated almost word for word at the close of the novel, creating a narrative loop. As David Trotter observes, 'the older Esther is the sum of the experiences which have shaped her appearance', and I would add that her box is the defining element of identification, as index to the weight of those 'experiences', but also to Esther's circular return to a life in service and a declined social situation at the end of the novel. David Trotter, *The English Novel in History 1895–1920* (London: Routledge, 1998), p. 120. George Moore, *Esther Waters* (1894; London: William Heinemann, 1932), pp. 1, 364–5.

28. Ibsen, *Hedda Gabler* (1891), in *Four Major Plays*, p. 170.

29. Married women would, in fact, gain the right to control their own wealth in Norway during the 1890s, shortly after Ibsen's play. Nevertheless, such associations would have endured well beyond legal reform.

30. Wynne, *Women and Personal Property*, p. 10.

31. Ibid., p. 35. Emphasis added.

32. Jules Verne, *Le tour du monde en quatre-vingts jours* (1873; Paris: Bookking International, 1994), p. 142. My translation. Bly does have casual chaperones and guides in passing, but she makes the round trip in its entirety on her own, and her adventure was publicised as such.
33. Nelly [*sic*] Bly, *Around the World in Seventy-Two Days* (1890; Rockville, MD: Wildside, 2009), pp. 5–6.
34. Alexandra Lapierre, 'Foreword' in *Women Travelers: A Century of Trailblazing Adventures*, by Christel Mouchard, trans. Deke Dusinberre (Paris: Flammarion, 2007), p. 4.
35. Emily Lowe, *Unprotected Females in Norway; Or, The Pleasantest Way of Travelling There, Passing Through Denmark and Sweden* (London and New York: G. Routledge & Co., 1857), p. 3.
36. 'The Lady Guide and the Tory Tourist', cartoon, *Fun*, 49.1249, 17 April 1889, p. 167.
37. According to Mary Chapman, American suffragettes would go on to use this tactic in the first decades of the twentieth century, boldly displaying their political messages on brightly-coloured news bags, which attracted significant media attention at the time and challenged gendered codes of conduct on the city streets. See Mary Chapman, *Making Noise, Making News: Suffrage Print Culture and U.S. Modernism* (Oxford and New York: Oxford University Press, 2014), p. 44.
38. Oscar Wilde, *The Importance of Being Earnest*, in *The Collected Works of Oscar Wilde* (Ware, Hertfordshire: Wordsworth, 1998), p. 559.
39. The New Woman in question was namely George Egerton, whose controversial *Keynotes* collection had appeared the previous year. The bespectacled woman is depicted with an open book in one hand and a raised latchkey in the other. 'Donna Quixote', *Punch* 106, 28 April 1894, p. 195.
40. Leigh Wilson, '"She in Her 'Armour' and He in his Coat of Nerves": May Sinclair and the Rewriting of Chivalry', in *Feminist Forerunners: New Womanism and Feminism in the Early Twentieth Century*, ed. Ann Heilman (London: Pandora, 2003), p. 179. Wilson centres her discussion on the work of May Sinclair and her particular response, both critically and artistically, to these wider debates.
41. George Gissing, 'The Poet's Portmanteau', in *Human Odds and Ends: Stories and Sketches* (1898; New York and London: Garland, 1977), p. 88. The story itself was first published in *The English Illustrated Magazine* in February 1895.
42. Robert Selig, '"The Poet's Portmanteau": A Flirtation that Dares not Speak its Name', *The Gissing Journal*, 36.1, January 2000, p. 30
43. Sarah Grand, 'The Undefinable', in *A New Woman Reader: Fiction, Articles, Drama of the 1890s*, ed. Carolyn Christensen Nelson (Peterborough, ON: Broadview, 2001), pp. 35–51; Ella D'Arcy, 'The Pleasure–Pilgrim', *The Yellow Book: An Illustrated Quarterly* 5, April 1895, pp. 34–67.
44. Gissing, 'The Poet's Portmanteau', p. 82.
45. George Egerton, 'Virgin Soil', in *Keynotes; Discords* (1893–4; London: Virago, 1983), pp. 145, 148.
46. Ibid., p. 148.
47. Ibid., p. 157.
48. Bly, *Around the World in Seventy-Two Days*, pp. 24–5.
49. Egerton, 'Virgin Soil', p. 148.
50. Ibid., p. 157.
51. Tony Tanner, *Adultery in the Novel: Contract and Transgression* (Baltimore: Johns Hopkins University Press, 1979), p. 15.
52. Ibsen, *Hedda Gabler*, in *Four Major Plays*, pp. 203–4. Egerton, in fact, lived in

Norway for a period and was strongly influenced by Ibsen. 'Virgin Soil' must be seen as a very conscious engagement with his work.

53. Egerton, 'Virgin Soil', pp. 155, 154.
54. Ibid., pp. 162, 150.
55. Ibid., pp. 157, 161.
56. Ledger, *The New Woman*, p. 191.
57. Egerton, 'Virgin Soil', p. 161.
58. Ledger, *The New Woman*, p. 192.
59. John Cowper Powys, *Dorothy Richardson* (1931; London: Villiers, 1974), pp. 8, 6. Emphasis in original. Powys's essay was first published in 1931.
60. Dorothy Richardson, *Pilgrimage,* vol. 1 (London: Dent and Cresset, 1938), pp. 10, 9. Each of the four volumes of *Pilgrimage* has the same publication details.
61. Powys, *Dorothy Richardson*, p. 36.
62. Richardson, *Pilgrimage,* vol. 3, p. 278.
63. This is a conflict which recurs in modernist women's writing, most prominently in the work of Jean Rhys. Her *Good Morning, Midnight* (1939), figures life outside the house of fiction as a form of exclusionary dispossession over and above a form of freedom: 'Walking in the night with the dark houses over you, like monsters . . . No hospitable doors, no lit windows, just frowning darkness.' Jean Rhys, *Good Morning, Midnight* (1939; London: Penguin, 1969), p. 28.
64. Richardson, *Pilgrimage,* vol. 1, p. 321.
65. Richardson, *Pilgrimage,* vol. 3, p. 453.
66. Richardson, *Pilgrimage,* vol. 1, p. 26.
67. Richardson, *Pilgrimage,* vol. 2, p. 90; vol. 1, p. 194; vol. 2, p. 110.
68. Richardson, *Pilgrimage,* vol. 1, p. 15. The Saratoga accompanies Miriam for most of *Pilgrimage* and is used interchangeably with other forms of travelling kit, for example a more lightweight Gladstone bag. The Saratoga is replaced in one of the very late chapters, *Clear Horizon*, by a cabin trunk. Incidentally, *Pointed Roofs* is not the only chapter to begin with the image of Miriam in transit with fore-grounded luggage. *Honeycomb* begins as Miriam unpacks in a new room at the end of a journey. The opening line of *The Tunnel* pictures Miriam with a 'heavy bag dragging at her arm'. Similarly, *Interim*'s opening line figures her 'thump[ing] her Gladstone bag down' on a doorstep. *The Trap* begins as Miriam is unpacking in a new flat, while *Oberland* finds her negotiating her luggage on a train station platform. See Richardson, *Pilgrimage,* vol. 2, pp. 11, 291.
69. Jean Radford, *Dorothy Richardson* (Hemel Hempstead: Harvester Wheatsheaf, 1991), p. 27. Christian's allegorical burden is most explicitly alluded to in *Backwater*:

> The list of questions for self-examination as to sins past and present in thought, word, and deed brought back the sense of her body with its load of well-known memories. Could they be got rid of? She could cast them off, feel them sliding away like Christian's Burden. (Richardson, *Pilgrimage,* vol. 1, pp. 262–3)

70. Gloria Glikin, 'Dorothy M. Richardson: The Personal "Pilgrimage"', *PMLA*, 78.5, December 1963, p. 593; Also corroborated by John Rosenberg in *Dorothy Richardson: The Genius They Forgot* (London: Duckworth, 1973), p. 55.
71. Richardson, *Pilgrimage,* vol. 1, p. 58.
72. Ibid., p. 23.
73. Ibid., p. 266; Powys, *Dorothy Richardson*, p. 35.
74. Katherine Mansfield, 'Three Women Novelists', in *Novels and Novelists*, ed. John Middleton Murry (London: Constable and Company Limited, 1930), p. 4.

75. Graham Greene, 'The Saratoga Trunk', in *The Lost Childhood and Other Essays* (London: Eyre and Spottiswoode, 1951), pp. 84, 85.
76. Leon Edel, 'Dorothy Richardson, 1882–1957', *Modern Fiction Studies* 4, Winter 1958, p. 168.
77. Stewart, *On Longing*, p. 26; Trotter, *The English Novel in History*, p. 80.
78. Richardson, *Pilgrimage*, vol. 1, p. 9.
79. See Linda Edelstein and Pat Morse, *Antique Trunks: Identification and Price Guide* (Iola, WI: Krause, 2003), pp. 10–11.
80. Richardson, *Pilgrimage*, vol. 1, pp. 74, 34.
81. Ibid., p. 208.
82. Ibid., p. 436.
83. Ford Madox Hueffer, 'The Woman of the Novelists', in *The Critical Attitude* (London: Duckworth, 1911), p. 168.
84. Richardson, *Pilgrimage*, vol. 1, p. 388.
85. Ibid., p. 74.
86. Gaston Bachelard, *The Poetics of Space*, trans. Maria Jolas (1958; New York: Orion, 1964), p. 81. Emphasis in original.
87. Sigmund Freud, *Fragment of an Analysis of a Case of Hysteria ('Dora')* in *Case Histories 1: 'Dora' and 'Little Hans'*, trans. Alix and James Strachey, ed. James Strachey, assisted by Angela Richards and Alan Tyson (London: Penguin, 1977), p. 99. Emphasis in original. The association of jewellery with female sexuality has a long history in literature, from Pamela's long-winded defence of her 'most precious of all jewels' in Samuel Richardson's eighteenth-century novel (1740) through to the erotically charged image of the ruby choker in Angela Carter's *The Bloody Chamber* (1979). The imaginative appeal of the jewel-case as indicator of a woman's intimate life is likewise a persistent one. To give one illustrative example, Isabel, in outlining her fast-growing familiarity with Mme Merle in James's *The Portrait of a Lady*, notes that 'it was as if she had given to a comparative stranger the key to her cabinet of jewels'. Samuel Richardson, *Pamela; Or, Virtue Rewarded* (1740; London: Penguin, 1980), pp. 46, 229; Angela Carter, 'The Bloody Chamber', in *The Bloody Chamber* (Harmondsworth: Penguin, 1979), pp. 7–41; Henry James, *The Portrait of a Lady* (1881; London: Penguin, 1997), p. 174.
88. Freud, *Fragment of an Analysis of a Case of Hysteria*, pp. 113–14.
89. Sigmund Freud, *The Interpretation of Dreams*, trans. James Strachey, ed. James Strachey, assisted by Alan Tyson (1900; London: Penguin, 1991), pp. 237–8, 275–6, 475. He refers, in part, to the work of Wilhelm Steker in making these associations and also draws attention to the German word for receptacle – 'Büchse' – which was in common use as a slang term for the female genitals.
90. Ilza Veith, *Hysteria: The History of a Disease* (Chicago: University of Chicago Press, 1965), p. 1. For another instructive outline of the long history of the 'disease paradigm' known as 'hysteria', see the opening chapters of Rachel P. Maines, *The Technology of Orgasm: 'Hysteria,' the Vibrator, and Women's Sexual Satisfaction* (Baltimore: Johns Hopkins University Press, 1999), pp. 1–48.
91. Freud, *Fragment of an Analysis of a Case of Hysteria*, p. 130.
92. Ibid., p. 104.
93. For one insightful reappraisal of Dora's case, which acknowledges the ground-breaking nature of the analysis, while challenging certain aspects of it in light of twentieth-century feminist criticism, see Nancy Armstrong, *Desire and Domestic Fiction: A Political History of the Novel* (1987; Oxford: Oxford University Press, 1989), pp. 225–50.

94. Freddie Rokem, 'Slapping Women: Ibsen's Nora, Strindberg's Julie, and Freud's Dora', in *Textual Bodies: Changing Boundaries of Literary Representation,* ed. Lori Hope Lefkovitz (New York: State University of New York Press, 1997), p. 237

95. Peter Gay, *The Bourgeois Experience: Victoria to Freud,* vol. 1 (New York: Oxford University Press, 1984), p. 167. The quotation is taken from a chapter entitled 'The Problematic Sex' (pp. 144–68), which, as a whole, provides an overview of the controversial discussions surrounding the nature of female sexuality in literature, from medical to imaginative, through the nineteenth century and into the twentieth.

96. Richardson, *Pilgrimage,* vol. 2, p. 221.

97. Richardson, *Pilgrimage,* vol. 1, p. 436.

98. Richardson, *Pilgrimage,* vol. 3, p. 246.

99. Richardson, *Pilgrimage,* vol. 2, p. 92.

100. DuPlessis, *Writing Beyond the Ending,* p. 143.

101. Richardson, *Pilgrimage,* vol. 1, pp. 183-4.

102. Kristin Bluemel, *Experimenting on the Borders of Modernism: Dorothy Richardson's Pilgrimage* (Athens: University of Georgia Press, 1997), p. 56. For a discussion of narrative in relation to masculine patterns of desire, see Joseph Allen Boone, *Tradition Counter Tradition: Love and the Form of Fiction* (Chicago: University of Chicago Press, 1987), p. 72. For a Richardson-specific discussion of the same, see DuPlessis, *Writing Beyond the Ending,* pp. 151–2.

103. Richardson, *Pilgrimage,* vol. 1, p. 349.

104. Ibid., p. 185.

105. Ibid., p. 284.

106. Ibid., p. 19.

107. See, for example, Sydney Janet Kaplan, *Feminine Consciousness in the Modern British Novel* (Urbana: University of Illinois Press, 1975), pp. 43–6; Elizabeth Podnieks, 'The Ultimate Astonisher: Dorothy Richardson's "Pilgrimage"', *Frontiers: A Journal of Women Studies* 14.3, 1994, p. 89; Radford, *Dorothy Richardson,* pp. 39–40. Tim Cresswell also makes a link between mobility and 'becoming' in *On the Move: Mobility in the Modern Western World* (New York: Routledge, 2006), p. 47.

108. Bryony Randall, *Modernism, Daily Time and Everyday Life* (Cambridge: Cambridge University Press, 2007), p. 91.

109. For a phenomenological reading of space and spatiality in *Pilgrimage* with a literary architectural emphasis, see Elisabeth Bronfen, *Dorothy Richardson's Art of Memory: Space, Identity, Text,* trans. Victoria Appelbe (Manchester: Manchester University Press, 1999).

110. Richardson, *Pilgrimage,* vol. 3, p. 87.

111. Elizabeth Fisher, *Woman's Creation: Sexual Evolution and the Shaping of Society* (New York: McGraw Hill, 1979), p. 56.

112. Fisher was partly nodding to the work of Sally Slocum here. Slocum had previously drawn attention to a male prejudice in anthropological accounts of evolution, spotlighting the equal importance of the woman's role as gatherer alongside the 'man as hunter' role. See Sally Slocum, 'Woman the Gatherer: Male Bias in Anthropology', in *Toward an Anthropology of Women,* ed. Rayna R. Reiter (New York: Monthly Review Press, 1975), pp. 36–50.

113. Fisher, *Woman's Creation,* p. 60.

114. Ursula K. Le Guin, 'The Carrier Bag Theory of Fiction', in *Dancing at the Edge of the World: Thoughts on Words, Women, Places* (New York: Grove Press, 1989), pp. 166–7. In formulating these theories, Fisher and Le Guin doubtless also owed

much to the ferment of thought surrounding *la différence féminine* in the 1970s and 1980s, spearheaded by Julia Kristeva, Luce Irigaray and Hélène Cixous, who, as Donna Stanton points out, broke with feminist predecessors like Simone de Beauvoir, in the 'valorization of the maternal', conceiving of a matrilineal aesthetics. Kristeva, in particular, honed in on womb-like imagery through the concept of the receptacle/*chora* as conceived by Plato in his dialogue concerning the origin of the universe, *Timaeus* (circa 360 BC). Interest in the 'feminine and maternal resonances' in Plato's account has, according to Emanuela Bianchi, re-emerged in the works of a number of more recent critics. See Donna Stanton, 'Difference on Trial: A Critique of the Maternal Metaphor in Cixous, Irigaray, and Kristeva', in *The Poetics of Gender*, ed. Nancy K. Miller (New York: Columbia University Press, 1986), p. 160; Julia Kristeva, 'Revolution in Poetic Language', in *The Kristeva Reader*, ed. Toril Moi (New York: Columbia University Press, 1986), pp. 89–136; Emanuela Bianchi, 'Receptacle/*Chōra*: Figuring the Errant Feminine in Plato's *Timaeus*', *Hypatia*, 21.4, Fall 2006, p. 124. See also Alison Stone, 'Against Matricide: Rethinking Subjectivity and the Maternal Body', *Hypatia*, 27.1, Winter 2012, pp. 118–38, and Irina Aristarkhova, *Hospitality of the Matrix: Philosophy, Biomedicine, and Culture* (New York: Columbia University Press, 2012).

115. 'Pour Les Dames', *The Bag, Portmanteau and Umbrella Trader and Fancy Leather Goods and Athletic Trades Review*, 4.126, April 1911, p. 10.
116. Katherine Mansfield, 'Je ne parle pas français' (1918), in *Collected Stories of Katherine Mansfield* (1945; London: Constable, 1980), p. 60.
117. Greene, 'The Saratoga Trunk', pp. 85–6.
118. Though my emphasis here will predominantly be on the appropriation and adaptation of masculine chivalric codes by suffragettes or New Women in the early twentieth century, it must be clarified at the outset that this was no straightforward issue. Other feminist campaigners thought it better to toe the traditional chivalric line in pursuit of their goals. Angela V. John, in discussing the often problematic engagement of a number of male literary figures (including H. G. Wells and John Galsworthy) in the suffrage cause, points out that '[w]omen suffragists also utilized the notion of female dependence on male protection as a strategy for gaining support'. The question of chivalry was thus a divisive one, even among women activists themselves. See Angela V. John, 'Men Manners, and Militancy: Literary Men and Women's Suffrage', in *The Men's Share?: Masculinities, Male Support and Women's Suffrage in Britain, 1890–1920*, ed. Claire Eustance and Angela V. John (London: Routledge, 1997), p. 89.
119. E. M. Forster, *A Room with a View* (1908; Harmondsworth: Penguin, 1978), pp. 221–2.
120. E. M. Forster, *The Feminine Note in Literature: A Hitherto Unpublished Manuscript*, ed. George Piggford (London: Cecil Woolf, 2001), p. 17. The two audiences were the Cambridge Apostles or Conversazione Society (men-only) and the Bloomsbury Friday Club (mixed).
121. Ibid., p. 17.
122. Virginia Woolf, 'Is Fiction an Art?' (1927), in *The Essays of Virginia Woolf*, vol. 4, ed. Andrew McNeillie (London: Hogarth Press, 1994), p. 457.
123. Richardson, *Pilgrimage,* vol. 2, p. 208.
124. Richardson, *Pilgrimage,* vol. 3, p. 218.
125. Ibid., p. 218.
126. To give an example, she expresses her admiration, on one occasion, for a new co-worker in terms of 'her way of gathering all spears to her own breast', a description which invokes the iconography of Joan of Arc. Joan of Arc was a figure commonly

held up by suffragette activists in the 1900s and 1910s, as the figurehead of a new chivalric mode tailored for women. Richardson, *Pilgrimage,* vol. 3, p. 485.

127. Rebecca West, 'The Girl Who Left Home' (1916), in *The Young Rebecca: Writings of Rebecca West 1911–1917*, ed. Jane Marcus (Bloomington: Indiana University Press, 1982), p. 323.

128. Mansfield, 'The Little Governess', in *Collected Stories*, p. 175.

129. Ibid., p. 185.

130. Ibid., p. 178. Emphasis in original.

131. Hamilton, *Marriage as a Trade*, p. 125.

132. If imaginative portraits are anything to go by, porters had a very poor reputation at this time. They are on the list of those 'blasted' in Wyndham Lewis's Vorticist journal in 1914 and portrayed as 'brutishly preoccupied ... figures moving in an evil dream' by Richardson later on in *Pilgrimage*. In a 1925 article published by the *LMS Railway Magazine*, affiliated to the railway company of the same name, the writer is compelled to defend the figure of the porter against such bad press, with a particular appeal to women travellers: 'There is no one in England more ready to help the solitary female passenger than the average porter.' See Wyndham Lewis, 'Manifesto – 1', *BLAST*, 1, 20 June 1914, p. 13; Richardson, *Pilgrimage*, vol. 4, p. 11; V. M. Green, 'Smiling at the Porter', *LMS Railway Magazine*, 2.9, September 1925, p. 279.

133. Mansfield, 'The Little Governess', p. 175.

134. Ibid., p. 184. Emphasis in original.

135. Ibid., p. 185.

136. Ibid., pp. 189, 176, 189. Emphasis in original.

137. Ibid., p. 176.

138. Pamela Dunbar, *Radical Mansfield: Double Discourse in Katherine Mansfield's Short Stories* (Basingstoke: Macmillan, 1997), pp. 62–4.

139. This is, of course, not always the case with Mansfield, and we find other examples of the woman's bag denoting something far more powerfully subversive: 'Something Childish But Very Natural' (1914) and 'The Stranger' (1920), for instance. Her work, as a whole, provides rich material for the study of women's relation to luggage, from a range of angles.

140. Virginia Woolf, *Jacob's Room* (1922; London: Penguin, 1992), p. 23.

141. See Anstey Guthrie, 'Bombs for Women!' *Punch*, 135, 8 July 1908, p. 26. A Dorothy handbag was a fabric bag with a drawstring, which served both as closing mechanism and handle. Such a delicate and 'feminine' form of bag was, no doubt, a tactical choice on the part of the suffragettes.

142. George Morrow, 'The Spread of Tango: Arrest of a Militant Suffragette', cartoon, *Punch*, 145, 26 November 1913, p. 458.

143. 'The Shop-Wrecking Mania', *The Bag, Portmanteau and Umbrella Trader and Fancy Leather Goods and Athletic Trades Review*, 5.175, March 1912, p. 4.

144. Wilson, '"She in Her 'Armour' and He in his Coat of Nerves"', p. 179.

145. 'The Deadly Hand-bag', *The Bag Portmanteau and Umbrella Trader and Fancy Leather Goods and Athletic Trades Review*, 11.453, July 1917, p. 25.

146. Woolf, *Jacob's Room*, p. 23.

147. Ibid., p. 23.

148. Virginia Woolf, *The Voyage Out* (1915; Harmondsworth: Penguin, 1992), pp. 200–1.

149. D. H. Lawrence, *Women in Love* (1920; Harmondsworth: Penguin, 1979), p. 467. Emphasis in original.

150. Ibid., p. 522.

151. D. H. Lawrence, 'Cocksure Women and Hensure Men' (1929), in *Selected Essays*

(Harmondsworth: Penguin, 1950), pp. 31–4. This essay, reiterating the bird imagery of *Women in Love*, sets up an opposition between the traditional intuitive power of the 'hensure' woman and what Lawrence regarded as a counter-intuitive 'cocksure' inclinations of the modern woman.

152. Kate Millett, *Sexual Politics* (London: Hart-Davis, 1971), pp. 237–93.
153. D. H. Lawrence, *Lady Chatterley's Lover* (1928; Harmondsworth: Penguin, 1994), p. 32.
154. Anne Fernihough, 'Introduction', in *The Cambridge Companion to D. H. Lawrence*, ed. Anne Fernihough (Cambridge: Cambridge University Press, 2001), p. 3. Emphasis added.
155. It is worth noting that the two words employed by Fernihough, 'bafflement' and 'fascination', occur themselves in *Women in Love*, in their variant forms, a total of nine and thirty-three times respectively. The kind of interpretative impasse exhibited in the passage under scrutiny is a consistent feature of the novel.
156. Rachel Potter, *Modernism and Democracy: Literary Culture, 1900–1930* (Oxford: Oxford University Press, 2006), p. 51.
157. Woolf, 'Mr Bennett and Mrs Brown', p. 74.
158. Ibid., p. 72.
159. Ibid., p. 72.
160. Ibid., p. 72.
161. Ibid., p. 73. Emphasis added.
162. Ibid., p. 74.
163. Ibid., p. 82.
164. Ibid., p. 84.
165. Virginia Woolf, *A Room of One's Own* (1929; London: Hogarth Press, 1959), p. 5.

3

'NO ONE IS SAFE FROM THE BEGGAR'S PACK': PORTABILITY AND PRECARITY

After an almost exclusive concentration on women and portability in Chapter 2, the scope of Chapter 3 will be more expansive and will loosely focus on the period between the two world wars. I have demonstrated the import of women's luggage as a subversive symbol for the New Woman and as a site of early modernist innovation. I have equally dwelt on figurations of the woman's bag as revelatory of the impedimental difficulties and pressures attending any endeavour to achieve an uncompromised form of freedom. The following more inclusive discussion of portable forms and experiences, both men's and women's, addresses the intensification of these issues during the interwar period. It is not my intention to imply that the turn-of-the-century preoccupation with women's bags directly incited a more general sense of the bag's symbolic potential, though this might well be true in some cases. It would be more accurate to say, rather, that the figure of the woman who carried her own bag embodied an exclusionary form of dispossession as well as a departure from or challenge to a proprietorial status quo, which came to be of driving importance for a range of modernist writers, whatever their sex. In other words, the emancipatory, disruptive, progressive, conflictual and ambiguous connotations of the woman's bag, as I have described, came to resonate more widely, making luggage-related forms and metaphors more widely applicable. The specific question of the freedom of the woman becomes a question of the freedom of the individual in the face of rising forms of authoritarian oppression in Europe between the wars, forms of totalitarian and bureaucratic power that subjected each and every person to external systems of control and rendered the condition of dispossession a more prevailing prospect. Luggage carries over as a vital metaphor through which to explore contradictory desires for freedom and security more broadly in literature of the 1920s and 1930s. It further carries over as a vital metaphor to probe the significance of the miniature, whether as subversive or vulnerable element, as set against gigantic, often unseen and unnameable forces, to re-invoke Susan Stewart's terms.

The chapter will begin by returning to depictions of modernist artistic exile. As discussed in Chapter 1, the most salient feature of modernist portability, as it is represented in an earlier phase of modernism, from Beerbohm through to Mansfield and Joyce, is its link to an ideal of artistic autonomy; either through facilitating a posture of political and aesthetic detachment, or through hinting at emergent possibilities of unfixed multiplicity and mobility inherent in the idea of a continually repackaged self within a new consumer culture. Further examples of both lines of representation will crop up throughout this chapter. However, my broader aim in the chapter as a whole is to show how such attributes of modernist portability are progressively problematised through the interwar period and into the 1940s. This is due, on one level, to a growing sense of the fragility of that modernist ideal of artistic autonomy in the context of escalating political anxieties and international tensions and, on another level, to the implied breakdown of the distance between the avant-garde artist and the marketplace. In other words, the figure of the modernist literary exile is, in late modernist work, overshadowed by the figure of the refugee, on the one hand, and undermined by the figure of the tourist, on the other. This gradual problematisation of portability is most evident in the reconstitution of its surrounding discourse in terms of precarity rather than individual freedom and possibility, especially conspicuous in the changing resonances of terms such as 'hasty packing' and 'travelling light'. Central to Judith Butler's recent theorisation of precarity is the acknowledgement of 'relationality', which serves to complicate understandings of human ontology in the liberal tradition, while also laying bare the degree to which humans are subject to forces of communality for better or worse: 'Loss and vulnerability seem to follow from our being socially constituted bodies, attached to others, at risk of losing those attachments, exposed to others, at risk of violence by virtue of that exposure.'[1] If earlier acts of hasty packing and travelling light can be figured as attempts to break away from forms of social constitution, portability increasingly comes to speak of loss, vulnerability, risk and exposure in the face of social and political entities which render naïve previous visions of artistic escape.

FREEDOM BY NECESSITY

To account for and understand the progressive complication of portability and portable forms from modernism to late modernism, we must begin with the

First World War. Beerbohm, though by no means a modernist himself in any straightforward sense, articulates an early modernist approach to luggage in conceiving of exciting new formal and narrative possibilities through his hat-box. This is an approach which is fortified after the First World War, but with this difference: the 'Pack Up Your Troubles' taint of wartime movement never entirely disappears from representations of luggage and packing thereafter. This is not least because certain aspects of the imposition of wartime restrictions upon mobility – the passport, for example – are retained after the armistice.[2] 'Pack Up Your Troubles' might be posited as an epitaph for the entire interwar period and not just 1914 to 1918. Bridget T. Chalk has highlighted a significant paradox in the literary output of the period in this respect: 'cosmopolitanism and international movement generated and characterize modernist literature, and yet the years between the two world wars were marked by strengthening technologies of mobility controls'.[3] We must also remember that the re-drafting of national boundaries after the First World War first gave rise to the phenomenon of the stateless, and therefore powerless, individual.[4] Thus, if 'fantasies of flight and freedom' can be found to pervade literature between the wars, as Fussell describes in *Abroad*, these fantasies are noticeably troubled by comparison with the visions of modern escape produced by prewar writers such as Beerbohm.[5]

Even Raoul Duquette's vision of unsettled portmanteaux, in Mansfield's 'Je ne parle pas français', carries the suggestion of freedom as a compromised ideal. Written in 1918, Mansfield's story cannot readily be removed from its wartime context. This becomes apparent if we place Duquette's image side by side with a strikingly similar passage from George Orwell's later *Coming Up for Air*, in which the protagonist George Bowling recalls his experiences of the First World War on the eve of the second in 1939:

> I don't believe in the human soul. I never have. I believe that people are like portmanteaux – packed with certain things, started going, thrown about, tossed away, dumped down, lost and found, half emptied suddenly or squeezed fatter than ever, until finally the Ultimate Porter swings them on to the Ultimate Train and away they rattle.[6]

> it didn't occur to them to try to escape. The machine had got hold of you and it could do what it liked with you. It lifted you up and dumped you down among places and things you'd never dreamed of, and if it had dumped you down on the surface of the moon it wouldn't have seemed particularly strange.[7]

On a first reading, the portmanteaux in Mansfield's story seem to epitomise the loosening of the modern subject from the defined parameters of a fixed place. The arbitrariness of their motions can be set in paradoxical relation to the final aspirational shift towards an 'Ultimate' design. Yet, considered in juxtaposition with Bowling's conception of wartime experience in terms of machine-controlled motion, it is the complete lack of agency of the portmanteaux in Duquette's vision, which comes to the fore most startlingly. They are 'packed', 'started', 'thrown', 'tossed', 'dumped', 'lost', 'found', 'emptied', 'squeezed' and finally swung. But by whom or what? It is certainly not on their own respective initiatives. Suddenly Duquette's 'Ultimate Porter' starts to look a little more sinister and insidious in influence. His portmanteaux become paragons of powerlessness in the hands of a modern machinery, which is stamped with the uniformed authority of officialdom. The sense of curtailed freedom, implicit in Duquette's vision, is made both explicit and ominous in Bowling's retrospective description, a description shaped by the prevailing anxieties of the late 1930s. That the illusion of freedom no longer exists is emphatically registered in Bowling's recollection: '*it didn't occur to them* to try to escape'. In other words, it doesn't now occur to anyone to think they are free. Moreover, in presenting the submission of the modern individual to a form of machine-like totalitarian authority, his description also has a pointed political dimension scarcely, if at all, perceptible in Duquette's. The luggage paradigm proposed in Mansfield's story still articulates a principle of freedom through modern flux; compromised though this principle might be (not least through its articulation by the dingy and rather suspect character of Duquette), it has no overt political bearing. It is the gradual politicisation of literary packing from 1918 to 1939 which this chapter seeks to chart.

Charting such a development necessarily calls for a reassessment of that well-established modernist exilic imperative, a reassessment which has already been initiated by a number of critics. For Chalk, the 'particular administrative conditions of modernist mobility' require further consideration in order to counter 'assumptions about the ease and exigencies of expatriate life'.[8] Similarly, Caren Kaplan has taken issue with the literary critical promulgation of the idea of modernist exile in ahistorical terms for the purpose of creating an exclusive category of aesthetic displacement:

> Like all symbolic formations, Euro-American modernist exile culls meaning from various cultural, political, and economic sources, including the lived experiences of people who have been legally or socially expelled from one location and prevented from returning ... The Euro-American formation 'exile', then, marks a place of mediation in modernity where issues of political conflict, commerce, labor, nationalist realignments, imperialist expansion, structures of gender and sexuality, and many other issues all become recoded.[9]

Kaplan is concerned with destabilising such a formation through demanding a more rigorous approach to the specificities of various and distinctive terms of displacement. She draws particular attention to the frequent 'conflation of exile and expatriation', together with the dismissal of tourism, by a number of modernist writers and critics.[10] Most importantly, she exposes the prevailing notion of 'aesthetic gain' through the 'imperative of displacement' as a very deliberate construction.[11]

Yet Kaplan's criticism of the mythologisation of modernist exile is, I would argue, already inscribed in certain late modernist texts through self-conscious acts of reworking earlier forms and fantasies of portability. Recent scholarship on the subject of late modernism has posited the phenomenon as a response to certain crystallised features of a recognised version of modernism as much as an anticipation of postmodernism. Indeed, the 'institutionalization of modernism began as early as the 1930s', and this must have had an effect on writers during this period.[12] As Tyrus Miller notes:

> the late modernist response to modernism is inseparable from its emergence as a *historically* codified phenomenon. Modernism had to have aged, had to have become in a way 'historical', had to have entered into a certain stage of canonization, for the kind of writing I discuss to be possible.[13]

For Marina MacKay, a vital facet of this response focuses on the idea of exile, highlighted by Kaplan: 'The enduring emphasis on cosmopolitanism, deracination, expatriation, and cultural exchange in accounts of the 1920s and 1930s starts to look more complicated toward modernism's closing years.'[14] She characterises the 'metaphor of the journey not made' as one key late modernist trope in direct contrast to the stress on mobility so characteristic of early modernism.[15] In a similar vein, Lyndsey Stonebridge identifies a late modernism 'responding to the dawn of the era of the refugee' as set against the affirmative cosmopolitanism of an 'earlier moment of modernism'.[16] Both MacKay and Stonebridge present a version of late modernism in which the ideal of the cosmopolitan subject is turned on its head through enforced stasis, on the one hand, and a politicised form of mobility on a mass scale, on the other. Correspondingly, late modernist writing is replete with images of stalled or still-standing luggage, luggage which begins, with mounting intensity through the 1930s, to signal obstructed flight rather than the prospect of escape. During the Second World War, Robert Graves and Alan Hodge characterised the interwar era as *The Long Week-End* (1940), the title of their social history of interwar Britain. The period framed between the two world wars is posited thus as an interim period, a 'long' weekend but a short-lived escape from the habitual run of things, from a more mundane and troubled reality. The phrase, by the same token, suggests a public form of holiday, a common experience, over and above the idea of a private retreat. In the 1930s, we find an increased recognition, not only of the short-lived nature of the interwar escape, the

imminent ending of the long weekend, but, equally, the impossibility of a previous model of aesthetic and political detachment. This new consciousness is
conveyed, most memorably, in Woolf's analogy of 'the leaning tower' in her
eponymous 1940 essay.[17]

Building on the observations of Chalk, Kaplan, Miller, MacKay and
Stonebridge, I submit that in the work of certain late modernist writers, conceptions of portable experience become negative inversions of those conceptions foregrounded in early modernism in a number of key ways. Primarily,
portability becomes reconfigured in terms of aesthetic *loss* rather than 'aesthetic gain', to rewrite Kaplan's phrase. One thing that is lost above all, in
this aesthetic scenario, is the certainty of an architectonic mode. 'We envy . . .
houses that are sure', W. H. Auden writes in his 1938 'Sonnet XVIII', a poem
which expresses some of the evolving concerns this chapter will go on to document.[18] The poem continues:

> But, doubtful, articled to error, we
> Were never nude and calm as a great door,
> And never will be faultless like our fountains:
> We live in freedom by necessity,
> A mountain people dwelling among mountains.[19]

The poem invokes a peculiar prewar, post-fall scenario (reminding us of the
pre- and post-lapsarian nature of the idea of the 'long week-end'). This is a
scenario in which lost innocence is equated with the architectural stability of a
previous time: 'But, doubtful, articled to error, we/ were never nude and calm
as a great door'. Architectural innocence is contrasted with the uncertainty of
freedom, but this, paradoxically, is figured as a 'freedom *by necessity*' (emphasis added), as if dwelling in motion is now an involuntary new reality rather
than an experience to aspire to. Similarly, portable forms in modernist writing
come to represent compromised ideals of artistic freedom, in which the choice
between house and case no longer exists in the same way, in which facility
becomes obstruction, in which the alluring possibility of the package becomes
the mundane interchangeability of the mass-market product, in which exciting
uncertainty becomes dangerous suspicion, in which a world gained becomes a
world lost and, most conspicuously, through which the figure of the escapee is
shadowed by the spectre of the refugee. In this compromised paradigm, we find
an acknowledgement of the rise of what Michael R. Marrus has described as
a 'radically new form of homelessness', whereby refugee status has come to be
equated with a sort of non-status, a complete deprivation of the rights allotted
by nation state.[20] 'In practically every way we can imagine', Marrus stresses,
'the First World War imposed on contemporaries the awesome power of the
nation-state.'[21] The interwar figure of the refugee thus exposes, first, the submission of the individual to increasingly pervasive forms of national security and,

second, the illusion of the freedom of the individual beyond the parameters of state-authorised, state-bound national identity and citizenship. Moreover, the refugee becomes emblematic of a wider all-inclusive crisis. As Hannah Arendt notes in 1943, 'the outlawing of the Jewish people in Europe has been followed closely by the outlawing of most European nations'.[22] Late modernist luggage gestures accordingly beyond the individual towards a collective dilemma and is provocatively poised on a knife-edge between the dream of escape and the nightmare of inescapability in the artistic imagination at this time.

COMPROMISED CASES OF FICTION

One particular manifestation of the reconfiguration of literary portability involves a perceptible change in the application and nature of portable analogues. Broadly speaking, such analogues come to be employed, not in relation to a literature of cosmopolitan possibility as before, but in relation to a 'literature of preparation', to borrow a term coined by Samuel Hynes in surveying the British literary output of 1939. His description of the impetus behind this kind of literature is interesting in the case of the present discussion:

> if you examined the past honestly, as a displaced person might examine his belongings before he fled his home, you might find what was worth saving; and if you imagined the future fully and without flinching, you might be able to survive it.[23]

In line with Hynes's account, portable models begin to come to the fore to describe forms of fiction which hark back to a lost stability. Such writings enact a reappraisal of the 'home' and thus the analogic model of the house, not as a model against which *cases* of fiction are set in productive opposition, but as a model whose dominance has been irremediably overtaken and cannot be redeemed. Luggage thus comes to figure towards the end of the interwar period in substitutive rather than contrastive terms and, as such, signals a feared rather than a desired state of uncertainty.

Aldous Huxley provides a good point of departure in tracing the transformative evolution of the portable analogue from modernism to late modernism as the ideal of aesthetic autonomy begins to looks a little frayed around the edges. He might have advocated a 'hold-all' of ideas, but this was not quite as straightforward as the image might imply. The main character of his 1921 novel *Crome Yellow,* an insecure young writer by the name of Denis Stone, carries the manuscript of the beginnings of his own novel in his luggage on his visit to Crome (a barely disguised version of Garsington Manor, famously presided over by literary hostess and patroness, Lady Ottoline Morrell). His literary luggage, in this case, goes hand in hand with his sense of artistic alienation and disenchantment. This is a state of mind wittily parodied by fellow guest, Mr Scogan, as he surmises the general outline of Denis's novel-to-be:

'I'll describe the plot for you. Little Percy, the hero, was never good at games, but he was always clever. He passes through the usual public school and the usual university and comes to London, where he lives among the artists. He is bowed down with melancholy thought; he carries the whole weight of the universe upon his shoulders. He writes a novel of dazzling brilliance; he dabbles delicately in Amour and disappears, at the end of the book, into the luminous Future'.

Denis blushed scarlet. Mr Scogan had described the plan of his novel with an accuracy that was appalling. He made an effort to laugh. 'You're entirely wrong', he said. 'My novel is not in the least like that'. It was an heroic lie. Luckily, he reflected, only two chapters were written. He would tear them up that very evening when he unpacked.[24]

Huxley satirises some of the wider imaginative preoccupations of the period, but it is the image of manuscript in suitcase to be unpacked and destroyed which I would highlight here. The forbidding structure of Crome symbolically serves to obliterate the value of Denis's artistic work on arrival. Yet the association of writing with luggage expresses a desire to depart from traditional forms and approaches to fiction, culminating, in *Crome Yellow,* in Denis's contrived escape from the '[s]evere, imposing, almost menacing' structure of the house itself at the end of the novel.[25] Despite his evident authorial failure and the satirical terms in which it is rendered, Denis's aspiration towards an innovatory point of artistic detachment reflects Huxley's own; *Crome Yellow* is, in subject and shape, not unlike the type of novel described by Scogan above. *Crome Yellow* represents, then, the kind of novel Denis fails to achieve in practice and an early example of Huxley's own conception of a hold-all of ideas. At the same time, the novel is directly modelled on the largely satirical nineteenth-century country-house novels of Thomas Love Peacock and, like many of Peacock's works, is named after the structure in which it is set.[26] Though Denis escapes from this structure, it is with a measure of reluctance and regret, and his departure is characterised as a death. This is a novel which appears to be caught between paradigms of house and hold-all.

Or is it an attempted synthesis of the two? In proffering the image of the bursting hold-all of ideas, Huxley must have been sensitive to the fact that even new ideas draw from what has gone before and that luggage stands, in essence, as an important point of symbolic contact between past and future, between tradition and modernity. It is within the contours of long-established Crome that Denis is overwhelmed by the unoriginality of his manuscript. If Huxley's novel is posited as a more successful holdall of ideas, it is one which succeeds through attempting to *hold* the past in unison with the present/future. Luggage moves forward, but it also carries forward. In the '[l]iving modernly's living quickly' vision of Lucy Tantamount in his later *Point Counter Point* (1928), he offers an expression of what might be seen as the apotheosis of a nomadic metaphysics, but this is by no means heralded as a triumphant realisation. For Lucy, in that novel, even hasty packing must theoretically be eliminated as an unnecessary impediment to independent movement of body and thought:

> 'When you travel by airplane you must leave your heavy baggage behind. The good old-fashioned soul was all right when people lived slowly. But it's too ponderous nowadays. There's no room for it in the aeroplane. [. . .] If you like speed, if you want to cover the ground, you can't have luggage. The thing is to know what you want and to be ready to pay for it. I know exactly what I want; so I sacrifice the luggage. If you choose to travel in a furniture van, you may. But don't expect me to come along with you, my sweet Walter. And don't expect me to take your grand piano in my two seater monoplane'.[27]

These pronouncements are made to her lover, Walter Bidlake, who desires more than a sensuous relationship. But Lucy, a manifestly negative incarnation of the modern woman, maintains a hard line of autonomous self-sufficiency in the face of Walter's tender advances. In an age of perpetual hurry, new ideas must be mobilised, and old ideas must be left behind, a principle Huxley himself is far from fully advocating. For Lucy, modernity means travelling light *and* travelling alone, and though she presents an extreme position here, it is intended as a commentary on a more prevalent tendency.

This is a tendency which must particularly be set and considered against the growth of a new consumer culture where 'travel light' was roundly embraced as a favourite promotional catchphrase between the wars. 'Nowadays we travel often – and we "travel light"; but more comfortably than before!' announces an advertisement for Mark Cross luggage in 1924, '[f]or the good reason that if we have learned to carry less, we have also learned to carry it properly'.[28] It is clear that modes of travel were changing at this time, with holidays becoming shorter and more frequent for those who could afford to go away. Air travel was paving the way for more compact and lighter forms of luggage, also the result of the development of fibre-based materials, as Graves and Hodge record.[29] Yet if people were 'learning' to travel differently, they were also following a course laid down by advertisers. To keep people in circulation was to keep money in circulation. Consequently, lessons on modern modes of travel were superimposed onto other forms of advertisement. Furthermore, if the idea of travelling light infiltrated the marketplace, this was partly an outcome of the development of disposable commodities for the benefit of those who sought to avoid sustained encumbrance. The catchphrase 'travel light' was used to advertise everything from crispbread – 'Vita-weat: The crispbread that lets your stomach travel light' – to soap.[30] Consider, for example, the tagline for a 1927 advertisement for LUX: 'The modern girl "travels light" on her holiday, yet she looks fresh and dainty everyday. How does she do it?'[31] The inclusion of 'travel light' in quotation marks here, as in the Mark Cross advert, denotes a phrase in popular currency. Moreover, the advent of portable radio and home cinematograph machines saw advertisers refer to them as 'suitcase' models, and tags, such as 'carry it like a suitcase!', were used as a marketing device.[32] Portability was foregrounded as a strong selling point for an assortment of products from torches to cooking ranges. Modernity is cast, whatever the product advertised, as the age of mobility, portability, disposability and renewal. Ironically, 'travelling light', while advocating, as a catchphrase, the repudiation of material ties, was employed to promote the accumulation of a wide range of products. This is a paradox wittily exploited by Evelyn Waugh in *A Handful of Dust* (1934) and in his later *Scoop* (1938). Both novels feature characters (Tony Last in the former, William Boot in the latter) ludicrously weighted down with unnecessary travel goods and products in the attempt to appropriately fulfil the respective roles of explorer and war correspondent abroad.[33]

I make this detour into consumer culture to show how the 'living modernly's living quickly' philosophy, proffered by modern woman Lucy Tantamount, merges unsettlingly with a capitalist ethos of mobility and replaceability. Lucy has no luggage because, in dispensing with a human 'soul' as Duquette does before her in his portmanteau analogy, she herself becomes a continually moving package in a soulless capitalist world. In this, she resembles a further character from Waugh's fictional world, American millioniairess Mrs Rattery in *A Handful of Dust*. This character is a living embodiment of capitalism, her person shown to move at the same rate as her money. Waugh tells us that Mrs Rattery is an 'American by origin, now totally denationalised, rich without property or possessions, except those that would pack in five vast trunks', and, a page later, that she 'never noticed houses much'.[34] In other words, she has liberated herself from the constraints of class and country, but also of responsibility. As with Lucy, a distrust of long-term material investment goes hand in hand with a distrust of lasting emotional investment. Her 'five vast trunks' are as deliberately expressive of her capitalist ethos as Hetton Abbey is of Tony Last's would-be feudal ethos in that novel.

Such representations disturb more elitist and rarefied notions of modernist portability, through the figure of the avant-garde artist with his/her singular *case* of fiction. In Chapter 1, I cited the packed manuscript of Edgar Naylor, in Cyril Connolly's *The Rock Pool*, as one more example of the many inter-war depictions of mobile authorship. Connolly's 1936 novel is presented as a revisitation of the mythologised continental bohemianism of the literati of the previous decade. From the standpoint of 1936, Naylor's packed manuscript must be seen as an attempt, conscious or unconscious, to tap into this nomadic mythology. Over the course of the novel, however, he is progressively shorn of his illusions, and that initial image of self-conscious authorial distinction corrodes into something altogether more tawdry and prosaic: 'He felt old and miserable, going through life trying to peddle a personality of which people would not even accept a free sample.'[35] Bohemian writer with manuscript in attaché case here becomes travelling salesman with a case of cheap samples. The artistic freedom generated through the pluralisation of packaged selves here leads to a loss of aura in line with Walter Benjamin's theories in 'The Work of Art in the Age of Mechanical Reproduction' (an essay, incidentally, published in the same year as Connolly's novel).[36] By the end of *The Rock Pool,* we are left with the image of Naylor's manuscript smeared with blood and Pernod just as modernist bohemianism has been tarnished with an air of commercial vacuousness in the novel. In Connolly's attaché case, we are a far cry from Beerbohm's hat-box or even Huxley's not-altogether-straightforward literary hold-all.

Yet if we pursue another interwar thread in the progressive complication of portability, we find that the concept of the autonomous, singular, *un*packaged, soul*ful* individual is brought to the fore, rather than obliterated through a kind of mass production. Let us return to 1924 and the immediate postwar era. The dystopian novel *We,* a precursor to Huxley's *Brave New World* and Orwell's *1984,* published in that year by Russian writer Yevgeny Zamyatin, propels us into a future dimension and the realm of the 'One State'. In this realm, individuality has been entirely subdued by a process of rational and collective systematisation, as the title implies. Citizens are identified by number, and, interestingly, the development of the state is described in terms of the ascendency of a sedentarist order:

> it is clear that the entire history of mankind, insofar as we know it, is the history of transition from nomadic to increasingly settled forms. And does it not follow that the most settled form (ours) is at the same time the most perfect (ours)? People rushed about from one end of the earth to the other only in prehistoric times, when there were nations, wars, commerce, discoveries of all sorts of Americas. But who needs that now? What for?[37]

Individuality is thus associated with a nomadic impulse which has been lost, and, in the current settled state, the very suggestion of a 'soul' is considered a 'dangerous' and 'incurable' malady.[38] The novel recounts the gradual awakening of the narrator, D-503, to his own irrational impulses and desires through his attraction to the alluring I-330, who is involved in the clandestine activities of a group of rebels, known as 'Mephi'. Through I-330, D-503 is drawn into the revolution, but is, in the end, subjected to an operation which quashes his imagination. Within this narrative, the object of the valise becomes a symbol for a repressed and primal nomadic impulse, imagination and, most importantly, the cultivation of a soul. D-503's friend, the State poet, R-13, is continually and rather curiously described as having a valise-shaped head: 'The back of his head is like a square little valise, attached from behind (I recalled the ancient painting, "In the Carriage").'[39] Though never explicitly stated, it is strongly suggested that R-13 is a member of the underground Mephi movement; he, too, is linked with I-330, and his room, though arranged in the same orderly fashion as all other rooms, becomes a scene of disproportional and displaced planes upon his entry, intimating a nonconformist bent.[40] There is also something about R-13 that the narrator cannot rationalise, and this inexplicability is deliberately related to 'that little box of his with its strange baggage that I did not understand'.[41] If D-503 does not fully understand R-13 – he, in fact, falls out with him due to a mutual attraction to I-330 – this only serves to magnify his own realisation that he does not fully understand himself. Before his eventual act of capitulation to the system, he makes a decision to depart into the 'unknown' in order to join the revolutionaries. This demands the formulation, in line with R-13, of his own figurative and strangely personal baggage, an acknowledged symptom of what he calls his 'soul sickness': 'I stand up and look around the room, the whole room; I hastily take with me, gather up into an invisible valise, all that I'm sorry to leave behind.'[42] Here we find a further instance of that emblematic act of interwar 'hasty packing', and it simultaneously dramatises the activation of D-503's authorial imagination through the use of figurative language. He notes, parenthetically, just prior to this passage, that his 'eyes are now like a pen'.[43] But this must be distinguished from the kind of hasty packing elevated by Fussell, on the one hand, and from a consumer-driven form of modern restlessness, on the other. Zamyatin, a former Bolshevik turned anti-Communist, is writing with an eye to the freedom of the artist in the context of the rise of a totalitarian state in post-Revolutionary Russia, a subject on which he wrote countless essays in the early 1920s.[44] He was, indeed, himself driven into exile in 1929 as a consequence of the publication of *We* in a Russian émigré journal in Czechoslovakia two years before, lending the above passage an air of the prophetic. The valise, in this contextual light, must, therefore, also be seen to stand for artistic spontaneity as set against the totalising force of a repressive organisation. In addition, as D-503's 'invisible valise' markedly attests, it is linked to the preservation of the memory of the individual as this corresponds to the preservation of the idea of an individual human soul. D-503's soul-recovering valise, imagined in singular, forms the foil to Duquette's soulless valises, imagined in plural.

In Zamyatin's *We*, self-preservation is figuratively aligned with packing as autobiographical authorship, and this is a distinctive and recurrent feature of work by political exiles and refugees between the wars. The modernist trend of depicting packing as a means of temporary reinvention must be offset with this equally prevalent trend of depicting packing as a means of self-preservation, just as any discussion of voluntary escape at this time must be counterbalanced by a discussion of forced flight. If the writing of this period is replete with images of packed manuscripts, these are as often the imaginative conceptions of displaced writers working in situations of constraint as of Fussell's interwar fantasists of flight and freedom. It is important to distinguish between the kinds of luggage analogue employed in either case. Thus, Viktor Shklovsky's perception that life is a 'well ordered *nécessaire*, but not all of us can find our places in it', as described in *Zoo, or Letters Not About Love* in 1923, in conjunction with his assertion that the modern writer must be seen as a 'nomad' rather than a 'ploughman' – 'It's impossible to write a book in the old way' – derives from his experience of unwanted exile in Berlin in the early 1920s: 'Let into Russia me and all my guileless luggage.'[45] This is a work abounding with textual luggage from a 'briefcase full of page proofs' to a 'suitcase filled with manuscripts and torn papers – everything so jumbled that it was impossible to tell research notes from pants'.[46] Yet textual luggage is something he would happily forgo in order to return unimpeded to his homeland: 'I am bound to Berlin but if I were told, "You can return", I swear by Opoiaz that I would go home without looking back, without taking my manuscripts.'[47] Not dissimilarly, when the fictional writer-figure and exile Fyodor Godunov-Cherdyntsev announces on the very first page of his autobiography in Vladimir Nabokov's *The Gift* (1937–8), written between 1933 and 1937, that 'in *my* suitcase there are more manuscripts than shirts', we must not forget that Nabokov had likewise been obliged to depart from Russia in the 1920s, like Zamyatin and Shklovsky before him, after the ascendency of the Bolsheviks.[48] Though there is a hint of the romance of exile surrounding this image of manuscript in suitcase, it is a claim which foregrounds a portability by necessity first and foremost. When his later Sebastian Knight, another fictional writer, from *The Real Life of Sebastian Knight* (1941), is shown to abandon his bags in flight from Moscow and to entitle his 'most autobiographical work' *Lost Property*, we must not lose sight of the figure of the real writer; Nabokov is purported to have written the book itself on a suitcase balanced upon a bidet in the bathroom of the one-bedroom Parisian apartment he occupied with his family during its composition.[49]

A comparable portable aesthetic is evident in works by Jewish writers in the 1930s and 1940s. In his seminal novel *The Death of Virgil* (1945), Hermann Broch conceives of the dying Roman poet, in transit with the Emperor Augustus from Greece to Italy, as 'driven by fate' and 'hunted . . . from the simplicity of his origins'.[50] On this journey, he manifests a continual anxiety about the safety of his manuscript-chest (containing the precious text of his *Aeneid*), the symbolic value of which is asserted again and again in the text. This conception must be read with a view to Broch himself who, as an Austrian Jew, began the work in a Nazi concentration camp in 1938 and completed it in exile in America in 1945. If luggage looms large in Irène Némirovsky's *Suite Française* (2004), in which the mass exodus from a Paris under siege is portrayed in terms of people 'clinging to their cases and hatboxes like shipwrecked men to their lifebelts', then we must see this in relation to the creation of the novel itself, written in transit during the Second World War and forming part of her own wartime luggage, much later rediscovered in a forgotten suitcase.[51] At the same time, the preserved literary luggage of Broch and Némirovsky only heightens the severity of the loss of Walter Benjamin's renowned briefcase during his ill-fated flight from the Nazis across the French-Spanish border. Lisa Fittko, in his company at the time, recalls:

> We walked slowly, like tourists enjoying the scenery. I noticed that Benjamin was carrying a large black briefcase which he must have picked up when we had stopped at the inn. It looked heavy and I offered to help him carry it. 'This is my new manuscript', he explained. 'But why did you take it for this walk?' 'You must understand that this briefcase is the most important thing to me', he said. 'I cannot risk losing it. It is the manuscript that *must* be saved. It is more important than I am'.[52]

This passage raises several significant points in the context of my broader discussion. Unlike earlier images of people as portmanteaux or as fast-paced interchangeable packages in an ever-moving commercialised modernity, here is an image not of case merging with person, but of textual case substituting person as unique legacy. (In an odd way, it conjures Beerbohm's image of his irreplaceable, luggage-stamped hat-box.) Benjamin's manuscript in briefcase can be seen, in retrospect, as a symbol of the fate of the work of art, as well as the fate of the individual, in the age both of mechanical reproduction and of mechanical devastation.[53]

Portability came to have palpably different resonances by the 1930s, and many works of this period adopt a disconcerting mode of interweaving conflicting lines of luggage imagery and thus discourses of mobility (from holiday-making to mass emergency exodus). One aspect of the above passage about Benjamin should be pinpointed in this light: the invocation of the leisurely moving tourist. This is an invocation which chimes with the descriptive ambiguity attending the characterisation of refugees in terms of their 'aimless wanderlust' in a 1939 *Times* article.[54] A similar blurring of lines occurs in *The Post Office Girl* by Stefan Zweig, another Jewish writer of Austrian origin. In this rather bleak novel, written during the 1930s but published posthumously, a young and downtrodden post-office employee, Christine Hoflehner, is unexpectedly invited to a high-class hotel in the Alps by an aunt, now married to a wealthy American. Christine, on taking up this invitation, is transformed and overwhelmed by her new and luxurious surroundings, realising happiness for the first time through the aristocratic persona of Christine von Boolen. This happiness is short-lived, however, and, upon discovery of Christine's back-ground by fellow guests, her aunt dismisses her in fear that her own lowly origins will alike be exposed. The remainder of the novel describes the damag-ing impact of this fleeting fairy-tale turned sour. I draw attention to this novel here because, throughout her time at the hotel, it is Christine's 'seedy little straw suitcase' which perpetually reminds her of the delusional nature of her adopted persona.[55] Christine is haunted by this suitcase. It is shown to swing with 'telltale lightness in her hand' upon arrival, unlike the heavy and opulent wardrobe trunks of the other guests.[56] It fills her with a detestable uncertainty as she stands in the hotel lobby, and, having unpacked her drab lower-middle-class belongings, she imagines the maid's ridicule of this new 'beggarly guest for the rest of the staff to hear'.[57] Once she has fully adopted her von Boolen persona, she packs her belongings in a cardboard box out of sight with the aim of forgetting her 'former, other, Hoflehner self'.[58] Her eventual discharge by her aunt – 'Sending me off like a package, express mail, special delivery' – enacts not only the death of Christine von Boolen but also the symbolic termi-nation of the figure of the leisured tourist:

> It's beginning, inescapably: the day, the end, the departure. Now she must pack her things, leave, be that other, Postal Official Hoflehner of Klein-Reifling, forget the one whose breath had quickened to see the finery that is now no longer hers.[59]

This novel cannot be read without taking account of Zweig's own prolonged experience of exile. Having left Vienna in 1934, he took up residence first in England, then in the United States, and finally Brazil, where he ended his own life in 1942. If Christine's seedy suitcase casts a shadow over the authenticity of her status as a lady of leisure, this has everything to do with the centrality of the suitcase as a symbol of 1930s dispossession.[60] In the years before the war, Zweig had relished the prospect of freedom from proprietorial responsibility: 'I don't want any possessions . . . Possessions make a man heavy, old, fat and sluggish. I want to be on the way somewhere, travelling light.'[61] He would, however, come to dread the prospect of hasty packing. 'As to our voyage', he writes to his in-laws from Rio de Janeiro in December 1940, 'we do not enjoy it to [sic] much, we would like to have a few month [sic] without packing and wandering around, but who has not this wish to have a quiet life in these ter-rible times.'[62] Only seven months later, this distaste for travelling light had evolved into outright aversion after a series of upheavals across South and North America: 'I hate the packing and unpacking.'[63] His autobiography, giving an unsparing account of his rise to and fall from grace as an established Austrian writer, expresses the 'cruel truth for every Jew' of the old Russian proverb that 'No one is safe from the *beggar's* pack and the jail'.[64] This rep-resents a dubious doubling-up of the term used in relation to Christine in his novel. This autobiography should be read as a companion piece to *The Post Office Girl* and serves to muddy the trope of tourism in the earlier fictional work.

The obfuscation of tropes of tourism and dispossession reoccurs alike in English writing in the late 1930s. 'Any typology of '30s travelling is bound to be a rickety construct', Valentine Cunningham remarks in opening a chapter on the subject of the 'pervasively escapist' aspect of this literary age in *British Writers of the Thirties*.[65] Cunningham's experience of typological inconsistencies can be attributed to the fact that travel, in itself, had manifestly become a 'rickety' concept over the course of the decade. In Christopher Isherwood's *Goodbye to Berlin* (1939), the well-to-do Jewish heiress Natalia Landauer disappears, 'smiling' and dreamy, in the middle of a party with the suggestion that she is to meet an admirer: 'all at once, she was in a hurry. She was late, she said. She'd got to pack. She must go at once.'[66] We are left in no doubt that this act of happy hasty packing serves to magnify the certainty of more unhappy displacements to come, as the narrator observes: 'I thought of Natalia: she has escaped – none too soon, perhaps. However often the decision may be delayed, all these people are ultimately doomed. This evening is the dress-rehearsal of a disaster.'[67] As if to corroborate this, Isherwood refers to the gathering as a 'party that didn't really "go"' (a description bearing a disquieting resemblance to the title and subject of Henry Green's *Party Going*, published in the same year).[68] Refugees intrude upon the English literary consciousness in ways that irreparably distort those cherished interwar fantasies of adventurous escape. When Auden portrays the poet 'rummaging into his living' in 'The Composer', the action is charged with the self-preserving, self-memorialising instinct of the displaced person who keeps what is significant close at hand, as the line that follows indicates: 'Rummaging into his living, the poet fetches/ The images out that hurt and connect.'[69] Even Robert Byron, a leading figure in Fussell's *Abroad*, is forced, in his travelogue *The Road to Oxiana* (1937), to set his own hasty packing – notably carried out by a servant – against a less glorified form.[70] Refugee imagery infiltrates the book several times; he encounters a boatload of Jewish refugees leaving for Palestine from Trieste and, later on, a home for Russian refugees in Tehran.[71] Despite his nomadic outlook, Byron dramatises his final homecoming as a form of obstructive collision which enacts the ultimate elevation of an architectural paradigm, overseen by a maternal figure:

> At Paddington I began to feel dazed at the prospect of coming to a stop, at the impending collision between eleven months' momentum and the immobility of a beloved home. The collision happened; it was 19½ days since we left Kabul. Our dogs ran up. And then my mother – to whom, now it is finished, I deliver the whole record; what I have seen she taught me to see and will tell me if I have honoured it.[72]

This conclusion points to the advent of late modernist obstruction, along Marina MacKay's line. It also implies a recognition both of the impossibility of previous forms of untroubled mobility and of the imminent threat to the immobile constancy of the beloved home.[73]

The beloved home reasserts its imaginative power towards the end of the 1930s, while travelling light starts to ring more than a little hollow as a catchphrase with the onset of another war. The phrase itself even becomes something of a precautionary tagline in British Railways notices about strategic travel during blackouts.[74] 'Refugees of necessity travel light', a May 1940 *Times* article informs the reader.[75] Only a few months later, as if in answer to that earlier 1922 editorial on 'travelling light', a more fraught version of the same theme appears in a December 1940 editorial entitled, with no small irony, 'The Happy Traveller':

> It used to be said of a distinguished traveller and administrator that a toothbrush was all the luggage he needed to take him from one side of Africa to the other. We may well envy him his ability to cut down extraneous equipment to the bone. But nowadays even the most settled and stable of us may find himself compelled to leave home at a moment's notice with nothing more than he happens to be standing or sleeping in at the time. As for voluntary travelling, the best advice is 'Don't', both in national interest and in one's own. But if travel cannot be avoided, then travel, as light, as patiently, and as cheerfully as you can.[76]

The compulsion to uproot smacks less here of irresistible urge and more of emergency procedure as well as national duty. The practice of cutting down 'extraneous equipment to the bone', of travelling light, has become, paradoxically, an enforced burden (*'may find himself* compelled'), largely because the beloved home is no longer guaranteed as a point of return.

Leaving home at a moment's notice and hasty packing on the spot form the subject of Rose Macaulay's short story, 'Miss Anstruther's Letters', first published in 1942. If Macaulay earlier identified packing as the standard stuff of the postwar dream in *Dangerous Ages* (1921), then this story serves to problematise that earlier dream like no other. Set in London during the Blitz, Miss Anstruther, one more fictional writer-figure, is given a fleeting opportunity to salvage some of the possessions in her flat before it burns to the ground on one 'wild, blazing hell of a night'.[77] Taking a suitcase, she furiously fills it with books and various other odds and ends, but discovers, when it is all too late, that she has overlooked the most valuable possession of all: crucially, letters from her lover (now dead), a collection spanning twenty-two years. The only remnant is a scrap of paper with the following unrepresentative and rather unfortunate words: 'leave it at that. I know now that you don't care twopence; if you did you would . . . '[78] This story describes the horror of rummaging into one's living, only to find you have left the most important objects behind, the horror of the bag all too hastily packed and the grim prospect of travelling, not light, but empty as a consequence, as the final words of the story convey:

> She was alone with a past devoured by fire and a charred scrap of paper which said you don't care twopence, and then a blank, a great interruption, an end. She had failed in caring once twenty years ago, and failed again now, and the twenty years between were a drift of grey ashes that once were fire, and she a drifting ghost too. She had to leave it at that.[79]

Macaulay's story presents a suitably disenchanted vision, both of the act of hasty packing and of the prospect of travelling light. If I have considered imaginative devaluations of and departures from household structures at various points in this book, these have largely been departures by choice and devaluations by design. Whether devalued or abandoned, the house is still shown to stand as a symbolic alternative. Here, on the contrary, we find an image of unwilled dispossession, unwanted luggage *and* domestic destruction. 'Miss Anstruther's Letters' presents a world in which there is seemingly no architectural alternative to the experience of portability. Luggage becomes the only viable structural metaphor. Moreover, Miss Anstruther – an example of the independent woman who, by the 1940s, has come to have a room of her own – is reminded by her luggage, first and foremost, of the magnitude of her proprietorial loss.[80] This is in stark contrast to earlier female figures of adventurous mobility from Miriam Henderson to Lucy Tantamount. Macaulay, in an unpublished piece of non-fiction written during the war, provides perhaps one of the best expressions of the conceptual transfiguration of 'travelling light' from a state of voluntary free play to a traumatic state of imposed reduction:

> As to one's possessions, recent experience has taught us all to sit light to these; they are so continually being torn from one's hands by the greedy visitants from the skies; safer, some think, to have none, there would be the less to grieve over.[81]

Extreme portability has now, paradoxically, become both more precarious *and* 'safer' than domesticity.

Elizabeth Bowen's Left Luggage

Elizabeth Bowen is one late modernist writer whose *oeuvre* maps the emerging paradoxes of portability in line with a renewed interest in architectural form. Her characters are perpetually caught in portable paradigms, which simultaneously signal architectural escape, in the tradition of Miriam Henderson, and architectural deficit, as in the case of Miss Anstruther. Her negotiation of the shifting significations of portability in relation to architecture is reminiscent of Forster, though the two writers diverge in terms of emphasis. If, in *Howards*

End, Forster sees the 'modern ownership of movables' as detrimental to the imagination, this is a development which, on the contrary, serves to enrich Bowen's creative output, providing material for novel and novel.[82] At the same time, her complicated embrace of the modernity so feared in Forster's work articulates a peculiar form of late modernist uncertainty.

Bowen's own engagement with Forster's writing started, in fact, with an appreciation of its architectural qualities. 'I arrived into it with a sense of homecoming', she recollects of her first encounter with his work as a school-girl, outlined in her introduction to a collection of essays marking his ninetieth birthday in 1969.[83] This work is projected both as a resting place retrieved and a final destination. The novelist-in-the-making is shown to arrive home and into the house of fiction through reading Forster. And yet, the young Bowen was, to all intents and purposes, just preparing to set out – not to settle down – as a novelist herself. Bowen's sense of 'homecoming' through the work of Forster is shot through with a recognition of eventual departure; this is a characteristic superimposition in her fiction.[84] As Karen Michaelis perceives on a visit to a dying aunt in Ireland in *The House in Paris* (1935), '[b]y having come, you already store up the pains of going away'.[85] While acknowledging Forster's profound influence on her development as a writer, she casts his work as a house she must also strike out from. Though well known for her render-ings of domestic spaces, I will contend here that Bowen's model is not primar-ily architectural. The house that pervades her work is most often a house left behind. She presents us, rather, with a *case* of fiction: the 'luggage left in the hall between two journeys as opposed to the perpetual furniture of rooms', to use her own formulation in 'Notes on Writing a Novel'.[86] It is a formulation I will look at more closely later in this analysis.

Bowen, like Forster, sketches the contours of a culture of portability. However, her conception of a more established portable culture within a 1930s context has radically different implications, implications Forster could never have envisaged in 1910. The difference between these representations can be understood through an observation made by Bowen herself in reflect-ing on Forster's work: 'The world of these novels is a world of conflict; its not being a world actually *in* conflict, fraught by battles and revolutions, makes the schisms within and oppositions between its people stand out more sig-nificantly and strongly.'[87] Unlike Forster, Bowen's novels feature an external world *in* conflict (or verging on conflict), which cannot but infiltrate the world of the personal. This is most evident, as I will show, in her 1935 novel *The House in Paris*, a pointed reconceptualisation of *Howards End* at a time when portability can no longer hide its precarious face.

The evident anxiety at the heart of *Howards End*, concerning the negative repercussions of a reversion to a 'civilisation of luggage', is certainly some-thing Bowen shared more generally. A writer with a 'conservative vision' on many levels, she clearly set great store by tradition.[88] The loss of tradition is frequently presented, in her writings, as something to be regretted in an age that is 'decentralised', a word used by Lady Waters in *To The North* (1932).[89] Writing on the subject of 'Manners' in 1937, she considers some of these negative repercussions:

> The lives of most people now, say, in their thirties have changed inconceivably since childhood. Tradition is broken. Temperament, occupation, success or failure, marriage or active nervous hostility to an original *milieu* have made nomads of us. The rules we learnt in childhood are as useless, as impossible to take with us as the immutable furniture of the family home.[90]

Overarching codes of behaviour cannot be sustained in a decentralised age. The essay was written at a late-1930s moment of acute anxiety as to wider security, the more so for the Anglo-Irish Bowen in an independent Ireland under Éamon de Valera. Central fragmentation implies the redundancy of that archetypal nineteenth-century central point of reference, the 'family home' with its 'immutable furniture'. The passage reeks of Forster. Here is a writer seemingly compelled to a metaphorical abandonment of the house against her will. Here we perceive a writer forced to join the 'civilisation of luggage' with some considerable reluctance.

However, in other essays, the very idea of dislocation is affirmatively foregrounded where the question of literary style is concerned. It becomes apparent that if Bowen metaphorically departs from the model of the house in her work, it is figured as a departure as much by choice as by compulsion. Ideal language must, she advised the would-be writer, in a much later essay on style and language, be 'clear as glass – the person looking out of the window knows there *is* glass there, but he is not concerned with it'.[91] Note that the person figured here is looking out of the window, unlike the internally focused 'individual vision' upheld in James's 'house of fiction' model.[92] In this model, James imagines an 'incalculability of range' in terms of the diversity of possible interior scenes.[93] For Bowen, such an incalculability of range depends upon change of *scenery* (upon movement, in other words). We would do well to imagine the individual in Bowen's vision to be looking out of a train or car window as opposed to a house. Her ideal language, clear as glass, is also mobile, and she saw stylistic 'mobility' as something to strive for: 'Our language must on no account be allowed to set or harden; all the time we must get it to extend its range, keep it on the move.'[94] This is also a trait she identifies in the works of writers she admires. 'Ever on the move', Katherine Mansfield's 'tentative, responsive, exploratory' approach, never settling into any single mode, is seen to be informed by her restless propulsion: 'She had no time to form a consistent attitude to any one finished story: each stood to her as a milestone passed, not as a destination arrived at.'[95] Likewise, the 'enormous sense of release' evident in Woolf's *Orlando* is, to Bowen's mind, 'partly an affair of effortless speed, mobility, action'.[96] This is a projection of style that cannot readily be contained within old forms, a projection of style as an act of breaking away.

Judging by a further postwar essay published in 1950, Bowen clearly saw the act of breaking away as necessary for authorial development. More interestingly, she conceived of it as a form of 'disloyalty', picking up on Graham Greene's use of the term. Such a term implies a personal betrayal. But who or what is Bowen purporting to betray here? She explains that to be disloyal is to recognise

> the danger to the writer of anything which may exercise a restrictive and ultimately blinding hold. His ideal is to be at once disabused and susceptible and for ever mobile. This is not easily come at; for, indeed, the writer has, in an even greater degree than his fellow man, the disposition to be attached – ideas, creeds, persons and ways of life first magnetise then begin to absorb him.[97]

While Forster ascribed 'imaginative poverty' to the modern nomad, as a facet of the detached state, Bowen suggests here that imaginative poverty must be seen as the outcome of excessive attachment.[98]

I would posit Forster, Bowen's literary antecedent, as one such attachment from which she saw that she must break away.[99] Indeed, her subject is the 'civilisation of luggage' he disparaged, her interwar work forming a compendium of 'case' studies, from holiday-maker Sydney Warren in *The Hotel* (1927) through to the displaced Portia Quayne in *The Death of the Heart* (1938). In favouring disconnection in her approach to writing, she is effectuating a necessary disloyalty to one key hereditary literary influence, a disloyalty she saw as vital for the intuitive writer:

> This crisis, simultaneously felt in his personal being (because of debts and affections) and his aesthetic being is the crux of the feeling writer's career. He cannot free himself from the hereditary influences without the sense of outraging, injuring and betraying them.[100]

To consider either Forster or his works with any degree of objectivity was something Bowen claimed to find extremely difficult, so immersed was she in his writing from adolescence.[101] A disloyalty to Forster was certainly personal as well as aesthetic and, as such, problematic.[102] In her birthday essay on his work, she recalls first coming upon *Howards End*, most likely a first edition of the book, in a 'half-empty valise in an attic at the top of an aunt's house'.[103] Here the very 'protracted crisis' of conflicting values, implicit in Forster's novel, is captured in miniature.[104] The contextual pertinence of this disclosure is so marked that one wonders if it is a later retrospective reconstruction on the part of a writer who admitted that her own 'tendency to attribute significance to places ... became warranted by its larger reflection in E. M. Forster'.[105] Bowen opens her essay on the same author with the comment: 'There was something to be said for first reading E. M. Forster when I did: 1915.'[106] There is clearly also something to be said for discovering Forster *where* she did: in an immobile valise in a house not her own. The subsequent loss of this particular copy is described as 'catastrophic': 'It doomed me to remain without *Howards End* for I don't know how long.'[107] If she arrived into the world of Forster with a sense of homecoming, she departed from it with a sense of homelessness.

Such a sense of homelessness would become the keynote of Bowen's revision of *Howards End* through *The House in Paris*.[108] In keeping with the idea of the 'catastrophic', my discussion of *The House in Paris* turns around the pronounced 'catastrophe' which arises from Leopold Grant-Moody's ill-fated handling of Henrietta Mountjoy's paper-leather dispatch case in the first part of the novel.[109] Leopold's mishandling of this dispatch case results in the sudden, 'crashing' distribution of Henrietta's overnight belongings – 'two apples, a cake of soap and an ebony-backed hairbrush' along with a sponge bag and some reading material – around and about Mme Fisher's Parisian salon.[110] The young Henrietta's reaction to this event is described as follows: 'For the first time this morning a smile twitched up her cheeks, then she laughed outright: she sat on the sofa excitedly laughing, pushing her hair back like a girl at a pantomime.'[111]

The catastrophe surrounding the dispatch case is presented as a form of pantomime on several different levels in the text. It enacts, in the first place, the epistemological crisis at the very heart of the novel in relation to Leopold's understanding of his own origins. It mimics, in the second place, the catastrophic sexual relationship between Karen and Max, played out in the middle part, which is shown to produce the illegitimate Leopold and culminates in Max's suicide. In the third place, it gestures outwards to more violent forms of historical upheaval in Europe in the mid-1930s.

To better grasp these varied implications, let us start, as Bowen herself does in the novel, with that paper-leather dispatch case. It is highlighted from the outset at Henrietta's feet in the taxi she shares with Naomi Fisher from the Gare du Nord on the way to Mme Fisher's house.[112] Why the unusual paper-leather material? Why a dispatch case (essentially a satchel-like carrier bag with two buckled straps) and not simply a small case or an overnight bag? These specific designations are important, not least because the paper-leather dispatch case is an object that Bowen pointedly returns to, again and again, throughout the novel.[113] It is, as Leopold himself perceives, the 'symbol of [Henrietta's] departure', but, within the broader scheme of the novel, it also becomes the symbol of Leopold's transgressive arrival.[114] Extending beyond the novel's direct scope, it indicates the predicament of the politically disenfranchised between the wars. The nominally insubstantial 'paper-leather' material of the case conveys a sense of semi-substance or semi-reality, correlating with Henrietta's perception of Paris as a 'cardboard city' and of Mme Fisher's abode as 'miniature, like a doll's house' with 'doll's-house furniture'.[115] The interactions between Henrietta and Leopold indeed produce a sort of pantomime of grown-up reality, accentuated by the repeated references to Lewis Carroll's *Alice in Wonderland*.[116] It is almost as if the case stands as a prop in a re-enactment of a grown-up world just out of their own sphere and, as we will see, an untold narrative just out of their ken. The word 'dispatch' points to the respective situations of both Henrietta and Leopold. The two (virtually) parentless children have been, quite literally, dispatched by their respective carers. It is as 'dispatches', a word tainted with a sense of superfluity, that they cross paths. But further to this, 'dispatch' is a word with connotations of violence and death. The threat of 'being dispatched', in the sense of being dealt a death-blow, casts a permanent shadow across the pages of this novel from Karen's visit to her dying aunt in Rushmore to the individual encounters of the children with the dying Mme Fisher. This is not to mention the central gruesome spectre of Max's act of suicide through slitting his own wrist. If, as Neil Corcoran has observed, *The Last September* is a 'novel full of holes', then *The House in Paris* is a novel full of blood, imagined as much as real.[117]

The incident surrounding the dispatch case might itself be characterised as an incident of epistemological blood-letting, or, to borrow a phrase used by Andrew Bennett and Nicholas Royle in their discussion of the novel, the occurrence of a sudden and bloody 'gash of knowledge'.[118] During Henrietta's interview with Mme Fisher, shortly after the incident, she is probed on the source of the recent disruptive noise: '"What has he been breaking? I heard something fall just now."'[119] This question, prompting a quick-fire exchange on the 'magnetic' subject of Leopold, swiftly leads to the startling and violently sudden revelation of Leopold's father's unfortunate involvement with Mme Fisher's daughter, Naomi:[120]

> 'Oh', Henrietta said, 'did you know his father too?'
> 'Quite well', said Mme Fisher. 'He broke Naomi's heart'.[121]

Bowen, consciously linking the 'breaking' sound of the dispatch case to the painful exposure of Naomi's broken heart (an image of emotional bloodshed), conceives thus of the 'gaping dispatch case' as the visual expression of a gaping epistemological gash.[122] It also represents the violent opening up of a Pandora's box with a life of its own. 'Its two clasps', we are told, 'indignantly sprang open.'[123] More than this, the gaping dispatch case nods to the epistemological gash of all gashes. To reiterate Mme Fisher's words with emphasis added: '"I heard something *fall* just now."' Bowen deliberately invokes the narrative of the original fall of man and woman through the will to greater knowledge. We must remember that Henrietta's dispatch case dispatches two apples, and it is one of these apples which leads Leopold into the temptation of an illicit investigation of his own origins through 'breaking' into Naomi's handbag: 'Set on driving Henrietta upstairs, [Miss Fisher] had forgotten the rubbed black Morocco bag sitting there by the apple. Leopold's eye lit on it with the immediate thought that inside there might be letters about him.'[124] The catastrophe surrounding Henrietta's dispatch case serves thus to open up the quintessential narrative of origins, original sin and epistemological longing.

But the fall of man is also a narrative about the emergence of a consciousness of sex, and the dispatch case catastrophe likewise has an important sexual dimension. The interactions between the children surrounding the case parody the adult interactions in the novel, particularly the relationship between Karen and Max. Both engaged to other people, their illicit relationship is, in effect, a relationship which is founded on and associated with luggage, visible or absent. Theirs is a love which has no place in any house, and Bowen will not permit us to forget this fact. When they fleetingly touch hands in the grass, it is next to an 'upturned packing-case' as makeshift tea table in the garden of Naomi's late aunt.[125] When they say goodbye shortly afterwards in a train carriage at Victoria station, they are momentarily locked into a crucial proximity by a baggage blockage on both sides of the narrow corridor in which they stand.[126] When they meet for a day in Boulogne, the illegitimacy of their relationship is rendered even more conspicuous through the complete lack of luggage on route: '[Karen] sat in the train in her thin dress; everyone else had luggage.'[127] Finally, on the way back from their brief trip to Hythe, during which they consummate that relationship, their separated suitcases announce the placelessness of their love and the impossibility of a union on fixed ground. Theirs is a love with no address:

> Karen stared at her suitcase on the opposite rack. Past midnight, that other train would crash into the Gare du Nord; Max getting out would be carrying *his* suitcase and the Folkestone mackintosh through the angry steam a French train makes. She thought suddenly: I don't know his address.[128]

Maud Ellmann has referred to Leopold, the product of this meeting, as a 'misdirected' letter, a letter, in other words, with the wrong *address*.[129] But a further useful way to think about Leopold would be as a bag without a label, a piece of lost or, perhaps more fittingly, left luggage: '"But look here"', Henrietta prods him, '"Who do you really belong to?"'[130] As the legacy of this relationship founded on luggage, he is himself later figured as part of the 'baggage' of his adoptive American parents by Mme Fisher, when she meets him late in the novel.[131] Thus his 'rough' handling of Henrietta's dispatch case – 'going across to pick up the dispatch case, [he] weighed it and swung it boastfully' – is really a rough handling of his own history.[132] The crash of the dispatch case belatedly enacts, in fact, an earlier luggage-related accident that does not happen, at the very moment Karen and Max part company: 'their parting had been voluntary and busy: the great thing had been for him to balance her suitcase so that, when her taxi started, it should not fall on her feet'.[133]

Bearing both Leopold and luggage (and Leopold as luggage) in mind, I would like now to suggest a number of interesting parallels and disjunctions between this novel and *Howards End*. We find a socially unsanctioned affair in both; affairs that end, in each case, with the death of the man (Leonard Bast and Max Ebhart) and the birth of a boy (Helen Schlegel's child and Leopold). We find an elderly woman with a palpable influence over the atmosphere of a house, benevolent in the early novel (with Mrs Wilcox) and malign in the later (with Mme Fisher). Moreover, the name 'Leopold' is, I would suggest, a reference to the character of Leonard in Forster's novel. Certainly, those two characters, Leopold and Leonard, share a thirst for knowledge, but inhabit a world which denies them any kind of fulfilment in this line. But Leopold, with his Jewish heritage, has also, quite rightly, been aligned, by Corcoran, with that 'most famous literary Jew written by a gentile – and, like Elizabeth Bowen, an Irish gentile – in the twentieth century'.[134] He alludes, of course, to Leopold Bloom in James Joyce's *Ulysses*, and this other alignment marks a vital point where Bowen departs from Forster and from *Howards End*. Corcoran draws upon Jean Radford's political and historical reading of *The House in Paris* in making his observation; both critics foreground the implications for Leopold of the introduction of the Nuremberg Laws in 1935, laws which rendered boys of his background exceptionally vulnerable.[135] Radford argues that Bowen's novel is representative of the modernist text of the 1930s, which sought to integrate 'personal and collective histories', thus positing the novelist, in V. S. Pritchett's words, as the 'historian of a crisis in a civilisation'.[136] Corcoran is a little more reticent than Radford in pressing the historical point of the novel, but, despite his reservations, he acknowledges that

> it is hard not to think of the child whom Ray considers 'this brittle little Jewish boy' . . . carrying his suitcase at the Gare de Lyon, without recall-ing those other brittle little Jewish boys who would, only a few years after the contemporary date on which this novel is set, also stand on European station platforms, but not in order to return to their mothers.[137]

As Bennett and Royle argue, anticipatory 'dread' permeates *The House in Paris*.[138] However, it is a present reality of European affairs, not just a future prospect of more serious situations of upheaval, which is reflected here. By 1935, vast numbers of people had already been set in motion for political reasons. That 'radically new form of homelessness', identified by Marrus, is certainly a troubling spectre in Bowen's novel.[139]

Like Forster, Bowen envisages a 'civilisation of luggage'. But it is one of involuntary refugees as much as voluntary exiles, and she does not attempt to bring them in under the narrative roof.[140] If *Howards End* begins and ends in a house, then *The House in Paris* begins and ends in and around a train station, and a continental train station at that. If Forster's novel concerns the 'condition of England', as is so often stressed, then Bowen's must be seen to concern the condition of Europe. If, in *Howards End*, English liberal values are at stake, in *The House in Paris*, these same values are critiqued through the representation of the blatant anti-Semitism of the Michaelis family.[141] The fate of England is bound up with that of Europe in Bowen's novel, as individual history is bound up with collective history. Leopold, poised between England and the continent, is also poised at the point where the two kinds of luggage civilisations meet. In light of this, the most important difference between the two novels lies in the fact that the illegitimate child in *Howards End* becomes heir to a house, while Leopold, abandoned by his own mother at birth, becomes the very embodiment of 1930s dispossession. Despite offering the suggestion of a possible reconciliation and homecoming beyond the ending, the novel leaves Leopold at a paradoxical point of still-standing transit. The reader is left in no certainty about his ultimate reinstatement and security. The question of whether or not his luggage will, in the end, be reclaimed hangs unanswered in the chilly Parisian air as the book draws to a close.

The politically charged representation of the 'civilisation of luggage' in *The House in Paris* lends a nightmarish quality to the 'Move Dangerously' slogan of the travel agency depicted in her earlier novel, *To The North*.[142] It also casts Bowen's emphasis on stylistic mobility in a new and somewhat more chequered light. This is not least because travelling light is figured more often within the realm of fantasy than that of possibility in her work. Her essay on 'Disloyalties', though upholding an ideal of mobile detachment on the part of the writer, also acknowledges that this is not always easy to achieve in practice, nor is it always desirable: 'In turning away from resting-places, from lighted doorways, to pursue his course into darker country, [the writer] carries with him a burden of rejected alternatives and troubling regrets.'[143] The writer portrayed in this image moves heavily, reluctantly, with regret. And it is his carried burden which hinders his progress. We must remember that luggage, while enabling mobility, also encumbers it. Indeed, the portable paradigm that Bowen presents as a literary architectural alternative, in her 1945 essay, 'Notes on Writing a Novel', is strangely static. Even more curiously, it is an image of *left* luggage:

> [The novelist] is forced towards his plot. By what? By the 'what is to be said'. What is 'What is to be said'? A mass of subjective matter that has accumulated – impressions received, feelings about experience, distorted

results of ordinary observation and something else – x. This matter is *extra* matter. It is superfluous to the non-writing life of the writer. It is luggage left in the hall between two journeys as opposed to the perpetual furniture of rooms. It is destined to be elsewhere. It cannot move till its destination is known. Plot is the knowing of destination.[144]

Bowen's left luggage suggests the dream of movement rather than movement itself, and this aptly corresponds to the characteristic experience of a Bowen novel. It also aptly corroborates MacKay's identification of the 'metaphor of the journey not made' as a key late modernist trope.[145] This state of suspension is epitomised in *The House in Paris*, and the above image might well describe Leopold's situation in that novel in fact. Driven by an 'anxiety to be elsewhere' but stalled at every turn, Bowen's characters are shown to be continuously in transit but also continually obstructed.[146] It is a quandary that numerous critics have highlighted and one reflected in her use of luggage imagery between the wars.[147] Luggage, in Bowen's work, conveys escapist mobility and paralytic detention in equal measure. Lois Farquar in *The Last September* (1929), coming upon some luggage left in the hallway of Danielstown (that of the newly arrived Marda Norton), is struck by the feeling of adventurous possibility that the accumulated luggage evokes beyond the enclosed domain of the Big House. Slipping on Marda's fur coat, Lois imaginatively escapes her surroundings: 'the blurred panes, the steaming changing trees, the lonely cave of the hall no longer had her consciousness in a clamp. *How* she could live, she felt.'[148] But if the very sight of luggage spells imaginative escape for Lois, it is an image applied, in turn, by Theodora Thirdman in *Friends and Relations* (1931), to denote a sense of social and physical stagnancy. '"But don't we want to *matter* in this place? Aren't we ever going to begin?"' She cries out to her woefully inadequate mother. '"you're like someone sitting for always on a suitcase in a railway station. Such a comfortable suitcase, such a magnificent station! *Eeooch!*"'[149] Lois's naïve fantasy and Theodora's lament exemplify two distinctive and oppositional Boweneque leitmotifs. Together they articulate the peculiar paradox of luggage in conjuring escape and obstruction at one and the same time. The luggage paradox is, in effect, the Bowen paradox. To my mind, she is to literary luggage what Henry James is to literary architecture.

I have suggested that luggage became emblematic of the search for a new kind of form for emerging modernist writers. To conclude this chapter, I would like to propose that luggage equally enunciated the nostalgic loss of a previous stable structure, embodied in the image of the house. This is particularly apparent in works by late modernist writers like Bowen. Forward- and backward-looking at one and the same time, luggage in Bowen's work exposes a certain late modernist ambivalence; the deliberate alienation from a previous architectural model in favour of a more mobile conceptual approach can be found to coexist disconcertingly with an enduring belief in the overarching force and importance of that previous model *in absentia*. In Bowen's interwar writing, this formal and stylistic ambivalence must be seen to be inextricably linked to the political context. By the end of the 1930s, 'the sense of crisis and of even greater crisis ahead was never out of men's minds ... [a]nd that constant consciousness of disaster must necessarily have had consequences for the forms that the imagination conceived'.[150] These words of Samuel Hynes apply equally to the work of women writers at this time. For one thing, that sense of crisis engendered a reappraisal of the stability encoded in traditional structures. For Bowen, as for many late modernist writers, the house no longer worked as an enclosing framework and yet the longing for an eventual destination, an ultimate resting place, is palpably felt throughout her work. A novelist of the nomadic horde, she admits in *Bowen's Court* (1942) that we have 'everything to dread from the dispossessed'.[151] If she advocates mobility in writing, it is in order to get somewhere. The pervading nightmare, subdued yet ever-present, revolves around the idea of an indefinite entrapment in a state of limbo, the suspension of progress or, as she puts it in *The Last September*, 'the sense of detention, of a prologue being played out too lengthily'.[152] This is the dilemma that her 1945 portable paradigm brings to the fore. It is a paradigm which acutely captures the contradictory nature of her engagements with modern life and modernist experiment.

In this regard, she is not unlike Forster, who had an 'awkward relationship to modernism'.[153] If Forster looks out at the 'nomadic horde' from the inside of a threatened structure in *Howards End*, Bowen looks in wistfully from the outside, as at a house of words no longer possible but imagined nonetheless. It might be said that Howards End/*Howards End* is the other house which haunts her work, the shadowy fictional third in her imaginative relation to the structure of Bowen's Court, her much-loved family estate in Ireland. Bowen's Court was itself a structure from which she was forced ultimately to part, due to the prohibitive expense of its upkeep. Sold in 1959, it was knocked down the following year, and these circumstances must, of course, be factored into a reading of her retrospective essay on Forster, written exactly ten years later. Howards End/*Howards End* forms the fictional counterpart to the real house left behind, but it is also the house projected at some fantastical future destination point. To reiterate the words of Margaret Schlegel towards the end of Forster's novel:

'This craze for motion has only set in during the last hundred years. It may be followed by a civilisation that won't be a movement, because it will rest on the earth. All the signs are against it now, but I can't help hoping, and very early in the morning in the garden I feel our house is the future as well as the past.'[154]

In her essay on Forster, Bowen claimed that his work became a 'landmark' for her during the Second World War, when all others 'were swept away'.[155] The essay itself is entitled 'A Passage to E. M. Forster', and I would suggest that Bowen's portable paradigm also represents, in effect, an inconclusive search for Forster's lost house, that literary house of the future as well as the past, a stable and historic landmark. Permanence, she once remarked, is an 'attribute of recalled places', and the projected destination in her work might be said to be the permanent place, the house recalled.[156] At the same time, that house is recalled, for Bowen, from a point of ineffaceable modernist experience (the experience of liminality, obstruction, transience, if you like), accentuated both by the Second World War and by the later very personal loss of Bowen's Court. To return to the wording of her portable model, notably formulated at the end of the Second World War: 'It is luggage left in the hall between two journeys as opposed to the perpetual furniture of rooms. It is destined to be elsewhere. It cannot move till its destination is known. Plot is the knowing of destination.' If plot is the knowing of destination, then modernism witnesses the collapse of the idea of traditional plot as the obliteration of the idea of a knowable end-point. Thus, that conception of luggage in the hall between two journeys above all sustains the illusion of a permanent resting-place (the luggage is 'destined to be elsewhere') known in practice (the luggage 'cannot move') to be irrecoverable, impossible.

Significantly, the year before Bowen's essay on Forster, her final novel, *Eva Trout* (1968), ends with the death of the most dislocated of all her characters, Eva, at the hands of her own adopted child, Jeremy. The child accidentally comes upon a revolver within Eva's luggage, accumulated 'like a fallen city' in a London hotel suite.[157] Jeremy himself is the proud young owner of a dispatch case of 'vermilion tartan' as if to signify, following *The House in Paris*, a final self-destructive, vengeful impulse on the part of the dispossessed, unwitting and innocent as the young Jeremy himself is in carrying out the act.[158] Much earlier in the novel, when probed on the question of what she is afraid of, Eva responds: '"That at the end of it all you'll find out that I have nothing to declare."'[159] She invokes, in this line, the standard interrogatory question of the customs official at customs control: 'Have you anything to declare?' The intentional irony of this early customs invocation is evident, given her later death as a result of the illicit component in her baggage. But her words also register the threshold anxiety of the displaced person under scrutiny, which harks back to the heightened nervousness of the interwar years. Edwin J. Kenney points out that the 'fear of customs officials was one of Miss Bowen's concerns as an outsider, an alien, and becomes a metaphor for all complex people'.[160] In harbouring this fear, Eva is no exception. The chapter to follow shifts attention to those numerous depictions of luggage in the *customs hall* between two journeys during the interwar period and to the complex, displaced person under scrutiny.

NOTES

1. Judith Butler, *Precarious Life: The Powers of Mourning and Violence* (London and New York: Verso, 2006), pp. 22, 20.
2. This is not to suggest that passports came into existence at this time. Passports, in various forms, have, indeed, a long history. However, during the nineteenth century, passport requirements were relaxed, sometimes even abolished, in countries throughout Europe in line with the growth of an increasingly complex railway network, allowing for ease of movement across national borders until the reintroduction of stricter forms of frontier control with the onset of the First World War. For further information on the history and effect of the passport, see John Torpey, *The Invention of the Passport: Surveillance, Citizenship and the State* (Cambridge: Cambridge University Press, 2000); Paul Fussell, *Abroad: British Literary Traveling Between the Wars* (New York: Oxford University Press, 1980), pp. 24–31; Michael R. Marrus, *The Unwanted: European Refugees from the First World War Through the Cold War* (Philadelphia: Temple University Press, 2002), p. 92.
3. Bridget T. Chalk, *Modernism and Mobility: The Passport and Cosmopolitan Experience* (New York: Palgrave Macmillan, 2014), p. 4. In drawing attention to this paradox, Chalk was prompted by remarks made by Raymond Williams in his lecture 'When Was Modernism?'
4. For an explanation of the phenomenon of the stateless as '[s]ymptomatic of the new refugee problem' arising between the wars, see Marrus, *The Unwanted*, p. 178.
5. Fussell, *Abroad*, p. 4.
6. Katherine Mansfield, 'Je ne parle pas français' (1918), in *Collected Stories of Katherine Mansfield* (1945; London: Constable, 1980), p. 60.
7. George Orwell, *Coming Up for Air* (1939; Harmondsworth: Penguin, 1976), p. 112.
8. Chalk, *Modernism and Mobility*, pp. 5, 7.
9. Caren Kaplan, *Questions of Travel: Postmodern Discourses of Displacement* (Durham, NC: Duke University Press, 1996), pp. 27–8.
10. Ibid., p. 36.
11. Ibid., p. 36.
12. Morag Shiach, 'Periodizing Modernism', in *The Oxford Handbook of Modernisms*, ed. Peter Brooker, Andrzej Gąsiorek, Deborah Longworth and Andrew Thacker (Oxford: Oxford University Press, 2010), p. 28.
13. Tyrus Miller, *Late Modernism: Politics, Fiction and the Arts Between the World Wars* (Berkeley: University of California Press, 1999), pp. 22–3. Emphasis in original.
14. Marina MacKay, '"Is your journey really necessary?": Going Nowhere in Late Modernist London', *PMLA*, 124.5, October 2009, pp. 1601–2.
15. Ibid., p. 1601.
16. Lyndsey Stonebridge, 'Refugee Style: Hannah Arendt and the Perplexities of Rights', *Textual Practice*, 25.1, 2011, pp. 72, 71.
17. Virginia Woolf, 'The Leaning Tower' (1940), in *The Moment and Other Essays* (1947; San Diego: Harcourt Brace Jovanovich, 1974), pp. 128–54.
18. W. H. Auden, 'Sonnet XVIII' from 'Sonnets from China', in *Collected Poems*, ed. Edward Mendelson (1976; London: Faber, 1991), p. 193.
19. Ibid., pp. 193–4.
20. Marrus, *The Unwanted*, p. 4. Asylum seekers, of one kind or another, have naturally always existed, but not on the mass scale witnessed in the twentieth century,

when the question of how to deal with refugees became a political problem. Marrus traces the 'emerging consciousness of a refugee phenomenon' (p. 9) back to the 1880s.

21. Ibid., p. 51.
22. Hannah Arendt, 'We Refugees' (1943), in *The Jewish Writings*, ed. Jerome Kohn and Ron H. Feldman (New York: Schocken Books, 2007), p. 274.
23. Samuel Hynes, *The Auden Generation: Literature and Politics in England in the 1930s* (London: Faber, 1979), p. 341.
24. Aldous Huxley, *Crome Yellow* (1921; London: Vintage-Random, 2004), p. 13.
25. Ibid., p. 50.
26. Peacock's novels had titles such as *Headlong Hall* (1815), *Nightmare Abbey* (1818) and *Crotchet Castle* (1831).
27. Aldous Huxley, *Point Counter Point* (1928; London: Chatto and Windus, 1934), pp. 282, 283.
28. 'Mark Cross', advertisement, *The Times*, 27 March 1924, p. 11.
29. Robert Graves and Alan Hodge, *The Long Week-End: A Social History of Great Britain 1918–1939* (1940; London: Faber, 1950), p. 232.
30. 'Vita-Weat', advertisement, *The Times*, 6 October 1939, p. 11.
31. 'Lux', advertisement, *The Times*, 18 August 1927, p. 9.
32. See, for example: 'M.P.A. Portable Sets', advertisement, *The Times*, 25 September 1926, p. 8.
33. Tony Last adopts the posture of explorer in order to escape an unpleasant reality (chiefly, his wife's infidelity) at home, yet his accumulated travel accessories – which are comically listed at some length – only serve to remind him of the inauthenticity of the posture. Waugh takes the joke a notch further in *Scoop*. William Boot is advised, by newspaper magnate Lord Copper, to 'Travel Light and Be Prepared', advice producing a kit which requires an 'additional aeroplane', putting the trappings of the earlier Tony in the shade. See Evelyn Waugh, *A Handful of Dust* (1934; Harmondsworth: Penguin, 1951), p. 155; *Scoop: A Novel About Journalists* (1938; Harmondsworth: Penguin, 1957), pp. 41, 45.
34. Waugh, *A Handful of Dust*, pp. 97, 98.
35. Cyril Connolly, *The Rock Pool* (1936; Oxford: Oxford University Press, 1981), p. 73.
36. Walter Benjamin, 'The Work of Art in the Age of Mechanical Reproduction', in *Illuminations: Essays and Reflections*, trans. Harry Zorn, ed. Hannah Arendt (1968; London: Pimlico, 1999), pp. 211–44.
37. Yevgeny Zamyatin, *We*, trans. Mirra Ginsburg (1924; New York: EOS-HarperCollins, 1999), p. 11.
38. Ibid., p. 89.
39. Ibid., p. 42.
40. Ibid., pp. 41–2.
41. Ibid., p. 61.
42. Ibid., pp. 194–5.
43. Ibid., p. 194.
44. See Mirra Ginsburg, 'Introduction', in *We*, by Yevgeny Zamyatin, trans. Mirra Ginsburg (1924; New York: EOS-HarperCollins, 1999), pp. v–xx.
45. Viktor Shklovsky, *Zoo, or, Letters Not about Love*, trans. Richard Sheldon (Normal, IL: Dalkey Archive Press, 2001), pp. 19, 23, 104. Emphasis in original. A *nécessaire* was a small case for personal effects.
46. Ibid., pp. 39, 42.
47. Ibid., pp. 53–4.

48. Vladimir Nabokov, *The Gift*, trans. Michael Scammell and Dmitri Nabokov (1938; London: Penguin, 2001), p. 11. Emphasis in original.
49. Vladimir Nabokov, *The Real Life of Sebastian Knight* (1941; London: Penguin, 1964), p. 6. For an account of the composition of the novel in the bathroom of his Parisian apartment, see Brian Boyd, *Vladimir Nabokov: The Russian Years* (Princeton: Princeton University Press, 1990), p. 496.
50. Hermann Broch, *The Death of Virgil*, trans. Jean Starr Untermeyer (1945; Oxford: Oxford University Press, 1983), p. 4. In the novel, Virgil finally comes to the decision to burn this manuscript.
51. Irène Némirovsky, *Suite Française* (Paris: Denöel, 2004), p. 109. My translation. It is also worth mentioning Edmund de Waal's *The Hare With Amber Eyes* (2010) here, which charts the discovery of a family history through an inherited set of Japanese netsuke, first preserved in the pocket of a servant and then within a 'little leather attaché case' transported from Vienna to England in 1945. See *The Hare With Amber Eyes: A Hidden Heritance* (2010; London: Vintage, 2011), p. 283.
52. Lisa Fittko, 'The Story of Old Benjamin', in *The Arcades Project*, by Walter Benjamin, trans. Howard Eiland and Kevin McLaughlin, prepared on the basis of the German volume, ed. by Rolf Tiedemann (Cambridge, MA and London: Belknap–Harvard, 1999), p. 948. Emphasis in original.
53. The range of examples cited here are, again, intended as representative, and there is clearly scope for a more comprehensive study of portability from the distinct angle of the refugee writer.
54. 'Refugees from Poland', *The Times*, 16 October 1939, p. 10.
55. Stefan Zweig, *The Post Office Girl*, trans. Joel Rotenberg (1982; London: Sort Of Books, 2009), p. 35.
56. Ibid., p. 35.
57. Ibid., p. 41.
58. Ibid., p. 93.
59. Ibid., pp. 132, 135.
60. The object of the suitcase continues to be employed as a powerful emblem for the refugee, judging from the titles of some recent books both on victims of the holocaust and on other situations of twentieth-century political displacement. See, for example, Karen Levine, *Hana's Suitcase: A True Story* (London: Evans, 2003) and Julie Mertus, Jasmina Tesanovic, Habiba Metikos and Rada Boric (eds), *The Suitcase: Refugee Voices from Bosnia and Croatia*, trans. Jelica Todosijevic (Berkeley: University of California Press, 1997).
61. Quoted in Erika and Klaus Mann, *Escape to Life* (Boston, MA: Houghton Mifflin Company, 1939), pp. 146–7.
62. Letter to Hannah and Manfred Altmann, Rio de Janeiro, 15 December 1940. See Stefan and Lotte Zweig, *Stefan and Lotte Zweig's South American Letters: New York, Argentina and Brazil, 1940–42*, ed. Darién J. Davis and Oliver Marshall (New York and London: Continuum, 2010), p. 95.
63. Letter to Hannah and Manfred Altmann, Ossining, c. 19 July 1941. See See Zweig, *Stefan and Lotte Zweig's South American Letters*, p. 121.
64. Stefan Zweig, *The World of Yesterday: An Autobiography* (1942; London: Cassell, 1943), p. 319. Emphasis added.
65. Valentine Cunningham, *British Writers of the Thirties* (Oxford: Oxford University Press, 1988), p. 377. The chapter I refer to, entitled 'Somewhere the Good Place?', gives a wide-ranging overview of 1930s tropes of travel and escape in British fiction (pp. 377–418).
66. Christopher Isherwood, *Goodbye to Berlin* (1939; London: Minerva, 1989), p. 217.

67. Ibid., p. 219.
68. Ibid., p. 218.
69. Auden, 'The Composer', in *Collected Poems*, p. 181.
70. '[W]ithout a servant', he remarks, 'one spends half every day packing and unpacking'. Robert Byron, *The Road to Oxiana* (1937; London: Penguin, 2007), p. 158.
71. Ibid., pp. 5, 142–3.
72. Ibid., p. 333.
73. A further thought-provoking fictional text in this regard is Francis Brett Young's *Mr Lucton's Freedom*, published a little later in 1940. It concerns the spontaneous escape of an established businessman and father from his work and family-related responsibilities. Taking refuge in obscurity, he pursues a vagrant pastoral course, mostly on foot, for several months but finds this fugitive obscurity increasingly difficult to maintain. Eventually, it is the prospect of the coming war which prompts him to relinquish what has become a troubled, if not an impossible, form of freedom: 'Try as he would, he could not insulate his mind from the high potential of anxiety that strained so many millions of human hearts and whose waves were propelled, hour by hour, through the insentient ether.' Freedom, in this context, has become a self-centred kind of irresponsibility. Francis Brett Young, *Mr Lucton's Freedom* (1940; London: The Book Club, 1941), p. 318.
74. See for example 'British Railways', advertisement, *The Times*, 8 October 1941, p. 3.
75. 'Reception of Refugees: An Invitation to Householders', *The Times*, 14 May 1940, p. 10.
76. 'The Happy Traveller', *The Times*, 28 December 1940, p. 5.
77. Rose Macaulay, 'Miss Anstruther's Letters', in *London Calling*, ed. Storm Jameson (New York: Harper and Brothers, 1942), p. 302.
78. Ibid., p. 307.
79. Ibid., p. 308.
80. The corrected proof of this story reveals that Miss Anstruther was originally allotted the name 'Miss Ashley', as if to emphasise the sense of proprietorial destruction, in the form of a reduction to 'grey ashes'. See '[Miss Anstruther's Letters, Corrected Proof]', ERM $5^{4\ (1–10)}$, Papers of Rose Macaulay, The Wren Library, Trinity College, University of Cambridge.
81. '[During the Second World War]', ERM $8^{15\ (1)}$, Papers of Rose Macaulay, The Wren Library, Trinity College, University of Cambridge.
82. E. M. Forster, *Howards End* (1910; New York: Signet-Penguin, 1992), p. 119.
83. Elizabeth Bowen, 'A Passage to E. M. Forster' (1969), in *People, Places, Things*, ed. Allan Hepburn (Edinburgh: Edinburgh University Press, 2008), p. 278. Written as the introduction to a collection of essays entitled *Aspects of E. M. Forster*, ed. Oliver Stallybrass, to celebrate Forster's ninetieth birthday.
84. There are a number of engaging critical discussions of what Andrew Bennett and Nicholas Royle call the 'Bowenesque temporality of arrival and departure'. See, for example, their own chapter on *Friends and Relations* and *To the North*, entitled 'Shivered', in *Elizabeth Bowen and the Dissolution of the Novel: Still Lives* (Basingstoke: Macmillan, 1995), pp. 23–41 (28). See also John Hildebidle, *Five Irish Writers: The Errand of Keeping Alive* (Cambridge, MA: Harvard University Press, 1989), pp. 89–124.
85. Elizabeth Bowen, *The House in Paris* (1935; London: Vintage-Random, 1988), p. 77.
86. Elizabeth Bowen, 'Notes on Writing a Novel' (1945), in *Pictures and Conversations* (London: Allen Lane, 1975), p. 169.
87. Bowen, 'A Passage to E. M. Forster', p. 278. Emphasis in original.

88. John Coates, *Social Discontinuity in the Novels of Elizabeth Bowen: The Conservative Quest* (Lewiston, NY: The Edwin Mellen Press, 1998), p. 5.
89. Elizabeth Bowen, *To the North* (1932; Harmondsworth: Penguin, 1986), p. 170.
90. Elizabeth Bowen, 'Manners' (1937), in *Collected Impressions* (1950; London: Longmans, 1951), p. 68. Emphasis in original.
91. Elizabeth Bowen, 'Advice' (1960), in *Afterthought: Pieces About Writing* (London: Longmans, 1962), p. 213.
92. Henry James, 'Preface to *The Portrait of a Lady*' (1908), in *The Critical Muse: Selected Literary Criticism*, ed. Roger Gard (Harmondsworth: Penguin, 1987), p. 485.
93. Ibid., p. 485.
94. Bowen, 'Advice', p. 212.
95. Bowen, 'Stories by Katherine Mansfield' (1957), in *Afterthought*, pp. 58, 57, 60.
96. Bowen, 'Orlando' (1960), in *Afterthought*, p. 45.
97. Bowen, 'Disloyalties' (1950), in *Afterthought*, p. 196. This term was initially used by Graham Greene during a three-way discussion on the subject of writing between Greene, Bowen and V. S. Pritchett.
98. Forster, *Howards End*, p. 119.
99. Nicholas Royle has pointed to the 'peculiar connection between Mrs Wilcox's will (and its revised version) and the novel itself as a kind of strange will, a Forsterian document bequeathed to us as readers and to an unforeseeable future'. One way we might look at Bowen's relation to Forster's novel is as a reluctantly refused inheritance. See Nicholas Royle, *E. M. Forster* (Plymouth: Northcote House, 1999), p. 50.
100. Bowen, 'Disloyalties', p. 198.
101. Bowen, 'A Passage to E. M. Forster', p. 283.
102. The pair were, indeed, personally acquainted. See Victoria Glendinning, *Elizabeth Bowen: Portrait of a Writer* (1977; London: Phoenix, 1993), p. 141.
103. Bowen, 'A Passage to E. M. Forster', p. 272.
104. The phrase 'protracted crisis' is Bowen's own. It comes from a recorded talk given on the BBC Home Service in 1956, in which she refers to Forster's novel as 'violent', despite its Edwardian surface. This is an effect, she implies, of acute ideological discord: 'What causes this protracted crisis? Conflicting values, opposing views of life.' See 'Truth and Fiction' (1956), in *Afterthought*, p. 132.
105. Bowen, 'A Passage to E. M. Forster', p. 276.
106. Ibid., p. 272.
107. Ibid., p. 273.
108. Certain critics have likewise interpreted Bowen's *The Hotel* as a re-writing of Forster's *A Room With a View*. See Maud Ellmann, *Elizabeth Bowen: The Shadow Across the Page* (Edinburgh: Edinburgh University Press, 2003), pp. 79–82.
109. Bowen, *The House in Paris*, p. 35.
110. Ibid., p. 35.
111. Ibid., p. 36.
112. Ibid., p. 17.
113. Ibid., pp. 17, 18, 35–6, 51,192, 235, 236.
114. Ibid., p. 35.
115. Ibid., pp. 19, 22, 26. For analyses of doll's house imagery in relation to Bowen's work, see Bennett and Royle, *Elizabeth Bowen and the Dissolution of the Novel*, p. 12, and Ellmann, *Elizabeth Bowen*, p. 78.
116. Bowen, *The House in Paris*, pp. 28, 36.
117. Neil Corcoran, *Elizabeth Bowen: The Enforced Return* (Oxford: Oxford University Press, 2004), p. 39. Bowen also makes allusions to forms of political

bloodshed through an early observation of Henrietta's: '[she] had heard how much blood had been shed in Paris'. Jean Radford uses the same line to show the 'links between Paris, violence and revolution', established from the beginning of the novel and evidence of Bowen's historical and political interests. Bowen, *The House in Paris*, p. 22; Jean Radford, 'Late Modernism and the Politics of History', in *Women Writers of the 1930s: Gender Politics and History*, ed. Maroula Joannou (Edinburgh: Edinburgh University Press, 1999), p. 40.

118. Bennett and Royle, *Elizabeth Bowen and the Dissolution of the Novel*, p. 57.
119. Bowen, *The House in Paris*, p. 51.
120. Ibid., p. 52.
121. Ibid., p. 52.
122. Ibid., p. 35.
123. Ibid., p. 35.
124. Ibid., p. 39.
125. Ibid., p. 104.
126. Ibid., pp. 121–2.
127. Ibid., p. 133.
128. Ibid., p. 168. Emphasis in original.
129. Ellmann, *Elizabeth Bowen*, p. 115.
130. Bowen, *The House in Paris*, p. 62.
131. Ibid., p. 206.
132. Ibid., p. 35.
133. Ibid., p. 167.
134. Corcoran, *Elizabeth Bowen*, p. 97.
135. Leopold, being without a Jewish mother, is not technically Jewish, but these laws served to obscure such distinctions as Radford explains:

> Under Jewish law, neither Max Ebhart nor Leopold Grant-Moody is Jewish ... The year in which *The House in Paris* was published was the year in which the Nazi Government in Germany introduced the Nuremberg Laws which defined the Jew in a more inclusionary sense – as anyone with a Jewish grandparent. All such persons were in 1935 legally deprived of German citizenship, made 'home-less' within the German homeland. (Radford, 'Late Modernism and the Politics of History', p. 42)

136. Radford, 'Late Modernism and the Politics of History', pp. 35, 39.
137. Corcoran, *Elizabeth Bowen*, pp. 97–8.
138. They note the word's appearance over forty times in the novel, about once every five pages. Bennett and Royle, *Elizabeth Bowen and the Dissolution of the Novel*, p. 61.
139. Marrus, *The Unwanted*, p. 4.
140. Refugee imagery abounds in Bowen's novels of the late 1930s and 1940s, *The House in Paris* (1935), *The Death of the Heart* (1938) and *The Heat of the Day* (1949) particularly. Max and Karen are, indeed, characterised as 'refugee' lovers in *The House in Paris* itself. Bowen, *The House in Paris*, p. 113.
141. Radford and Corcoran both draw attention to this. See Radford, 'Late Modernism and the Politics of History', p. 41; Corcoran, *Elizabeth Bowen*, pp. 96–7.
142. Bowen, *To The North*, p. 23.
143. Bowen, 'Disloyalties', p. 196.
144. Bowen, 'Notes on Writing a Novel', p. 169. Emphasis in original.
145. MacKay, '"Is Your Journey Really Necessary?"', p. 1601. MacKay explores this trope, in part, in relation to Bowen's *The Heat of the Day*.
146. Bowen, *To the North*, p. 64.

147. Hildebidle neatly sums up this typical quandary in one rather memorable line: 'It is as if Bowen's characters must, in the end, choose between the rather airless spare room of someone else's house or the front seat of a speeding vehicle.' See Hildebidle, *Five Irish Writers*, p. 115.
148. Elizabeth Bowen, *The Last September* (1929; London: Vintage-Random, 1998), p. 77. Emphasis in original.
149. Elizabeth Bowen, *Friends and Relations* (1931; London: Penguin, 1946), p. 26. Emphasis in original.
150. Hynes, *The Auden Generation*, p. 300.
151. Elizabeth Bowen, *Bowen's Court* (1942; New York: The Ecco Press, 1979), p. 455.
152. Bowen, *The Last September*, p. 118.
153. Alistair M. Duckworth, *Howards End: E. M. Forster's House of Fiction* (New York: Twayne, 1992), p. 137.
154. Forster, *Howards End*, p. 268.
155. Bowen, 'A Passage to E. M. Forster', p. 274.
156. Bowen, 'Pictures and Conversations', in *Pictures and Conversations*, p. 44. This comprises two chapters of a longer intended autobiographical work that Bowen was unable to complete before she died.
157. Elizabeth Bowen, *Eva Trout or Changing Scenes* (1968; Harmondsworth: Penguin, 1987), p. 253.
158. Bowen, *Eva Trout*, p. 254.
159. Bowen, *Eva Trout*, p. 64.
160. Edwin J. Kenney Jr, *Elizabeth Bowen* (Lewisburg: Bucknell University Press, 1975), p. 98.

4

'HAVE YOU ANYTHING TO DECLARE?': PORTABLE SELVES ON TRIAL

> Chests, especially small caskets, over which we have more complete mastery, are objects *that may be opened*. When a casket is closed, it is returned to the general community of objects; it takes its place in exterior space. But it opens![1]

In discussing Freud's *Fragment of an Analysis of a Case of Hysteria* in Chapter 2, I alluded to Gaston Bachelard's phenomenological appraisal of hiding-places in *The Poetics of Space*, his study of the 'topography of our intimate beings' as mapped out in the structure of the house.[2] Some of his further remarks on this subject make for a suggestive starting-point for the chapter to follow. Bachelard sees small containers as concentrated points of intimate expression, evidence of the human *'need for secrecy'* but also of the human need to uncover secrets; these containers, we are told, are 'unforgettable for us but also unforgettable for those to whom we are going to give our treasures'.[3] This chapter will focus on the dynamics of containment and disclosure enacted through the more specific framework of the *portable* casket or case, often foregrounded as a source of intrigue in modernist writing in offering a point of access to a character in transit. Part of what made luggage an apposite index of character was its frequent fabrication, during this period, from the skin of an animal, whether cowhide or crocodile skin. This was a disconcerting human affinity certain writers hinted at and one neatly articulated by early-twentieth-century French diplomat, writer and perpetual traveller Paul Morand: 'When

I die, I'd like them to make a trunk from my skin.'[4] Luggage can be seen thus to represent both the materialisation *and* the mobilisation of the private space of the self in a number of modernist texts, capturing the intimate being in motion but also under an unpredictable form of public scrutiny. Intrigue is the keynote in the game of concealment and revelation recurrently played out. The luxury luggage designer Louis Vuitton astutely exploited the playful aspect of this game of intrigue in the slogan 'Montre-moi tes bagages et je te dirai qui tu es'/'Show me your luggage and I'll tell you who you are', used for a 1921 advertising campaign.[5] In a related vein, the chapter will trace the emergence of the figure of the Customs Official in interwar literature, a figure frequently aligned with the psychoanalyst, poised in a position of judgement over the 'case' in question. It will argue that those taglines 'travelling light' and 'pack up your troubles' are accompanied by the refrain 'Have you anything to declare?' at this time.

But a playful form of case-related intrigue is only one side of the story to be recounted here. Taken outside of the poetic but also protective space of Bachelard's house and placed in motion, the casket of the individual secret self might be liberated, but, by the same token, the 'complete mastery' of the subject over this casket is relinquished. From the 1920s to the 1930s, that borderline customs exchange transforms from light-hearted game into aggressive interrogation, in line with the gradual complication of the modernist trope of the escapist journey. The 'fate of individuality', to refer to the title of Michael Levenson's study of the relationship between character and form in modernism, hangs in the balance in those later interrogatory confrontations.[6] Levenson points to a prevailing paradox which undercuts the notion of liberating instability in the range of fictional works he discusses in this study: 'part of what makes these novels so tense and nervous is that they pursue their formal disruptions of character even as they so often sustain nostalgic longing for a whole self'.[7] Such a conflict comes to a head in the mid-to-late 1930s, as the question of the fate of individuality takes on a critical and political significance, particularly notable in the work of Henry Green. The overarching aim of this chapter, then, is to account for the progressively sinister aspect of the figure of the Customs Official, and to show that, when it comes to late modernism, suspicion overtakes intrigue as the keynote in that typical modernist encounter between strangers.

Contraband Psychology

'For who in this world can give anyone a character? Who in this world knows anything of any other heart – or of his own?' John Dowell exclaims midway through Ford Madox Ford's *The Good Soldier* in 1915.[8] 'It's appalling', Mr Wimbush says in Huxley's *Crome Yellow*, 'in living people, one is dealing with unknown and unknowable quantities'.[9] A few years later, Peter Walsh is shown to recall a youthful conversation with Clarissa Dalloway on the subject of the 'dissatisfaction' arising from 'not knowing people; not being known' in Woolf's 1925 novel.[10] These are representative expressions of a sentiment repeated again and again in modernist fiction, and it has now become something of a truism to say that the 'unknown' as well as the 'unknowable quantities' of the human psyche become an area of obsessive interest for modernist writers. But the localisation of epistemological questions of accessibility in and around the object of the portable case is entirely undocumented and adds an illuminating dimension to an ongoing discussion. I have touched upon this idea of accessibility in my consideration of the figure of the self-sufficient woman, her bag frequently serving to signal a female interiority outside of masculine and/or domestic control. As Nancy Armstrong has argued, the 'modern individual was first and foremost a woman', and I agree with her to the extent that the 'turn-of-the-century preoccupation with the unconscious arose in response to the question of what women want'.[11] Correspondingly, the modernist literary fascination with a secreted interiority, implied rather than fully (if at all) revealed through luggage, owes much to those earlier figurations.

From the 1910s onwards, instances of this fascination became more prolific. Mansfield, to give one early modernist example, turns the spotlight back upon the man in her 1910 short story 'The Baron'. The female narrator, guest at a German pension, is struck by the mysterious figure of the story's title. The Baron is a fellow guest but remains conspicuously aloof from the main pension contingent. His aristocratic status aside, a large part of the enigma surrounding this figure for the narrator is the black bag he carries with him at all times: 'I wondered where he was going, and why he carried the bag.'[12] The narrator's fascination only increases with time:

> Days lengthened into weeks. Still we were together, and still the solitary little figure, head bowed as though under the weight of the spectacles, haunted me. He entered with the black bag, he retired with the black bag – and that was all.[13]

Finally, the narrator comes into contact with the mysterious Baron and is granted a seeming insight into his elusive character. But, interestingly, he only volunteers '*some* information': '"I fear", he said, "that my luggage will be damp. I invariably carry it with me in this bag – one requires so little – for servants are untrustworthy."'[14] The Baron suggests reasons for why he carries this single black leather bag with him at all times, but gives no further indication as to its contents. Both narrator and reader remain largely in the dark. The bag, in effect, publicises inaccessibility. At the same time, it intimates a secret essence, however much its discovery is denied to the narrator/reader. To add to this, titillation is faintly touched with the macabre in this story. The solitary Baron admits to a voracious appetite, requiring him to eat alone in public and to 'imbibe nourishment' in his room during the day in private, a revelation of a form of gluttony which is as unnerving as it is eccentric.[15] Does the Baron distrust, we are led to ask, the covetousness of his servants, or their curiosity? In other words, does his bag contain something of value to protect or something of the illicit to conceal?

Luggage brings to the fore what David Trotter has identified as two fundamental impulses in the 'psychopathology of modernism': desire and disgust.[16] These impulses can be reformulated more specifically here as the desire to know and disgust at finding out. Luggage has long been recognised as a device to incite speculative curiosity, and, with the emergence of modernism, this evocative quality takes on a self-consciously hermeneutic function. The malleability of meaning is one important aspect of the appeal of Beerbohm's hatbox, as he outlines in 1900:

> You must know that I loved my labels not only for the meanings they conveyed to me, but also, more than a little for the effect they produced on other people. Travelling in a compartment, with my hat-box beside me, I enjoyed the silent interest which my labels aroused in my fellow-passengers. If the compartment was so full that my hat-box had to be relegated to the rack, I would always, in the course of the journey, take it down and unlock it, and pretend to be looking for something I had put into it. It pleased me to see from beneath my eyelids the respectful wonder and envy evoked by it. Of course, there was no suspicion that the labels were a carefully formed collection; they were taken as the wild flowers of an exquisite restlessness, of an unrestricted range in life.[17]

Beerbohm knowingly manipulates fantasy through a well-rehearsed set of provocative gestures in this passage, and it is worth paying some attention to the terms and figures of desire employed; interest, arousal, unlocking, the prospect of discovery and the seductive power of the unseen 'something'. The hat-box triggers 'wonder and envy' first and foremost as an object 'that may be opened', to return to Bachelard's description of the small casket. And in this act of opening up, the *meaning* of the 'carefully formed collection' is pitted against the *effect* of the 'unrestricted range' it evokes (a turn of phrase which tellingly pre-dates James's attribution of an 'incalculability of range' to his 'house of fiction').[18] Here we find a tension between unity and disunity along the lines suggested by Levenson; this hat-box can narrate any story, depending on the perspective of the spectator, while it is the material apotheosis of one single story, that of the owner. We also find an early example of the classic modernist train carriage encounter between unfamiliar passengers, and it is rendered in performative terms. Beerbohm elaborates on this theme at some length in his essay, going on to ask: 'The love of impressing strangers falsely, is it not implanted in all of us?'[19] Such a rhetorical question is far from surprising from the man who penned that other most notorious of essays, 'A Defence of Cosmetics', in the very first issue of *The Yellow Book* in 1894, an essay which loudly proclaims that 'the day of sancta simplicitas is quite ended'.[20]

The implied sense of a new and unholy complexity brings us back to desire's modern counterpart, disgust. The unholy is also the impure, the unsavoury. The projection of Beerbohm's labels as the 'wild flowers of an exquisite restlessness' offers only one side of a double-edged luggage fantasy. There is equally the dreaded prospect of what a case might conceal, as realised, to give one rather graphic illustration, in the mock-horrific discovery of the body of Maisie Maidan in Ford's *The Good Soldier*:

> [Leonora Ashburnham] had not cared to look round Maisie's rooms at first. Now, as soon as she came in, she perceived, sticking out beyond the bed, a small pair of feet in high-heeled shoes. Maisie had died in the effort to strap up a great portmanteau. She had died so grotesquely that her little body had fallen forward into the trunk and it had closed upon her, like the jaws of a gigantic alligator.[21]

Alligator skin was used in the manufacture of a more extravagant and expensive type of luggage, and though the material of Maisie's portmanteau is unspecified, it is tempting to see in this an image of a trunk not simply coming to life but coming *back* to life with a vengeance. More prosaically, trunks would become a common motif in golden age detective fiction, often employed for stowing corpses. Indeed, Ford may well have been drawing on a relatively recent trend in the above episode. As far back as 1878, in Robert Louis Stevenson's 'Story of the Physician and the Saratoga Trunk', Englishman Dr Noel comes to the aid of American, Silas Q. Scuddamore, who has happened upon the body of a dead man in his Parisian hotel-room bed. Surveying the room in search of a solution to this rather unfortunate dilemma, Dr Noel's eye falls upon what he refers to as 'one of those monstrous constructions which your fellow–countrymen carry with them into all quarters of the globe – in a word, a Saratoga trunk'.[22] He observes that 'the object of such a box is to contain a human body'.[23] The Saratoga trunk is duly employed for that purpose. Luggage enters into detective fiction vocabulary in this 'monstrous' capacity more prominently in the twentieth century, owing perhaps, in part, to certain high-profile murder cases involving trunks of various kinds.[24] It becomes particularly popular as a motif in the 1930s. Ian Carter explains that, following the requirement by Parliament that railways become common carriers, trunks, trains and left luggage offices provided an innovative solution to the age-old problem of how to dispose of a body.[25] As a literary device, the trunk, with its 'grisly' deposit, replicates that 'key device in detective fiction', the 'tiny sealed room'.[26] It also, of course, replicates the coffin, an association which recurs in fiction at this time, disclosing the blind spot at the end of the archetypal modernist journey.[27] Furthermore, the exposure of buried corpses is frequently related to the interpretative process in modernism – we need only think of T. S. Eliot's 1922 vision of graveyard agitation as textual agitation at the end of 'The Burial of the Dead' section of *The Waste Land* – and it is remarkable how often the search for the skeleton in the closet becomes the search for the skeleton in the suitcase.[28]

These double-edged luggage fantasies can be set in the context of changing approaches to psychology, as well as parallel developments in interpretative processes from the late nineteenth century. Allon White has made a convincing case for a connection between the tendency towards textual obscurity in modernist writing and the cultivation of a more intrusive mode of what he calls (after Louis Althusser) 'symptomatic reading', that is to say the attempt to probe beneath a surface statement in order to get at its underlying import. According to White, readers were becoming more visibly distrustful towards the end of the Victorian period and symptomatic reading, correspondingly, more sophisticated in technique: 'Its intrusion indelibly inscribed itself on the sensibilities of modern writers. With subtlety and violence it continually transgressed their defensive privacies, provoking in its turn renewed attempts at evasion.'[29] Textual obscurity or difficulty was, as such, a response to forms of transgressive curiosity on the part of the reader, and it consequently became an end in itself:

> The obscurity of modernism is not susceptible to simple de-coding. It is usually not a matter of information suppressed or omitted which the critic can patiently recover. It is rather that, despite a remarkable diversity of intent and effect, modernist difficulty signifies in and by the very act of offering resistance.[30]

This might be said to be the point of 'The Baron', for instance; obscurity, a word indeed invoked by Mansfield, is the threat the story attempts but fails to overcome. It is the fear that the Baron will 'drift into obscurity' before his mystery is uncovered which so bothers the narrator; that this is, in fact, what happens – 'Next day the Baron was gone', we are told quite simply at the end – is testament to this evasive modernist imperative.[31] Similarly, Beerbohm invites at the same time as he resists a symptomatic interpretation of his identity through his semi-revelatory hat-box, and it is the interplay between the two urges which is shown to foster imaginative 'range'.[32] Ideas of symptomatic reading and resistance (and of desire and disgust) immediately conjure Freudian theories of the unconscious.[33] Figurations of identity through luggage in the interwar period can frequently be seen to draw from psychoanalytic models; certain unfixed cases of modernist selfhood are *cases* of a distinctly and often deliberately Freudian hue. We might even say that those trunks of a more macabre nature, inducing disgust over and above desire, can be said to go beyond the pleasure principle in exemplifying the death drive, even before Freud himself articulates it in 1920.[34]

Customs inspection analogies for acts of symptomatic character reading and concomitant acts of resistance abound in writing after the First World War. The interwar time context in which these analogies most often occur is important, but the Freudian influence on such conceptions is equally marked. Carl Jung drew attention to a dream of his, situated on the Swiss–Austrian border and featuring the 'ghost of a customs official' who appears 'peevish, rather melancholy and vexed' and pays no attention to him.[35] This dream occurred in 1909, shortly before his intellectual and personal rift with Freud. It was also while he was working on *Psychology of the Unconscious*, which marked his departure from Freud's psychoanalytical model towards a model which incorporated mythological elements while disputing Freud's emphasis on the centrality of the sexual instinct. His own analysis of this dream gives us an insight into the suitability of the portable case for the representation of the unconscious, as well as making a direct link with Freud himself:

> I set about analysing this dream. In connection with 'customs' I at once thought of the word 'censorship'. In connection with 'border' I thought of the border between consciousness and the unconscious on the one hand, and between Freud's views and mine on the other. The extremely rigorous customs examination at the border seemed to me an allusion to analysis. At a border suitcases are opened and examined for contraband. In the course of this examination, unconscious assumptions are discovered. As for the old customs official, his work had obviously brought him so little that was pleasurable and satisfactory that he took a sour view of the world. I could not refuse to see the analogy with Freud.[36]

Jung's early connection between Freud as analyst and the persona of the customs official anticipates figurations of customs inspections as acts of character judgement in literature. The suitcase stopped at border control proved an apt means of conveying, not only a mind under scrutiny, but also a mind with the suggestion of something to hide. But Jung's dream is fascinating for another reason too. It had a crucial second section, in which he envisaged the 'contrasting' persona of a 'knight in full armour' on a busy modern city street.[37] He interpreted this as a reference to the holy grail quest and as a reflection upon his own early sense of a 'great secret' behind that myth, a secret and a quest with wider and, by the same token, deeply personal implications: 'My whole being was seeking for something still unknown which might confer meaning upon the banality of life.'[38] Though both dream figures are externally visualised, Jung implicitly posits himself as the knight with the spiritual quest as set against Freud's 'sour' customs official on the hunt for the contraband content and censored areas of the unconscious. He is thus positioned both as subject of analytical examination on the customs border and as analytical explorer by turn. However, the difference between the two forms of analysis, as represented in the dream, is of significance here in that it reasserts once again that tension in the approach to character in modernist writing, as construed by Levenson: character as dislocated, inherently untrustworthy and without a centrally definable essence, on the one hand, and a more unified conception of a sort of transcendental, holistic self to be preserved or discovered, on the other. The customs official, seeking to locate the corrupt, undermines the knight's quest for purity and, in adopting a posture of suspicion, poses a threat to the very idea of a unified essence or selfhood. We are left in little doubt about the reductive nature of this principle of interrogatory suspicion for Jung in contrast to the protective principle embodied by the knight. The knights of the holy grail are linked, after all, to guardianship as much as questing. But Jung's is perhaps itself a reductive approach to the idea of suspicion. Nathalie Sarraute, in classifying the modern period as the 'age of suspicion', offers an alternative take on the idea. She sees suspicion as enacting the destruction of 'character and all the obsolete apparatus which ensured its power', but characterises this destructive suspicion as a creative force, impelling the writer towards novelty as a self-defensive reflex.[39]

Jung's dream in its entirety, together with Sarraute's comment, gives some indication of the dilemma addressed through the literary invocation of customs control, in that suspicion is shown to demand either a protective or a destructively creative response. 'Have you anything to declare?' The stock phrase of the customs official becomes a question relating to what character means in a modern context: a sacred essence to be shielded from the disruptive intrusion of modernity or an identity to be created and performed in order to conceal something more unsavoury or, even worse, the unknown. Two examples bring these various and conflicting facets to light. The first returns us to Duquette's portmanteaux in Mansfield's 'Je ne parle pas français', and the second is taken from Woolf's *Orlando* of 1928:

> Not but what these portmanteaux can be very fascinating. Oh, but very! I see myself standing in front of them, don't you know, like a Customs official.
>
> 'Have you anything to declare? Any wines, spirits, cigars, perfumes, silks?'
>
> And the moment of hesitation as to whether I am going to be fooled just before I chalk that squiggle, and then the other moment of hesitation just after, as to whether I have been, are perhaps the most thrilling instants in life. Yes, they are, to me.[40]

> Orlando now performed in spirit (for all this took place in spirit) a deep obeisance to the spirit of her age, such as – to compare great things with

small – a traveller, conscious that he has a bundle of cigars in the corner of his suit case, makes to the customs officer who has obligingly made a scribble of white chalk on the lid. For she was extremely doubtful whether, if the spirit had examined the contents of her mind carefully, it would not have found something highly contraband for which she would have to pay the full fine.[41]

To be fooled or not to be fooled, to fool or not to fool; in the juxtaposed passages, we have the customs/character inspection from an external and an internal point of view. The extension of Duquette's portmanteaux vision moves us from the issue of the freedom of the individual to the issue of the nature of the individual, and character judgement is represented as a kind of hermeneutic game. We must remember that Duquette does not 'believe in a human soul', and this encounter is characterised as performative on both sides. There is no suggestion of any kind of sacred essence beneath the 'fascinating' lids. Moreover, the pleasure is in the guessing game of judgement itself, not in the accuracy of the squiggled decree. *Orlando* is a novel in which character is rendered inherently unstable, yet shown to aspire towards a unified ideal, 'what is called, rightly or wrongly, a single self, a real self'.[42] In the above rather ambiguously phrased passage, we see suspicion of the other turned back upon the self. Orlando seems both 'conscious' and 'doubtful' about the mode of her own psychic censorship, and so uncertainty is internalised here. The 'moment of hesitation' in confronting character, exhibited on the outside in Duquette's case, is exhibited from within in *Orlando*. The passage appears in the context of a discussion of authorship in the nineteenth century. Orlando, now both a Victorian woman and a writer, has recently married and must publicly conform to the expectations of the age in order to continue writing:

> She had just managed by some dexterous deference to the spirit of the age, by putting on a ring and finding a man on a moor, by loving nature and being no satirist, cynic or psychologist – any one of which goods would have been discovered at once – to pass its examination successfully.[43]

It is clear that the spirit of this age has no interest in delving into the murky depths of psychology, as long as there is outward conformity. That the customs metaphor itself is shown to be a product of a retrospective 1928 standpoint suggests that the spirit of the age has markedly altered, following the genesis of Freudian explorations of the unconscious, towards an ethos of symptomatic suspicion, engendering a culture in which the human mind is conceived as an unfixed object arbitrarily at the mercy of passing interrogatory examination. With the advent of the 1930s, however, such passing and playful interrogatory examinations take a decidedly darker turn.

DECLARING NOTHING OR EVERYTHING: THE 1930S

The figure of the customs official as a literary construct came to the fore between the wars, often as the allegorical nemesis of the escapee/refugee, but equally as a sign of the normalisation of suspicion in any dealings with strangers. Indeed, over the course of this period, suspicion became something of a knee-jerk response to the unknown in a climate of increasing state scrutiny and simmering national tensions. Though Sarraute, like White after her, traces the growth of a climate of suspicion back through Joyce, Freud and Proust to the late nineteenth century, it was in the aftermath of the First World War that suspicion was given a more politically legitimised edge, and a protective posture became widely adopted side by side with a performative posture as a necessary response to a sense of the public intrusion upon the private. To borrow the words of George Dangerfield, the war 'started nothing', but it 'hastened everything'.[44] One thing it hastened was the formalisation of administrative restrictions on mobility following the extension of the Defence of the Realm Act in 1915, which made it necessary to carry a passport on the move. This change brought about an inescapable imaginative awareness of state-authorised border control between countries, serving to accentuate the sense of imaginative frontiers between individuals, between public and private, between conscious and unconscious mental states (in line with Jung's intuitive interpretation of his dream frontier earlier on). 'However limited or eccentric such preoccupations', Marrus notes of the reaction to new forms of systematised regulation, 'there is no doubt that they marked an important change.'[45] And he adds: 'Travel was no longer the free and easy passage that it was ... Citizenship, once an irrelevant issue for European travelers, now assumed cardinal importance.'[46] By extension, the mobile visions of modernist writers, as Bridget T. Chalk has recently argued, manifest 'perpetual tension' between 'national identity and geographical cosmopolitanism'.[47]

Though Duquette and Orlando are far from openly betraying anxiety in their respective customs analogies (for both there is a certain enjoyment in the game of hide and seek), other examples in the immediate aftermath of the Great War sound a more obviously ominous note. Hope Mirrlees's 'Paris', an experimental poem depicting the impressionistic journey of a flâneuse through a Parisian cityscape and published in 1919 by the Hogarth Press, brings art into overt relation with the customs office in a disjointed and corpse-strewn postwar scene:

> The ghost of Père Lachaise
> Is walking the streets;
> He is draped in a black curtain embroidered with the
> > letter H,

He is hung with paper wreaths,
He is beautiful and horrible and the close friend of
Rousseau the official of the Douane.
The unities are smashed,
The stage is thick with corpses . . . [48]

Mirrlees's pointed reference here to Henri Rousseau, a Post-Impressionist painter who died in 1910, has much to do with the artist's all-too-suggestive nickname. He was dubbed 'Le Douanier' (The Customs Official) for his work in the Parisian toll office.[49] Once again, a 'close' association between death (through the Père Lachaise cemetery) and luggage is implied in this example, but the custom-house is also aligned with art (through the invoked Rousseau) as well as with a postwar artistic sense of smashed unities. Death and art and state-sanctioned taxation and intrusion are brought into uncomfortable proximity here. Significantly, Freud is later named directly in the poem – 'Freud has dredged the river, grinning horribly/ Waves his garbage in a glare of electricity' – linked to the earlier graveyard ghost by the 'horrible'/'horribly' repetition.[50] We might say that Freud is a friend of the 'close friend' of the official of the Douane by association, and the subject for artistic as well as psychoanalytic interrogation, by implication, is shown to have become the refuse or wasteland of the postwar mind projected onto a corpse-ridden urban stage.

The mention of the 'official of the Douane' in connection to postwar art, as well as psychology in this instance, is an early indicator of a more pronounced frontier-oriented fear for the fate of art, as much as the fate of individuality in the face of restrictive forms of interwar officialdom. The 'consciousness of frontiers', in Fussell's words, comes into play in fiction after the First World War – 'unknown before 1915 is that ritual occasion for anxiety so familiar to the modern person, the moment one presents the passport at a frontier' – but becomes an even more persistent feature of 1930s literature, something most critics of the period observe.[51] Valentine Cunningham pays particular heed to that variety of anxiety induced by the frontier for 'anyone with anything to hide or lose', observing that 'ordinary worrisomeness' is shown to rise 'dramatically' in such circumstances.[52] As such, the peculiar customs-oriented branch of frontier fixation also produced many comic and satirical interpretations, not least in relation to the dubitable (not to say dutiable) contents of the authorial bag. In Evelyn Waugh's *Vile Bodies* in 1930, the main protagonist Adam Fenwick-Symes is stalled on the border by his admission that he is carrying books: '"Yes", said the Customs officer menacingly, as though his worst suspicions had been confirmed, "I should just about say you had got some books."'[53] When it is further revealed that among these books is the typescript of his memoirs, he is taken aside for a more serious cross-examination, his typescript ultimately confiscated. Likewise, Robert Byron records one customs encounter in similar terms in *The Road to Oxiana*: '"Do you write books?" asked the customs officer, scenting an author of dutiable obscenities. I said I was not Lord Byron, and suggested he should get on with his business.'[54] What is most interesting about both of these examples (as well as the example from *Orlando,* itself a tongue-in-cheek account, not too long before) is that they either come from or are about autobiographical work, so that what we find here are depictions of a comic tension between authored and authorised forms of selfhood. Yet these humorous episodes only serve to emphasise the prevalence of a concern for privacy and for artistic freedom, at a time when totalitarian forms of public authority, whether left-wing or right-wing, Communist or Fascist, are on the rise throughout Europe. Looking back on the decade, George Orwell drew attention to the impact of an intensifying atmosphere of competing ideological demands upon the individual, an atmosphere which fostered anxiety as to how exactly to author an authorised version of the self:

> It was a time of labels, slogans and evasions. At the worst moments you were expected to lock yourself up in a constipating little cage of lies; at the best a sort of voluntary censorship ('Ought I to say this? Is it pro-Fascist?') was at work in nearly everyone's mind.[55]

In the 1930s, the customs official no longer simply represents an intrusive analyst with sophisticated symptomatic reading skills, but a far more perturbing and not so easily identifiable form of public surveillance.

Further, the political orientation behind certain acts of surveillance is not necessarily always itself 'declared'. Another customs-related dream, this time from 1936 rather than 1909, will illustrate the shift in emphasis from psychoanalytical to political invasiveness in the use of the customs analogy:

> I dreamed once that, like Clarence, I had 'pass'd the melancholy flood, with that grim Ferryman that poets write of', and that when we reached the other side, there was a Customs House and an official who had inscribed in golden letters on his cap *Chemins de fer de l'Enfer*, who said to me, 'Have you anything to declare?' And he handed me a printed list on which, instead of wine, spirits, tobacco, silk, lace, etc., there was printed Sanskrit, Hebrew, Greek, Latin, French, Italian, German, Spanish, Scandinavian, Chinese, Arabic and Persian, and it was explained to me that this list referred to the literary baggage I had travelled with during my life, and I need only declare those things of which I had a permanent record either in my memory or in written notebooks. There, sure enough, on the counter before me appeared two boxes, one labelled *Memory*, the other *Notes*. The Customs House official gave me a look, and said: 'Small Latin and less Greek?'
> And then I woke up.[56]

This dream description forms the opening to Maurice Baring's 1936 collection of miscellaneous reading notes and 'literary odds and ends'; it is cited as the stimulus for the ensuing declaration of what he refers to as his 'literary baggage' for the benefit of other readers.[57] What makes his introduction (of which the above dream forms part), notable is that, although outwardly light and untroubled in tone, it yet admits an inadvertent pitch of anxiety. Indeed, in response to the dream, Baring remarks only upon a newly awakened 'desire to make a declaration of such luggage as I have travelled with and kept, or discarded', completely ignoring the more disquieting elements: the interrogatory nature of the scene, the sense of an impasse and of being ultimately tested, the hellish inscription on the Customs official's cap, the note of insinuation and superciliousness in the final question, the hint of Babelian chaos in the list of languages, the association of the written word with the contraband.[58] In retrospect, Baring's unconscious vision is very much of its time and, as such, politically charged. Looking back on the course of events leading up to the Second World War, Samuel Hynes pinpoints 1936 as the 'peripeteia, the point where the action turned'.[59] Among other important developments, he refers to the beginning of the Spanish Civil War and Hitler's reoccupation of the Rhineland, signalling the failure both of the Versailles Treaty as well as the League of Nations, and paving the way (with the kind of inevitability only perceptible with hindsight) for the events of 1939. In this sense, Baring's dream position at a border is fitting, corresponding to a kind of spatial peripeteia. As Graham Greene was to observe three years later, '[t]he border means more than a customs house, a passport officer, a man with a gun. Over there, everything is going to be different; life is never going to be quite the same again.'[60] The border represents the gateway to hell in Baring's dream and in 1936, 'hell' was another word for 'war'.

By extension, 'customs official' became another term for warmonger. Christopher Isherwood drew attention to the 'fairly sinister air of leisure which invests the movement of officials at frontier stations', making them 'not unlike prison warders', in *Mr Norris Changes Trains* (1935).[61] This characterisation calls to mind the unsettling late-1930s tendency to confuse tropes of leisure and forced flight, highlighted in Chapter 3. War is repeatedly figured as a day of borderline judgement, in more ways than one. Hitler himself was known to be the son of a prominent Austrian inspector of customs. Referring to Rebecca West's record of a journey through Yugoslavia in 1937, *Black Lamb and Grey Falcon* (1941), Fussell comments that 'Hitler is considered a phenomenon more or less understandable once it is remembered that he was literally "the child of one of those parasites on our social system, a douanier"'.[62] Correspondingly, war is considered a phenomenon more or less understandable in a customs-controlled world. In his 1939 novel, *Coming Up For Air*, Orwell imaginatively reaches out beyond the moment of borderline judgement, and his conception of what follows is one of a brutal form of invasiveness: 'War is coming. 1941, they say. And there'll be plenty of broken crockery and little houses ripped open like packing cases.'[63] For Orwell, the day of judgement, the coming of war, amounts to a destructive intrusion upon the realm of the private, and it is rendered here in terms of an aggressive frontier customs inspection. The implications of this allusion to that culminating outcome of frontier suspicion should neither be underestimated nor overlooked. Orwell was of a generation which was, as has been well documented, acutely conscious of frontiers. His image of the ripped open house as ripped open packing case signals the obliteration of those earlier modernist fantasies of escape, as well as registering an assault on the topography of the intimate being, to echo Bachelard's phrase.[64]

But if customs control had become a byword for aggression in the 1930s, so too had the figure of the portable stranger with a case, a case which was palpably losing that earlier aura of wonder, envy and intrigue. The beginning of *Mr Norris Changes Trains*, in which the narrator, William Bradshaw, first encounters the Mr Norris of the title in the carriage of a train on route to Germany, marks this change. The opening line – 'My first impression was that the stranger's eyes were of an unusually light blue' – invokes a clichéd signifier of honesty only to subvert it.[65] Such a cliché is introduced in order to expose the farcical nature of former conceptions of honesty. Duplicitousness is now so much the norm that Bradshaw, upon perceiving Mr Norris's evident nervousness on approaching the frontier, suspects him to be 'engaged in a little *innocent* private smuggling'.[66] 'Probably a piece of silk for his wife or a box of cigars for a friend', he muses, in terms that recall Orlando's representation of her own internalised contraband.[67] Innocence now comprises an innocuous form of duplicitousness. Mr Norris is engaged, it is later insinuated, in somewhat more shady activities and, though hardly a dangerous individual, nonetheless presents a compromised version of the enigmatic earlier modernist *anonyme* within a train carriage. He is still an intriguing individual, but not in a way conducive to personal fantasy. His are secrets one would rather not discover, adventures in which one would rather not partake.

This waning of the stranger's aura of intrigue can be viewed against a background of failing diplomatic negotiations in Europe from the end of the First World War, negotiations very much played out in the public eye. The Versailles Treaty of 1919 and the 1925 Locarno Agreement (which worked to resolve differences arising from Versailles) served to stabilise the European political scene through diplomatic cooperation in the 1920s, lulling all concerned into a false sense of security. When diplomatic relations fall into decline through the 1930s, this decline is more often than not construed in terms of a breach in trusting and honest relations. Yet honesty and transparency are portrayed, in an age of suspicion, as all-too-naïve and simple-minded and, consequently, dangerous. 'Have you anything to declare?' became a highly charged political

ALL QUIET ON EVERY FRONTIER.

M. Briand (*International Optimist*). "ANYTHING TO DECLARE?"
Commercial Traveller. "NOTHING. I'M A EUROPEAN."
M. Briand. "PASS. FRIEND!"

Figure 4 Leonard Raven-Hill, 'All Quiet on Every Frontier', cartoon, *Punch*, 177,
18 September 1929, p. 323.
Reproduced with permission of Punch Ltd, www.punch.co.uk.

and diplomatic question of the day. From the late 1920s onwards, *Punch* regularly features cartoons which show an alignment between the political interests of a diplomatic negotiator and the packed contents of his case (Figure 4), but, increasingly, the idea of readily declaring those contents is characterised as a form of political artlessness (Figure 5).[68] Indeed, later cartoons depict Nazi negotiators as they are hospitably embraced and welcomed by British politicians, while the tightly closed, swastika-embossed cases of those negotiators suggest ulterior motives which entirely elude their hosts (Figure 6).[69] Such cartoons together sketch a general loss of trust, both in the opposition and in

ALL ABOVE BOARD.

Mr. Ramsay MacDonald *(to Mr. J. H. Thomas, who, fresh from his Transatlantic experiences, is kindly assisting his Chief to pack).* "DON'T FORGET THE CARDS, JIM."

Mr. Thomas. "CARDS?"

Mr. MacDonald. "TO LAY ON THE TABLE. NONE OF THE OLD SECRET DIPLOMACY FOR US."

Figure 5   Leonard Raven-Hill, 'All Above Board', cartoon, *Punch,* 177, 25 September 1929, p. 351. Reproduced with permission of Punch Ltd, www.punch.co.uk.

political leadership at home, over the course of the interwar period, and this development is hardly confined to Britain. Stefan Zweig, for example, observes a difference between the 'childish naive credulity' attending the First World War and the fatalism accompanying the arrival of the Second:

> In 1939 . . . this almost religious faith in the honesty or at least in the capacity of one's own government had disappeared throughout Europe. Diplomacy was despised, since one had seen with bitterness how the possibility of a lasting peace had been betrayed at Versailles.[70]

A PRESENT FROM BERLIN.

Mr. Eden. "THE GENTLEMAN FROM GERMANY TO SEE YOU, SIR."
John Bull. "OH, BUT I KNOW HIM WELL; SHOW HIM IN, EDEN. HOPE HE'S COME TO STAY."

[Herr von Ribbentrop, Herr Hitler's "Ambassador at large," has now been appointed Ambassador in London.]

Figure 6 Bernard Partridge, 'A Present from Berlin', cartoon, *Punch*, 191, 10 August 1936, p. 211. Reproduced with permission of Punch Ltd, www.punch.co.uk.

The increasingly farcical depictions of diplomacy, in the popular press, in terms of the breakdown of a naïve hospitality, respond to a wider sense of the necessity of viewing any case 'carried in an unsuspicious manner' (Figure 7) as inherently treacherous and a harbinger of danger, forcing ordinary citizens to assume the perspective of the customs inspector in relating to the unknown other. The figure of the enemy alien entered into fiction with a dubious case in hand with the onset of the war, a dual arrival anticipated in W. H. Auden's 1938 poem 'Gare du Midi':

"CARRYING A SUIT-CASE IN AN UNSUSPICIOUS MANNER."

Figure 7 Ernest H. Shepard, 'Carrying a Suit-case in an Unsuspicious Manner', cartoon, *Punch*, 185, 9 August 1933, p. 151. Reproduced with permission of Punch Ltd, www.punch.co.uk.

A nondescript express in from the South,
Crowds round the ticket barrier, A face
To welcome which the mayor has not contrived
Bugles or braid: Something about the face
Distracts the stray look with alarm and pity.
Snow is falling. Clutching a little case,
He walks out briskly to infect a city
Whose terrible future may have just arrived.[71]

Such a projected scenario would come to fruition in Graham Greene's *The Ministry of Fear* (1943), in which the main protagonist is asked by a stranger to carry a suitcase on his behalf, purportedly full of books but, in fact, containing a bomb which subsequently explodes.[72] Yet the necessity for adopting an attitude of suspicion in the face of the stranger '[c]lutching a little case' was in conflict with the hospitable impulse arising from the realisation of a growing European refugee problem. How to distinguish between the enemy alien and the genuine asylum seeker?[73] Genuine or not, it is clear that the figure of the stranger had come to suggest something very different by the outbreak of the war. During the war itself, intriguing question marks become 'little dark menacing question mark[s]', to use Greene's own expression for unfamiliar individuals in his earlier novel *The Power and the Glory* (1940), a novel also teeming with suspicious-seeming strangers.[74]

What are the implications of these developments for our broader understanding of portable selfhood, as it evolved into the late modernist period? Let me approach this question through a surrealist work of art by René Magritte entitled 'The Key of Dreams', created in 1936, that temporal turning-point identified by Samuel Hynes (Figure 8).[75] One of the most striking aspects of the painting is that 'the valise', despite being the only object correctly labelled, does not declare its contents. This is a work largely understood as a statement on the nature of the relationship between visual images and language, invoking museum display case and children's vocabulary book, transparent window and blackboard, as well as the title of Freud's seminal psychoanalytic work. It forms a surrealist vision of dreamlike disorientation. The painting has been seen to disorientate because, with the exception of the valise, word and image do not appear to correlate. In the words of Laurie Edson, 'Magritte has presented the reader with a series of conflicts between word and image that invite us to re-evaluate the assumptions we make about the relationship between the two'.[76] Contrary to the standard interpretation of a conflict between reading and viewing, it is my contention that the most disorienting element in this painting is, in fact, the correctly labelled item, the single point at which reader and viewer coalesce, where image and word correspond. The semantic disruption is crucially caused by the inscription of 'the valise' *for* the valise in this artwork, and this is not least because the word 'valise' itself is derived from another language.

An alternative way to see the painting would be as a commentary on both the functioning and failure of metaphor, which I. A. Richards defined that very same year as a 'borrowing between and intercourse of thoughts, a transaction between contexts'.[77] As a whole, Magritte's work can be described as enacting a 'transaction between contexts'; the visual and written/verbal, most obviously, but also childhood and adulthood, the domestic and natural, internal and external spheres, and so on. However, upon closer inspection, we find a

Figure 8 René Magritte, 'The Key of Dreams', 1936. Private Collection.
Reproduced by permission of ADAGP and SACK © René Magritte / ADAGP,
Paris – SACK, Seoul, 2016.

form of interaction on the level of the individual examples of seemingly disjunctive juxtaposition too. The word 'wind' conjures the *winding* of a clock.
By the same token, time itself has long been construed in terms of wind – the
winds of time – and we might even say that the clock hands are shown to
slant forward in the same direction as the written script, as if at the whim of a
gust. Likewise, the jug is noticeably bird-like in shape, the rim of its opening
pointed like a beak, its handle protruding like a tail. We might even stretch this
correlation to the onomatopoeic 'jug jug' of the nightingale, brought to the
fore in Eliot's *The Waste Land* the previous decade.[78] In other words, in each

of these examples, the two elements merge to create another kind of meaning. While these ostensibly arbitrary juxtapositions invite imaginative interpretation, the correctly labelled figuration of the valise paradoxically wards off definition and understanding. It is inherently resistant but not, I would suggest, in a way that incites experimental interpretation, as in White's model of modernist obscurity. If the figure of the case can be said to correspond to the concept of metaphor (in that the very word 'metaphor' derives etymologically from an original sense of 'bearing' or 'carrying'), that final image presents a metaphor which does not immediately divulge its semantic load. It is a metaphor which fails to complete its contextual transaction, reflecting a sense of the failure of contextual transactions on all fronts during this period. Symptomatic interpretation (like diplomatic or political negotiation) is stopped short. We, the viewers, are posited as interrogators before Magritte's 'valise'. 'Have you anything to declare?' we ask. The valise says nothing. We remain in a state of uncertainty, of suspicion. In thinking about small boxes, chests and caskets, Bachelard, as mentioned, made the observation that '[w]hen a casket is closed, it is returned to the general community of objects'. However, the valise, as I hope to have shown, was, by 1936, no ordinary object. It could not simply return unobtrusively to that general material community. Does the valise, in Magritte's image, have something to declare, we are forced to ask, and, if so, what kind of declaration can it be? Is the valise another emblem of treachery, in line with the title of his earlier most famous image of a pipe, 'La Trahison des Images' or 'The Treachery of Images'? Is it, on the other hand, an image of vulnerability at a time of pending crisis? Does it conceal the remnant of an essential self to be protected? Is it the 'tough case of something labelled fragile', to again borrow an expression used by Greene to describe a character, this time in *The Lawless Roads* (1939)?[79] Or does it have nothing whatsoever to declare? Does it announce a rejection of the symptomatic mode altogether? Is it a late modernist premonition of a postmodern aesthetic of surface value? Does it declare the absence or negation of interiorised meaning?

By posing these questions, I would like to suggest that Magritte's painting conveys the quandary faced by writers and artists at a point when the fate of the modern individual was being put to the test, along with the idea of symptomatic interpretation. While the difficulty of modernism might indeed have arisen as a form of resistance to symptomatic intrusiveness, I agree with Alan Wilde that 'what is at issue is the same epistemology of the hidden'.[80] We might say that the modernist conception of character both withstands and cultivates symptomatic interpretation at one and the same time, and the idea of a unified essence which might be discovered beneath the layers of obscurity is not entirely lost (as Levenson also highlights.) The effect of this is a sort of impervious ambiguity. By contrast, a major reason for the pertinence of that recurring line, 'Have you anything to declare?', in the 1930s, is that it demanded an unambiguous stand – a yes or no (there is no getting away with a 'maybe' at customs control) – and it was a question which could be mapped onto matters of aesthetic and political alignment.

One way of responding to this predicament of having to take account of one's position was, indeed, to take an unambiguous stand. It is no coincidence that this was the era when the documentary style, or the 'new vernacular', in Cyril Connolly's phrase, came into vogue, in line with the foregrounding of a politically committed art, on the part of emerging left-wing artists and writers.[81] The new vernacular was represented as a means of reaching out to the proletarian masses, as well as a response to early modernist obscurity (what Connolly labels, as set against the 'new vernacular', the 'mandarin' style, espoused by writers 'whose tendency it is to make their language convey more than what they mean').[82] However, the new vernacular must be considered, just the same, as a reaction, though of a very different kind, to the prevailing air of suspicion, as if the only way to counteract intrusiveness is to get rid of hiding-places altogether. Isherwood, one of the lead proponents of the documentary style, himself saw it in terms of a rejection of figurative ambiguity for the sake of a mode of textual portability that is unimpeded. In describing an earlier failed novelistic effort, he diagnoses the problem in retrospect in *Lions and Shadows* (1938) as follows:

> As usual, I was trying to pack a small case with the contents of three cabin trunks: my little comedy of bohemian life was, by this time, so overloaded with symbolism; the interplay of *motifs* (to use a very favour-ite word of mine, just then) was so complex and self-contradictory, that the book, had it ever been actually written, would have been merely a series of descriptions of the effects which I had hoped in vain, to be able to produce.[83]

Mandarin ambiguity is cast as an over-packed bag, at odds with the transpar-ency required of the vernacular school.

But, on the opposite end of the scale, we find an embrace of excess, equally conveyed through a portable paradigm. This was also the era of the 'inside the whale'/back to the womb approach, famously identified by Orwell. With this approach, by contrast, the retreat to an ultimate form of private hiding-place was the ideal. Consider the following representative passage from Lawrence Durrell's *The Black Book* (also 1938), which features the retirement of the narrator, Lawrence Lucifer, also a writer-figure, with his emotional freight:

> Forgive my imprecision, but it is as if I were packing to go on a long journey. Hilda lies open like a trunk in the corner of the room. There is room for everything, the gramophone, the records, the cottage piano, the microscope, the hair restorer, seven sets of clean clothes, manuscripts,

a typewriter, a dictionary, a pair of jackboots, skates, an ice pick, a crash helmet, a sheath knife, a fishing rod, and the latest Book Society Choice. There is even room for a portable God, if you rope it up among the canvasses. With these labels to assure me of my distinct and unique personality, I step down into the red tunnel, to begin my journey. For the purposes of simplification, let me be known as Jonah.[84]

If, as I have established here, luggage provided a metaphorical framework for the space of the unconscious, an unconscious liable to be publicly exposed, this reads like a complete retreat through the trunk into a protected womb-like unconscious zone with no intention of return or of public exposure. The narrator continues along these lines at some length. This is excess baggage at its most excessive: 'there is room for everything'. It is almost as though the loss of any one item will serve to detract from the complete essence of the individual, and so all must be accounted for and transferred to the self-contained, enclosed space of the trunk/womb.

Deborah Cohen remarks that '[a]mid the turmoil and sacrifices of the war, possessions became both less and more important to their owners', in that the emergency forced people to select the most essential, the most sacred personal objects, while belying the importance of any object when life itself was at stake.[85] Cohen's remark is penetrating in a number of ways but primarily for highlighting the extreme positions the wider crisis forced upon the individual, extremes which also come into play through that question, 'Have you anything to declare?' It was a question which highlighted, not least, a material dimension in the construction of selfhood, which is shown to come under strain during a period of conflict. We find, during this period, the expression of a renewed belief in the need to safeguard the essential self cast into doubt by modernists, a response which can be witnessed, not only in the popularity of the 'back to the whale/womb' motif, but also in the range of autobiographies which appeared late in the decade, all proclaiming a need to preserve the self through 'declaring' everything before the onset of disaster.[86] But we find, at the same time, a wartime impetus to obliterate this idea of the plumbed or unplumbed depths of a private unconscious in favour of a surface transparency, on the one hand, or a model of absolute performativity, on the other, induced by the same threatening circumstances. Hannah Arendt exposes the latter as a desperate form of desire in her well-known account of the refugee experience:

A man who wants to lose his self discovers, indeed, the possibilities of human existence, which are infinite, as infinite as is creation. But the recovering of a new personality is as difficult – and as hopeless – as a new creation of the world. Whatever we do, whatever we pretend to be, we reveal nothing but our insane desire to be changed, not to be Jews.[87]

'Have you anything to declare?' It seems that in the late 1930s political climate, only two answers presented themselves to this resonating question: 'Nothing' or 'Everything'. For the remainder of this chapter, I will discuss the wartime work of Henry Green as one late modernist attempt to negotiate these extremes.

HENRY GREEN'S AUTOBIOGRAPHICAL BAG

It seems fitting to conclude this study by considering the particular example of Henry Green (born Henry Vincent Yorke), with his retrospective and, at the same time, forward-looking outlook, both in his 1939 novel *Party Going* and in his autobiographical *Pack My Bag* (1940). Luggage features very prominently in his work around the outbreak of the war, and packing is also intimately related to the writing process. In this book, I trace the evolution of a portable modernist paradigm, and Green's work in the late 1930s and early 1940s, like Elizabeth Bowen's, is at once an affirmation and an interrogation of this kind of approach. As such, all of the associated issues explored in previous chapters are addressed and reappraised in this work; the emergence and *raison d'être* of the 'civilisation of luggage'; the use of the case as a substitute for the house as a formal analogue; the distinctive expression of female interiority through luggage; the politics of packing (the very title *Party Going* itself has potent political connotations); the envisioned plight of interwar refugees and asylum seekers from an English perspective; not to mention the unresolved problem of that fraught relationship between freedom and property. It is worth reiterating the words of Marina MacKay on the subject of late modernist impasse once again here, as she partly had Green in mind: 'The enduring emphasis on cosmopolitanism, deracination, expatriation, and cultural exchange in accounts of the 1920s and 1930s starts to look more complicated toward modernism's closing years.'[88] In *Party Going* and *Pack My Bag*, texts which I intend to read as companion pieces here, the image of the packed bag – as thematic motif and, more specifically, as analogic textual model – marks one critical locus where modernism attains a measure of self-reflexiveness, principally through the disjunctive invocations of various and conflicting tropes of mobility. No less importantly, Green's packed bag enacts the formulation of a late modernist response to what I would call the crisis of the intimate being; that is to say, the pressure placed upon the individual to take an unambiguous stand – to declare everything or nothing – at a time of emergency.

Green's most direct use of a portable analogue was in the title of his autobiographical *Pack My Bag*, published in 1940 but written between 1938 and 1939 (thus hot on the heels of *Party Going*, which was composed between 1931 and 1938). While some attention has been given to his somewhat unusual subtitle of 'Self-Portrait', as opposed to the more obvious alternatives of 'autobiography' or 'memoir', little sustained analysis has been given to the rich implications of the main title itself.[89] Green purportedly had some difficulty in choosing a name for his work, as Jeremy Treglown relates in his biography of the writer; he opted, in the end, for the final words of philosopher F. H. Bradley on the advice of John Lehmann, words which, as Treglown notes, 'in their new context hinted at wartime exigencies as well as picking up the morbid strain that runs through the book'.[90] We are, on the surface, a far cry from early modernist portability here. His textual endeavour is throughout conveyed as an act of hasty packing that is a deeply personal account of the intimate being, incited by the threat of war. 'That is my excuse', he writes on the opening page, 'that we who may not have time to write anything else must do what we now can.'[91] He later adds: 'everything must go down that one can remember, all one's tool box, one's packet of Wrigley's'.[92] This is material, we are told, which in less constrained circumstances 'would be used in novels'.[93] *Pack My Bag* is thus outwardly projected as an exercise in self-exposure. The bag is, by the same token, posited as a substitutive form at a time of crisis, in line with Hynes's definition of a late 1930s 'literature of preparation'.[94] Hynes further explains this literary tendency in terms of a forward-backward-looking dynamic: 'In such a time one might expect that the imaginations of writers would turn away from the immediate present ... They would turn instead backward, toward nostalgia, and forward, toward apocalypse.'[95] A form of apocalyptic nostalgia is certainly palpable throughout *Pack My Bag*, and the authorial bag then is proffered as a mobile archive of the past self as much as it stands as an unmistakeable sign of future emergency withdrawal or flight. As in those works examined in the previous chapter, from Isherwood's *Goodbye to Berlin* to Zweig's *The Post Office Girl,* we can perceive a shift from an application of a portable paradigm in relation to a literature of modernist cosmopolitan possibility towards its application in relation to a wartime literature of preparation, and this negative inversion is the most salient aspect of the luggage analogue as it is presented in *Pack My Bag.*

This very pointed conception of the packed autobiographical bag with an eye to imminent evacuation, a portable model reconfigured in terms of aesthetic loss rather than aesthetic gain, must be taken into account in any consideration of the phenomenon of stalled portability in his novel of the previous year, *Party Going.* In brief, the novel describes the congregation of a group of frivolously rich young Londoners in an unnamed train station (most likely Victoria), all packed and set for a continental holiday. They are hosted and funded by the wealthiest among them, a man by the name of Max. As fog descends, the trains are held up. The bright young set retreat to rooms in the station hotel, soon separated, by the crash of a steel barrier, from the accumulating masses of lowly office workers below. In the hotel, the group gossip (mainly about the escapades of a figure known as Embassy Richard) and squabble amongst themselves. There are cocktails aplenty. From time to time, they peer down at the increasingly impatient and clamorous crowd from the balcony and come to feel more than a little edgy themselves as the novel progresses. The women, joined midway through by a renowned beauty by the name of Amabel, compete for Max's attention. The reader is treated to sexual intrigue and boredom by turn. Edward Stokes pertinently invokes a line from Eliot's *Four Quartets* to express the prevailing mood: 'Distracted from distraction by distraction.'[96] Meanwhile, the servants take charge of the luggage on the station floor. An aunt, who has come upon and taken responsibility for a dead bird, falls ill and must be nursed in another bedroom, subject to feverish nightmares. An unidentified man with a shifting accent, thought to be the hotel detective, circulates throughout. Finally, the fog lifts and the trains begin moving again, just as the group is joined by the infamous Embassy Richard in person. Mrs Hilary's dream of '[p]acking; missing trains; meeting people; and just nonsense that means nothing', in Rose Macaulay's earlier *Dangerous Ages*, would make a concise description of this novel, except that, in *Party Going*, this is nonsense that is shown to mean nothing and everything at once, an 'untrivial treatment of triviality', as Stokes articulates it.[97]

We are clearly in *Vile Bodies* territory here, but why resurrect these vile bodies in 1939? Significantly, critics vary considerably in attributing particular dates to the events narrated, setting the novel anywhere between the late 1920s and the late 1930s, but this temporal opacity is part of the point.[98] *Party Going* offers, in effect, an impressionistic vision of the long interwar weekend, but with the climax as yet unwritten. The accumulated luggage of the party-goers at the centre of the station forms the important vanishing point at the centre of this picture. Written almost entirely in the past tense, there is a single momentary shift into present tense around twenty-one pages into the novel:

> So now at last all of this party is in one place, and, even if they have not yet all of them come across each other, their baggage is collected in the Registration Hall. Where, earlier, hundreds had made their way to this station thousands were coming in now, it was the end of a day for them, the beginning of a time for our party.[99]

Ostensibly drawing a distinction between the type of journey undertaken by office worker and party-goer, there is something inherently ominous about this passage from a late 1930s standpoint, especially the last line in its emphasis on mounting activity and stages of process. What exactly is beginning for this party? What is it that is ending for those surrounding them? And why does the very idea of baggage amassed in a Registration Hall ring so portentously here?

I would like to consider these questions in relation to a passage from Zweig's autobiography, briefly invoked earlier in relation to his novel *The Post Office Girl*.[100] Fittingly entitled *The World of Yesterday*, his autobiography was written during the Second World War and, in some ways, falls into the 'Literature of Preparation' category in its combination of nostalgic reassessment with apocalyptic fatalism.[101] For Zweig, as a fleeing Jewish writer, however, this was more a literature of post-preparation. His bag had already been packed in material rather than metaphorical terms. Having taken up residence in England in the mid-1930s in reaction to Hitler's growing influence, he looked back on the period immediately following the 1938 Munich agreement (which served to accentuate the refugee crisis in Europe) and made this rather telling observation:

> [The English] were generous to the refugees who now came over in hordes, they showed the most noble sympathy and helpful understanding. But a sort of invisible wall grew between them and us, it was here, there and everywhere; *the thing that had already happened to us had not yet happened to them.* We understood what had occurred and what was to occur, but they still refused – partly against their inner conviction – to understand ... Thus those of us who had been subjected to trial and those who as yet had been spared it, the immigrants and the English, spoke different languages. It is no exaggeration to say that besides a negligible number of Englishmen we were then the only ones in England who did no delude ourselves about the extent of the danger.[102]

I would like to isolate one particular line here – 'the thing that had already happened to us had not yet happened to them' – in order to assert that Green's *Party Going* is an evocation of this very scenario, of this invisible wall. In his discussion of 'latent' and 'manifest' senses in *The Genesis of Secrecy*, Frank Kermode takes *Party Going* as a specific case study, and his terms are useful in the context of my own discussion.[103] By this I mean that the figure of the refugee, that persistent 1930s spectre,[104] is latent in the manifest figure of the party-goer in *Party Going*. Similarly, the prospective is latent in the retrospective in a novel which, as I am contending, forms an impressionistic vision of the interwar period as a whole. If Zweig's 'invisible wall' refers to the psychological divide between the innocent and the experienced, it might equally be seen as a temporal divide between past and future, and *Party Going* sits on this cusp. It is in the shift to present tense in the above passage that this temporal wall becomes momentarily visible. On one side, we see the leisured 'civilisation of luggage' at a late-1920s height of interwar restlessness, held up in their pursuit of pleasure due to a heavy fog. But, with his foot in an imagined future, Green might also be said to look across and envision the other side. There we encounter the prospect of a party held up in its troubled flight from pain. The train station is, accordingly, a very strategic choice of setting. The railways, 'our gates to the glorious and the unknown', as Margaret views them in *Howards End*, were also seen to be of central importance to the war effort and were, in fact, shortly to be used to evacuate civilians in unprecedented numbers, just after Green had published *Party Going* and probably while he was writing *Pack My Bag*.[105] The collected and abandoned luggage in *Party Going* is likened on more than one occasion to an 'exaggerated grave yard' implying a pending fate which, for all their frivolity, the party-goers cannot escape, a sense of detention aggravated moreover by the purgatorial imagery throughout.[106] In MacKay's words, the novel 'describes a festivity turning into a funeral', and her emphasis here on a transformational process – 'turn*ing*' – rather than a final outcome picks up on that sense of detention.[107] The vile body is resurrected in this luggage-constructed graveyard only to be marked or – should we say? – registered. And 'hasty packing'? What dread that phrase must be seen to implicitly engender in this context, in line with Green's own autobiographical bag, hurriedly assembled in the light, as he puts it, of 'imminent death'.[108]

This interpretation of *Party Going* is informed by Green's overt employment of a reconfigured portable analogue in *Pack My Bag*, an analogue suggesting self-preservation rather than a modernist 'make it new' initiative. Yet just as a reading of the manifest qualities of *Pack My Bag* can be shown to inform a reading of the latent qualities in *Party Going*, so too can the manifest in *Party Going* lead us to the latent in *Pack My Bag*. For the remainder of this discussion, I intend to unsettle my own initial analysis of Green's act of autobiographical packing, drawing on elements from his novel. Treglown's perception of an undertone of wartime exigency and morbidity in the title of Green's autobiographical work accurately pinpoints one obvious aspect of its relevance, but it is a title which resists precise definition, just as the work itself is well known to obfuscate almost as much as it reveals about Green as a man.[109] To begin with, the phrase '*Pack My Bag*', in its imperative form, emphatically announces a particular class affiliation, markedly aligning Green with the smart set portrayed in his earlier novel.[110] 'I was born a mouthbreaker with a silver spoon in 1905', runs the well-known opening line.[111] The aristocratic Green was, in the early days of his marriage to Dig Biddulph, a wealthy man about town himself, and he was, in fact, a guest on a trip not unlike that depicted in *Party Going*, hosted by none other than Aly Khan, playboy son of the Aga Khan, in 1932.[112] His friend and fellow writer Evelyn Waugh, coined the tag 'Bright Young Yorkes' for the newly married couple.[113] Might there be a veiled reference in the title *Pack My Bag* to the main protagonist of Waugh's *Vile Bodies,* Adam Fenwick-Symes, who, at the beginning of that novel, is interrogated at Customs for carrying the manuscript of his own autobiography in his suitcase, a manuscript subsequently seized by the authorities?

Speculations and biographical insights aside, the title patently asserts in and of itself a privileged social status. Comparison with the memoir title of working-class writer William Holt, first published the year before Green's in 1939, makes this startlingly clear. Holt's was called *I Haven't Unpacked: An*

Autobiography.[114] In his title and subtitle, it is almost as if Green was deliberately setting his own title against Holt's: a juxtaposition of the two makes the imperative form of *Pack My Bag* difficult to ignore. It is a phrase which might well have been addressed by any one of the elite party-goers to his or her servant in *Party Going*. Max, incidentally, in his tardy decision to join the party, comes closest to voicing that order – 'pack my bag' – directly, but we learn that there is no need. His Edwards is 'too good a servant to leave things so late', and so, with the arrival of his car, we are given instead a post-hasty-packing command: 'My bags in? Yes, then come on, I'm in a hurry.'[115] The accumulated luggage in *Party Going* is emblematic of an elite class, even more so when it is abandoned to the servants. In 1930, the year before he began work on *Party Going*, Green wrote a short story entitled 'Excursion' (unpublished during his lifetime) along similar thematic lines, set at a train station and featuring a delayed train.[116] Conspicuous in its absence, in this story, is the luggage. This, however, is the story of a working-class group taking off for a bank holiday. We might well surmise that holiday luggage is taken to be for the leisured classes only and packing reserved for the servants.

Yet it might equally be argued that the image of the packed bag aligns Green, with the same force, with his left-leaning 1930s contemporaries. 'The younger sons were packing their bags', Cunningham writes of this generation, 'kicking over traces, leaving home'.[117] In this, he is picking up on a common motif, explicitly echoing the opening line of Cecil Day-Lewis's *A Hope for Poetry* from 1934, a line which seems to contain the kernel of Green's title within it:

> In English poetry there have been several occasions on which the younger son, fretting against parental authority, weary of routine work on the home farm, suspecting too that the soil needs a rest, has *packed his bag* and set out for a far country.[118]

It is no coincidence that C. Northcote Parkinson entitled his later 1967 survey of the rise and fall of British socialism *Left Luggage*.[119] The packed bag was a key indicator of the socialist interests of the 'Auden Generation', a generation of writers who attempted to leave their social origins behind in their acts of 'going over' the class border. These attempts were mostly unsuccessful, and, as Cunningham wryly notes, their bags were 'perpetually packed for the journey back'.[120] But 'going over' was undoubtedly one more 1930s literary watchword. Cunningham has himself noted the invocation of that very phrase, 'going over', along with the idea of party politics in the title of *Party Going*.[121] Carol Wipf-Miller, among other recent critics, has made a strong case for 'relocating Green in the contexts of 30s leftism and the new realism', as much as situating him at the tail end of high modernism.[122] Indeed, *Pack My Bag* itself betrays a degree of class guilt on Green's part, and makes his own act of 'going over', in working on the floor of his father's factory in Birmingham for two years, a central point of focus. This was an experience which provided the inspiration for his second novel, *Living*, in 1929, a novel which adopts a working-class idiom and which Christopher Isherwood called the 'best proletarian novel ever written'.[123] I don't myself think that the act of 'going over' is intentionally inscribed in Green's packing metaphor. However, the expression of class guilt within the body of the text does serve to undercut the upper-class assertion of his title, making us doubt the authenticity of the identity foregrounded.

Indeed, if we overlook Green's conspicuous definition of his portable model along the lines of a literature of preparation, we will find that it is an indeterminacy of identity which the image of the packed bag conjured for him more broadly. Green was attuned to the fact that packing a bag creates a fiction of the self, one that can be rewritten as his later intention to compose a follow-up memoir entitled *Pack My Bag Repacked* intimates. (This particular book never materialised, though William Holt did manage to produce his own *I Still Haven't Unpacked* by 1953, and again the difference in title here, though only projected in Green's case, tells us much about his own distinctive authorial approach by contrast.) In *Party Going,* various characters are shown to compose narratives of self through their luggage.

> Squatting down apart [Julia] opened this case. Everything was packed in different coloured tissue papers. They were her summer things and as she lifted and recognised them she called to mind where she had last worn each one with Max. She often went away weekends to house parties and it often happened that he was there. If she had no memory for words she could always tell what she had worn each time she met him. Turning over her clothes as they had been packed she was turning over days.
> Her porter sighed. He had enjoyed what he had seen of her things.[124]

Julia's clothes are her words, her case is her book, a lavishly illustrated book with tissue separating the pages. Not so lavish, however, as that of her main rival, Amabel, who, having joined the party unannounced, promises a more compelling narrative: 'So she is coming after all, Julia thought, maid and all and six cabin trunks full of every kind of lovely dress.'[125] Green was well aware of the special significance of bags and luggage for women and for those seeking to gain a feminine insight, as evidenced by another posthumously published story entitled 'Mood'. In this story, a man's glimpse at the handbag of an elegant young lady produces a yearning for an 'exquisite transparency, like a seashell in the sea, where her thumb branched off from the palm of her hand'.[126] Yet if bags generate narratives of desire in Green's work, they generate disgust in equal measure. Clive Hart, one critic who has devoted some attention to the abundance of baggage in *Party Going* (and this back in 1971), interprets the accumulated trunks as 'symbols of the corruption of the spirit' of the party-goers, as 'surrogates for the people to whom they belong', and, as such, he brands these trunks 'parcels of falsity'.[127] To some extent, I agree with Hart, but I would be less inclined to view these parcels of falsity in purely negative terms. Green had, after all, great sympathy with the impetus behind the masquerade, Henry Green itself being a pseudonym. He owned, in *Pack My Bag*, to a period of lying 'outrageously' to strangers in train carriages and advocated reticence above complete exposure in human relations:

> surely shyness is the saving grace in all relationships, the not speaking out, not sharing confidences, the avoidance of intimacy in important things which makes living, if you can find friends to play it that way, of so much greater interest even if it does involve a lot of lying.[128]

This description goes some way to account for the technique, as well as the appeal of *Pack My Bag* as a text, its elusiveness despite the continual claims of self-exposure, leading critics such as John Russell to take issue with the promise embedded in the title itself: 'If the reader of this book were to expect a kind of carefully stowed bag of remembrances and self-evaluations, he would discover that Green left the bag unpacked.'[129]

It also reminds us that that the bag itself is less important than the position allotted to the reader in relation to the bag. Green's autobiographical impulse in packing a narrative of self is not unlike that of Julia's, and whether either case is a parcel of falsity or not is beside the point. The point here is access. Like the porter eyeing Julia's case, the reader is only really granted a fleeting glimpse of the contents of Green's bag. Furthermore, just as it is more the idea of Amabel's six cabin trunks which stimulates Julia's imagination as well as envy, so Green was well aware that the bag that does not fully declare its contents often feeds the imagination more provocatively than the bag that does. On the subject of his preference for obscurity, his son, Sebastian Yorke, recalled a trip taken by his parents to New York in 1950 to settle a tax question. With a view to remaining incognito, the Yorkes travelled as 'Mr and Mrs H.V. Yonge, the initials matching the initials on their luggage'.[130] 'It was also about this time that he started to insist on being photographed only from the back', he adds.[131] This is obscurity, but only partial obscurity, and of a playful kind. It is an anecdote which should likewise alert us to the importance of the half-truth in a consideration of his fictional bag. His approach to masquerade is as a flirtation with different roles, but always from the basis of the known, an approach critics such as Andrew Gibson have equally highlighted on the level of his narrative style. '[H]is narrative idiom', Gibson remarks, 'is not so much a new one as a familiar one that is constantly . . . yielding to other idioms'.[132]

Tyrus Miller has described late modernism as the reassembly of 'fragments into disfigured likenesses of modernist masterpieces', and Green's late modernist luggage might be viewed on these terms.[133] It is for this reason that he makes such a compelling concluding example in this study. It can certainly be said that his is a disfigured version of an early modernist *case* of fiction, in that it is a model unavoidably compromised by historical circumstances and political realities. Hasty packing in Green's work is far from engendering the kind of excitement Fussell has in mind in *Abroad*. At the same time, we cannot entirely take the alternative preparative model he puts forward at face value in its more than wistful nod to the experimental escapism of a previous age of literary bohemianism. Green is indeed the master of the semi-escape and, correspondingly, the semi-distortion of the recognisable through the often disconcerting interplay of latent and manifest elements. The peculiar intensity of this interplay in the works I have looked at here owes everything to their composition on the brink of war, as he himself so eloquently explained:

> [A]s I see it people are taking a last look around. Picking, fingering, saying good-bye to what they could use to drape their hearts where everyone now wears his in the stress of the times, on his sleeve, not naked as hearts will be when the war comes, still covered but in a kind of strip-tease with rapidly changing, always fewer and ever more diaphanous clothes.[134]

In Green's novel and memoir, the packed bag is used as an analogue for a form of self-fiction which serves to strip and tease in equal measure, and, as such, presents a semi-solution to the crisis of the intimate being in the 'stress of the times'.

NOTES

1. Gaston Bachelard, *The Poetics of Space*, trans. Maria Jolas (1958; New York: Orion, 1964), p. 85. Emphasis in original.
2. Ibid., p. xxxii.
3. Ibid., pp. 81, 84. Emphasis in original.
4. Quoted in Pierre Léonforte, '100 Legendary Trunks', in *Louis Vuitton: 100 Legendary Trunks*, by Pierre Léonforte, Éric Pujalet-Plaà with the collaboration of Florence Lesché and Marie Wurry, trans. Bruce Waille (New York: Abrams, 2010), p. 237.
5. 'Montre-moi tes bagages et je te dirai qui tu es', advertisement, reprinted in *Louis Vuitton: 100 Legendary Trunks*, p. 364. Louis Vuitton also patented and promoted its own failsafe luggage locks from the 1890s. Their advertising campaigns cleverly appealed to the human need for privacy, as much as to the human inclination to posture. See Pujalet-Plaà, 'The Trunk in All Its States', in *Louis Vuitton: 100 Legendary Trunks*, pp. 454–5.
6. To reiterate the full title of Levenson's study: *Modernism and the Fate of Individuality: Character and Novelistic Form from Conrad to Woolf* (Cambridge: Cambridge University Press, 1991).
7. Ibid., p. xiii. The novels in question in Levenson's study are: Conrad's *Heart of Darkness*, James's *The Ambassadors*, Forster's *Howards End*, Ford Madox Ford's *The Good Soldier*, Wyndham Lewis's *Tarr*, Lawrence's *Women in Love* and Woolf's *To the Lighthouse*.

8. Ford Madox Ford, *The Good Soldier* (1915; Manchester: Carcanet Press, 1996), p. 139.
9. Aldous Huxley, *Crome Yellow* (1921; London: Vintage-Random, 2004), p. 158.
10. Virginia Woolf, *Mrs Dalloway* (1925; London: Vintage-Random, 2004), p. 134.
11. See Nancy Armstrong, *Desire and Domestic Fiction: A Political History of the Novel* (1987; Oxford: Oxford University Press, 1989), pp. 8, 224.
12. Katherine Mansfield, 'The Baron', in *Collected Stories of Katherine Mansfield* (1945; London: Constable, 1980), p. 703.
13. Ibid., p. 704.
14. Ibid., p. 704. Emphasis added.
15. Ibid., p. 705.
16. David Trotter, *The English Novel in History 1895–1920* (London: Routledge, 1998), pp. 195, 197.
17. Max Beerbohm, 'Ichabod' (1900), in *Yet Again* (1909; London: Heinemann, 1928), pp. 126–7.
18. Henry James, 'Preface to *The Portrait of a Lady*' (1908), in *The Critical Muse: Selected Literary Criticism*, ed. Roger Gard (Harmondsworth: Penguin, 1987), p. 485.
19. Beerbohm, 'Ichabod', p. 127.
20. Max Beerbohm, 'A Defence of Cosmetics', *The Yellow Book: An Illustrated Quarterly*, 1, April 1894, p. 65.
21. Ford, *The Good Soldier*, p. 73.
22. Robert Louis Stevenson, 'Story of the Physician and the Saratoga Trunk' (1878), in *New Arabian Nights* (1882; London: Heinemann, 1927), p. 45.
23. Ibid., p. 46.
24. I refer here particularly to the Crossman trunk murder of 1904, in which the remains of a woman's body were found packed in a trunk and embedded in cement at Kensal Rise, and the Devereux trunk murder of 1905, in which the bodies of a woman and her twin children were disposed of in a tin trunk and left at a warehouse in Harrow. The husbands of the two women were culpable in both cases, and, in the latter, the man admitted to using the Crossman case as a precedent. The later popularity of luggage murders in fiction around the 1930s had much to do with the Charing Cross Station case of 1927 and the two famous Brighton trunk murders of 1934. In two of these three later cases, body parts were found in trunks in railway station cloakrooms. See 'Supposed Murder and Suicide at Kensal-Rise', *The Times*, 25 March 1904, p. 9; 'Central Criminal Court, July 28', *The Times*, 29 July 1905, p. 4; 'Trunk Murder Charge', *The Times*, 30 June 1927, p. 14; 'Trunk Crime', *The Times*, 16 July 1934, p. 14; Trunk Crime No. 2', *The Times*, 18 July 1934, p. 14.
25. Ian Carter, 'The Lady in the Trunk: Railways, Gender and Crime Fiction', *The Journal of Transport History*, 23.1, March 2002, pp. 46–59.
26. Ibid., p. 47.
27. This blind spot is periodically glimpsed through the bringing together (and sometimes merging) of images of coffin/grave and trunk. Miriam Henderson, for instance, in the 1916 *Backwater* chapter of *Pilgrimage*, is disturbed to find her sisters chattering carelessly next to one of their open trunks: 'Did they see that it was exactly like a grave?' she asks herself, catching a prospective glimpse of the inevitable interruption of her own journey. Joanna Bannerman, the main protagonist of Catherine Carswell's *Open the Door!* (1920), is likewise forced to acknowledge this association through juxtaposition upon the death of her mother. Called to her deathbed in a remote Scottish village, she finds that 'everything' recalls 'the unforgettable journeys of childhood ... with piles of

luggage'. Soon after this, on transporting her mother's body back to Glasgow in the company of her brother, the idea of the unforgettable childhood journey is brought up against the idea of the undeniable final destination: 'On the steamer, the coffin having been slung on board from the ferry like any other piece of heavy luggage, Linnet and Joanna felt as if they were the sharers in a shameful secret.' Such a shameful secret underlies the modernist journey at all times, and it is a secret unremittingly divulged in depictions of the journey in late modernist writing. 'Life, seen whole for a moment, was one act of apprehension, the apprehension of death', Lois suddenly grasps in Bowen's *The Last September*, in a line which rewrites the Arnoldian/Forsterian 'see life steadily and see it whole' equation and goes some way to elucidate this figurative luggage/coffin/journey amalgamation. See Dorothy Richardson, *Pilgrimage*, vol. 1 (London: Dent and Cresset, 1938), p. 305; Catherine Carswell, *Open the Door!* (1920; Edinburgh: Canongate, 1996), pp. 345–6, 352; Elizabeth Bowen, *The Last September* (1929; London: Vintage-Random, 1998), p. 202; Matthew Arnold, 'To A Friend', in *Selected Poems of Matthew Arnold* (London: Macmillan and Co., 1882), p. 4; E. M. Forster, *Howards End* (1910; New York: Signet-Penguin, 1992), p. 212.

28. T. S. Eliot, *The Waste Land*, in *The Norton Anthology of Poetry*, ed. Margaret Ferguson, Mary Jo Salter and Jon Stallworthy (New York: Norton, 1996), pp. 1236–48 (p. 1238).

29. Allon White, *The Uses of Obscurity: The Fiction of Early Modernism* (London: Routledge and Kegan Paul, 1981), p. 3.

30. Ibid., p. 16.

31. Mansfield, 'The Baron', p. 705.

32. A further casket-related expression of thwarted symptomatic inquiry can be found in E. M. Forster's much later review of Joseph Conrad's *Notes on Life and Letters* in 1921:

   These essays do suggest that he is misty in the middle as well as at the edges, that the secret casket of his genius contains a vapour rather than a jewel; and that we need not try to write him down philosophically, because there is, in this particular direction, nothing to write.

   The quote appears in an extract from Forster's review in Norman Sherry (ed.), *Joseph Conrad: The Critical Heritage* (London and New York: Routledge, 1973), p. 346.

33. White, though acknowledging Freud, locates the beginnings of the rise of modernist obscurity somewhat earlier. He points, for example, to the growing interest in irrational states of mind as a facet of artistic creativity in the work of Cesare Lombroso, Max Nordau and J. F. Nisbet, among others. See White, *The Uses of Obscurity*, pp. 44–9.

34. Sigmund Freud, *Beyond the Pleasure Principle and Other Writings*, trans. John Reddick, ed. Adam Phillips (1920; London: Penguin, 2003).

35. Carl Jung, *Memories, Dreams, Reflections*, trans. Richard and Clara Winston, ed. Aniela Jaffé (1963; London: Flamingo, 1990), p. 186.

36. Ibid., p. 187.

37. Ibid., pp. 189, 188.

38. Ibid., p. 189.

39. Nathalie Sarraute, *L'ère du soupçon: essais sur le roman* (Paris: Gallimard, 1956), p. 79. My translation.

40. Katherine Mansfield, 'Je ne parle pas français' (1918), in *Collected Stories of Katherine Mansfield*, p. 61.

41. Virginia Woolf, *Orlando: A Biography* (1928; London: Hogarth Press, 1964), p. 239.
42. Ibid., p. 282.
43. Ibid., p. 239.
44. George Dangerfield, *The Strange Death of Liberal England* (1935; New York: Capricorn, 1961), p. viii.
45. Michael R. Marrus, *The Unwanted: European Refugees from the First World War Through the Cold War* (Philadelphia: Temple University Press, 2002), p. 93.
46. Ibid., p. 93.
47. Bridget T. Chalk, *Modernism and Mobility: The Passport and Cosmopolitan Experience* (New York: Palgrave Macmillan, 2014), p. 12.
48. Hope Mirrlees, *Paris: A Poem* (London: Hogarth Press, 1919), p. 11.
49. Rousseau never undertook the role of customs official in actuality, though he was popularly perceived to be in that particular line of work.
50. Mirrlees, *Paris*, p. 21.
51. Paul Fussell, *Abroad: British Literary Traveling Between the Wars* (New York: Oxford University Press, 1980), pp. 32, 30. For Samuel Hynes, the border can be seen to represent the 'edge of the unknown and the beginning of uncertainty' for the Auden generation, and this obsession is manifested particularly in the idea of 'going over' the class border for that set of writers. Valentine Cunningham writes more generally about 'threshold anxieties' and perceptively identifies the ambiguity of the border's meaning during this decade:

    The ancient taboos of the threshold – the place where the excitement of leaping across into the new is chequered by the fear of being stuck on the border, suspended in no-man's-land, dangerously exposed, fearfully indeterminate ... – are inevitably focused at very many of the '30s huge roster of thresholds.

    Cunningham also briefly discusses the 'border traumas of Europe's political refugees'. See Samuel Hynes, *The Auden Generation: Literature and Politics in England in the 1930s* (London: Faber, 1979), p. 56; Valentine Cunningham, *British Writers of the Thirties* (Oxford: Oxford University Press, 1988), pp. 366, 364, 372.
52. Cunningham, *British Writers of the Thirties*, p. 371.
53. Evelyn Waugh, *Vile Bodies* (1930; Harmondsworth: Penguin, 1951), p. 24.
54. Robert Byron, *The Road to Oxiana* (1937; London: Penguin, 2007), p. 15. This was in Palestine. Customs officials are invariably rendered throughout Byron's travelogue in disdainfully comic terms. Their inherent corruption is taken for granted. A further encounter in Persia is recounted as follows:

    the Persian officials offered us their sympathy in this disgusting business of customs and kept us three hours. When I paid duty on some films and medicines, they took the money with eyes averted, as a duchess collects for charity. (Byron, *The Road to Oxiana*, p. 41)

55. George Orwell, 'Inside the Whale' (1940), in *The Collected Essays, Journalism and Letters of George Orwell*, vol. 1, ed. Sonia Orwell and Ian Angus (London: Secker and Warburg, 1968), p. 519.
56. Maurice Baring, *Have You Anything to Declare? A Notebook With Commentaries* (1936; London: Heinemann, 1951), p. 1. Emphasis in original.
57. Ibid., p. 2.
58. Ibid., p. 1. The trope of the ultimate test is one that recurs in writing of the 1930s, as both Hynes and Cunningham point out, attributing its development to the younger 'Auden' generation of writers who had missed out on the First World

War and felt the need to prove themselves. Baring himself did participate in the Great War, but I would argue that his use of the customs analogy picks up on and shows the influence of these circulating ideas and motifs. Baring, moreover, involuntarily exhibits the kind of frontier anguish of the person with something to hide, typical of this period as remarked upon by Cunningham, even if he does not show a conscious awareness of it. His lack of awareness is an even greater testament to the prevalence of this imagery in a 1936 context. See Cunningham, *British Writers of the Thirties*, pp. 170–1; Hynes, *The Auden Generation*, pp. 127, 244.

59. Hynes, *The Auden Generation*, p. 193.
60. Graham Greene, *The Lawless Roads* (1939; London: Vintage-Random, 2002), p. 23.
61. Christopher Isherwood, *Mr Norris Changes Trains* (1935; London: Hogarth Press, 1969), p. 15.
62. Fussell, *Abroad*, p. 31. The source of the Rebecca West quotation is: *Black Lamb and Grey Falcon: The Record of a Journey Through Yugoslavia in 1937*, vol. 2 (1941; London: Macmillan, 1942), p. 501.
63. George Orwell, *Coming Up for Air* (1939; Harmondsworth: Penguin, 1976), p. 223.
64. This image also corroborates David Trotter's recent discussion of interwar renderings of customs examinations in terms of obscene bodily 'violation'. See David Trotter, *Literature in the First Media Age: Britain Between the Wars* (Cambridge, MA and London: Harvard University Press, 2013), p. 256.
65. Isherwood, *Mr Norris Changes Trains*, p. 7.
66. Ibid., p. 11. Emphasis added.
67. Ibid., p. 11.
68. Aristide Briand, in Figure 4, was President of France in 1929 and had been central in negotiating the Locarno Treaty in 1926, for which he was awarded a Nobel Peace Prize. Ramsay MacDonald, in Figure 5, became the first Labour Prime Minister in 1929. J. H. Thomas was the Lord Privy Seal. The latter cartoon refers to a visit undertaken by the Prime Minister to the United States in September of that year. For a further example of a pictorial alignment between packed case and political interest from the mid-1930s, see Leonard Raven-Hill, 'St. George for Merrie Europe; Or, Chivalry Begins Abroad', cartoon, *Punch*, 188, 24 April 1935, p. 451.
69. Anthony Eden, in Figure 6, was the foreign secretary in 1936. For a similar 1936 cartoon including Hitler himself, see Charles Grave, 'Diplomatic Exchanges (Unofficial)', cartoon, *Punch*, 191, 9 September 1936, p. 283.
70. Stefan Zweig, *The World of Yesterday: An Autobiography* (1942; London: Cassell, 1943), p. 175.
71. W. H. Auden, 'Gare du Midi', in *Collected Poems*, ed. Edward Mendelson (1976; London: Faber, 1991), p. 180.
72. Graham Greene, *The Ministry of Fear* (1943; London: Heinemann and Bodley Head, 1973), pp. 95–117. The chapter in which this incident is described is entitled 'A Load of Books'.
73. According to Marrus, Britain adopted a cautious posture towards refugees throughout the 1930s, and the numbers of incoming immigrants were low for much of the decade. After 1938, under pressure to admit greater numbers of asylum seekers, a more open policy was somewhat reluctantly taken up, and refugee entry accelerated. But hospitality was accompanied by a 'deep-seated anxiety' about illegitimate and potentially threatening aliens, an anxiety leading to rounds of internments:

In Britain, 27,000 enemy aliens (including some merchant seamen) found themselves behind barbed wire. British intelligence officers and other officials then began the sometimes clumsy efforts to ascertain whether the internees were, in fact, dangerous enemy agents. (Marrus, *The Unwanted*, pp. 152–3, 204–5)

74. Graham Greene, *The Power and the Glory* (1940; Harmondsworth: Penguin, 1983), p. 35. This is a phrase which recurs in various forms to refer to strangers throughout the novel.

75. This is a late third addition to a series of similarly structured works beginning in 1927, all entitled 'La Clef des Songes' or 'The Key of Dreams'. This last 1936 version is the only one in this series constructed through the English language.

76. Laurie Edson, *Reading Relationally: Postmodern Perspectives on Literature and Art* (Ann Arbor: University of Michigan Press, 2000), pp. 45–6.

77. I. A. Richards, 'Metaphor', in *Philosophical Perspectives on Metaphor*, ed. Mark Johnson (Minneapolis: University of Minnesota Press, 1981), p. 51. Emphasis in original. The essay was first published in *The Philosophy of Rhetoric* in 1936.

78. Unlike the earlier francophone images in the 'Key of Dreams' series in 1927 and 1930, this 1936 version is deliberately anglicised, thus authorising the use of an English literary frame of reference.

79. Greene, *The Lawless Roads*, p. 109.

80. Alan Wilde, 'Surfacings: Reflections on the Epistemology of Late Modernism', *boundary 2*, 8.2, Winter 1980, p. 210.

81. Cyril Connolly, *Enemies of Promise* (1938; London: André Deutsch, 1996), pp. 70–84.

82. Ibid., p. 25.

83. Christopher Isherwood, *Lions and Shadows: An Education in the Twenties* (1938; London: Methuen, 1979), pp. 128–9.

84. Lawrence Durrell, *The Black Book* (1938. New York: Dutton, 1963), pp. 177–8.

85. Deborah Cohen, *Household Gods: The British and Their Possessions* (New Haven, CT: Yale University Press, 2006), p. 199.

86. For an account of the sudden burst of autobiographical writing at the end of the 1930s and into the 1940s, see Jonathan Bolton, 'Mid-Term Autobiography and the Second World War', *Journal of Modern Literature*, 30.1, Fall 2006, pp. 155–72.

87. Hannah Arendt, 'We Refugees' (1943), in *The Jewish Writings*, ed. Jerome Kohn and Ron H. Feldman (New York: Schocken Books, 2007), p. 271.

88. Marina MacKay, '"Is your journey really necessary?": Going Nowhere in Late Modernist London', *PMLA*, 124.5, October 2009, pp. 1601–1602.

89. Marius Hentea points out that few works were entitled 'self-portraits' during this period, and he provides an elucidating interpretation of the deliberate distinction made by Green in characterising his work as a form of portraiture. Marius Hentea, 'A Guilty Self-Portrait: Henry Green's *Pack My Bag*', *The Cambridge Quarterly*, 40.1, 2011, pp. 36–52.

90. Jeremy Treglown, *Romancing: The Life and Work of Henry Green* (London: Faber, 2000), pp. 130, 310 (note 36). Other possibilities, recorded by Treglown, were 'Henry Green by Henry Green', 'Before a War', 'Taking Stock' and 'A Chance to Live'.

91. Henry Green, *Pack My Bag* (1940; London: Hogarth Press, 1952), p. 5.

92. Ibid., p. 12.

93. Ibid., p. 5.

94. Hynes, *The Auden Generation*, p. 341.

95. Ibid., pp. 340–1.
96. Edward Stokes, *The Novels of Henry Green* (London: Hogarth Press, 1959), p. 144.
97. Rose Macaulay, *Dangerous Ages* (London: W. Collins, 1921), p. 109; Stokes, *The Novels of Henry Green*, p. 82.
98. To give some examples, John Lehmann is known to have assumed a 1929–31 timeframe, as recounted by Stokes. Similarly, Tim Parks takes it to be set in the late 1920s. On the other hand, Frank Kermode surmises that it must be 'at some date ... in the Thirties', while Marina MacKay supposes the timeframe of the novel to correspond with the time of its composition just before the Second World War. See Stokes, *The Novels of Henry Green*, p. 149; Tim Parks, 'Introduction', in *Party Going*, by Henry Green (1939; London: Vintage-Random, 2000), p. v; Frank Kermode, *The Genesis of Secrecy: On the Interpretation of Narrative* (Cambridge, MA: Harvard University Press, 1980), p. 6; MacKay, '"Is your journey really necessary?"', p. 1603.
99. Green, *Party Going*, p. 21.
100. Green's *Pack My Bag* is often usefully read in relation to other memoirs of the period by British writers from a public school background – Christopher Isherwood's *Lions and Shadows* (1938) and Cyril Connolly's *Enemies of Promise* (1938), among others – but I believe a comparison with autobiographical writing by refugees from continental Europe can offer equally fruitful, sometimes more interesting, lines of enquiry. Although I can only touch on such a comparison here, there is certainly material for a lengthier comparative study of the memoirs of Green and Zweig. For accounts of Green's work in relation to other British memoirs of the late 1930s, see Bolton, 'Mid-Term Autobiography and the Second World War', pp. 155–72, and Rod Mengham, *The Idiom of the Time: The Writings of Henry Green* (Cambridge: Cambridge University Press, 1982), pp. 56–7.
101. In Zweig's case, this temporal double bind ultimately proved too much. He committed suicide shortly after he finished the autobiography, along with his wife, in exile in Brazil in 1942.
102. Zweig, *The World of Yesterday*, pp. 314–15. Emphasis added.
103. Kermode, *The Genesis of Secrecy*, p. 3.
104. By using the term 'spectre' here, I do not mean to impose the quality of the spectral upon real refugees who were experiencing the actuality of displacement at this time, but to draw attention to the fact that the figure of the refugee palpably haunts the English literary imagination in the mid-to-late 1930s (as touched upon in Chapter 3), often most acutely in texts which are not explicitly concerned with refugee characters. Even a cursory overview of British press coverage of the mass movements of peoples around Europe in the late 1930s establishes that this was very much an issue at the forefront of the public consciousness.
105. Forster, *Howards End*, p. 10. British Railways ran a promotional campaign during the war with the tagline 'The Lines Behind the Lines' (for example, 'Your Parcels and Letters Depend on the Lines Behind the Lines'.) The railways were pivotally involved in the mass evacuation from London of 1–4 September 1939, described by *The Railway Gazette* at the time as 'the greatest civilian mass movement in history'. This was to be trumped by the mass exodus of civilians from Paris upon Nazi occupation the following year (June 1940), which, as Marrus records in retrospect, was the 'greatest single upheaval of the entire war in Europe', comprising 6–8 million escapees. This evacuation is the subject of Irène Némirovsky's *Suite Française*, a novel which might be read as *Party Going's* fictional correlative (just as *The World of Yesterday* might be read as *Pack My Bag's* in the life-writing line). See 'Your Parcels and Letters Depend on the Lines

Behind the Lines', poster, Imperial War Museum Online Collection, <http://www.iwm.org.uk/collections/item/object/32539> (last accessed 27 April 2016); 'Some L.M.S.R. Evacuation Statistics', *The Railway Gazette*, 71.17, 27 October 1939, pp. 559; Marrus, *The Unwanted*, pp. 200, 201.

106. Green, *Party Going*, p. 21.
107. Marina MacKay, *Modernism and World War II* (Cambridge: Cambridge University Press, 2007), p. 93.
108. Green, *Pack My Bag*, p. 207.
109. *Pack My Bag* is widely held to go against the grain as an autobiographical work. Rod Mengham describes the memoir as the 'autobiographical form unlearned' in its resistance to the expectation that an autobiography should aim to provide a clear account of the self. Hentea likewise casts it as an 'autobiography that, in many ways, does not conform to expectations', and further asserts that it is a work 'informed by a wholesale hesitancy about writing and authorship'. See Mengham, *The Idiom of the Time*, p. 63; Hentea, 'A Guilty Self-Portrait', pp. 38, 50.
110. The imperative form of the title *Pack My Bag* is worth noting for its anomalous status alone when positioned within the wider body of Green's oeuvre. Most of his titles strikingly take the gerundive form (*Living, Party Going, Loving, Nothing, Concluding, Doting*) with a small number of other exceptions, none imperative (*Blindness, Caught, Back*). For an attempted interpretation of these titles *en masse*, see John Russell, *Henry Green: Nine Novels and an Unpacked Bag* (New Brunswick, NJ: Rutgers University Press, 1960), pp. 16–17.
111. Green, *Pack My Bag*, p. 5.
112. See Treglown, *Romancing*, p. 107.
113. Ibid., p. 101.
114. Holt's autobiography charts his rise from humble origins. Not unlike Green's, it concerns, in large part, his experiences of the First World War (though Holt was old enough to fight). The style as well as the use of the luggage metaphor in the journey-of-life mode is, in contrast to Green, unremarkable, though the record is interesting on its own terms. See William Holt, *I Haven't Unpacked: An Autobiography* (1939; London: The Book Club, 1942).
115. Green, *Party Going*, p. 18.
116. Henry Green, 'Excursion', in *Surviving: The Uncollected Writings of Henry Green*, ed. Matthew Yorke (London: Harvill-HarperCollins, 1993), pp. 64–74.
117. Cunningham, *British Writers of the Thirties*, p. 112.
118. Cecil Day-Lewis, *A Hope for Poetry* (1934; Oxford: Basil Blackwell, 1936), p. 1. Emphasis added.
119. See C. Northcote Parkinson, *Left Luggage: From Marx to Wilson* (London: John Murray, 1968).
120. Cunningham, *British Writers of the Thirties*, p. 249.
121. Ibid., pp. 9–10.
122. Carol A. Wipf-Miller, 'Fictions of "Going Over": Henry Green and the New Realism', *Twentieth Century Literature* 44.2 (Summer 1998), p. 137. For another interesting discussion of Green and the politics of class identity which delves into ideas of cross-dressing and masquerade, see Peter Hitchcock, 'Passing: Henry Green and Working-Class Identity', *Modern Fiction Studies*, 40.1, Spring 1994, pp. 1–31.
123. Quoted in Hitchcock, 'Passing', p. 6.
124. Green, *Party Going*, p. 25.
125. Ibid., p. 99.
126. Green, 'Mood', in *Surviving*, p. 45. It is believed that this extended story was written around 1926.

127. Clive Hart, 'The Structure and Technique of *Party Going*', *Yearbook of English Studies* 1, 1971, pp. 195–6.
128. Green, *Pack My Bag*, p. 126.
129. Russell, *Henry Green*, p. 5.
130. Sebastian Yorke, 'A Memoir', in *Surviving : The Uncollected Writings of Henry Green*, by Henry Green, ed. Matthew Yorke (London: Harvill-HarperCollins, 1993), pp. 286–302 (p. 299).
131. Ibid., p. 299.
132. Andrew Gibson, *Reading Narrative Discourse: Studies in the Novel from Cervantes to Beckett* (New York: St Martin's Press, 1990), p. 126.
133. Tyrus Miller, *Late Modernism: Politics, Fiction and the Arts Between the World Wars* (Berkeley: University of California Press, 1999), p. 14.
134. Green, *Pack My Bag*, p. 186.

CONCLUSION

'My dear Henry', Aunt Augusta said, 'if you had been a young man I
would have advised you to become a loader. A loader's life is one of
adventure with far more chance of a fortune than you ever have in a
branch bank. I can imagine nothing better for a young man with ambition except perhaps illicit diamond digging . . . '

'Sometimes you shock me, Aunt Augusta', I said, but the statement had
already almost ceased to be true. 'I have never had anything stolen from
my suitcase and I don't even lock it'.

'That is probably your safeguard. No one is going to bother about an
unlocked suitcase. Wordsworth knew a loader who had keys to every
kind of suitcase. There are not many varieties, though he was baffled
once by a Russian one'.[1]

In Graham Greene's *Travels With My Aunt* (1969), the elderly Aunt Augusta
of the title advises her more conservative ex-banker nephew, the novel's narrator, who is later revealed as her son, on the profession of luggage loading.
This novel is, in many ways, a nostalgic homage to an earlier epoch of travel,
and both characters are, in their own ways, somewhat anachronistic. The
septuagenarian Aunt Augusta, a woman who is pointedly shown to travel
light and of an age to number among those first women who carried their
own bags, is shown to cling onto a past full of adventurous escapades. Henry,
on the other hand, attempts to recover a past life that never quite took off

through embarking on a range of belated escapades in her company. I quote the above passage here because it reminds us that luggage and, correspondingly, a portable aesthetic, came to prominence in a literary age both of upheaval and of suspicion. However sour and destructive suspicion is shown to become, it was still the illicit allure of luggage – the cultivation of a collection of symptomatic keys and the bewilderment at the one case which yet resisted, the exhilaration at standing judgement over a locked case and the corresponding exhilaration at unlocked bluffing under scrutiny, the inscribed promise of transgressive discovery and of unsanctioned 'adventure' – that engaged creative attention.

Luggage has, indeed, been central to this exploration of modernist portability and has been encountered in all manner of guises, from shapeless hold-alls and diminutive dispatch cases to colossal wardrobe trunks and intricate Saratogas. The book has also attended to luggage in various conditions and situations: well kept or careworn, basic or elaborately designed, located at home or abroad, empty or overflowing, unassuming or label-smothered, open or closed, lost or found, personal or functional, heavy or lightweight, set in the hall between two journeys or in transit on the journey itself. We have grappled with the remarkable expressive capacity of luggage as well its significatory complexity. Luggage casts forwards and backwards at once. It nods towards an uncertain future, forms a material connection to the past, but, most of all, captures the transitional moment. It implies a departure from the home as well as an inability to fully detach. It exhibits but it also harbours, deceives as much as it exposes, declares nothing as often as everything. It obstructs and it facilitates. It points to dispossession and loss but equally to liberation and experiential abundance. It can mean deprivation, but it can equally mean privileged, moneyed mobility. It generates fantasy and collects memories. It announces solitary movement, but can likewise form the focal point of social interaction and exchange, whether as an object of intrigue, conflict or interrogation. It encapsulates the gigantic potential of the miniature in motion, on the one hand, and the insignificance of the mobilised miniature in the face of gigantic external forces, on the other. It outwardly speaks of life's journey but covertly communicates death's end.

Most intriguingly, luggage identifies a prevailing symbolic form which writers and critics to date have only gone so far as to negatively determine *not* to be a house.[2] In attempting a 'survey, even the freest and loosest, of modern fiction' in 1925, for instance, Woolf describes a rebellious questioning of a literary architectural framework of the kind 'so well constructed and solid in its craftsmanship that it is difficult for the most exacting of critics to see through what chink or crevice decay can creep in'.[3] 'And yet', she adds, 'if life should refuse to live there?'[4] She thus acknowledges a domestic departure – 'Life escapes' – but does not offer an alternative symbolic paradigm.[5] This book takes up where Woolf leaves off here by establishing that alternative paradigm as portable, a portable paradigm capturing life's refusal to live in the house of fiction and calling the integrity of centralised meaning into doubt by virtue of its centrifugal proclivity as well as its emphasis on a decentralised, wide-ranging plurality. 'Is it not the task of the novelist', Woolf goes on to ask, 'to convey this varying, this unknown and uncircumscribed spirit, whatever aberration or complexity it may display, with as little mixture of the alien and external as possible?'[6] Luggage offers the modern novelist a model for the conveyance of the varying, unknown and uncircumscribed spirit in all its aberrations and complexities while, contrary to Woolf's last supposition, *allowing for* a mixture of the 'alien and external', the kind of materialistic approach she sets out to disparage in her essay. Life escapes, yes; but it escapes with certain things, belongings, objects. Luggage draws attention to a materialism which cannot quite be left behind at the house of fiction door, even if this is a kind of materiality which fosters a liberating irregularity, a materiality which does not confine or pin down in the same way. Luggage gives a material form to the escaping spirit, anchoring an aspiration towards total lightness just as the 'extraordinary, irreplaceable' trapeze artist in Franz Kafka's 1921 short story 'First Sorrow' is shown to occupy the luggage rack on 'inevitable' train journeys to performance venues as a 'miserable substitute . . . but nevertheless a substitute' for his usual vertiginous and gravity-defying mode of existence.[7] It is the compromised quality of the modernist escape – the proprietorial underpinnings to its immaterial longings – that this study of portability reveals more than anything else.

Portability is thus never unproblematic, as this book makes clear, but neither is modernism. The contradictions and paradoxes are there from the outset. Indeed, it is telling that portable forms and experiences are often most fully envisioned in the works of those writers with a demonstrably uncomfortable relationship to modernism – Forster, Bowen, Green, for example – as if luggage looms largest for those most attuned to the abiding complications. In many ways, the narrative I recount here is that of intrinsic problems becoming gradually more unavoidable and difficult to ignore. The book, at glance, seems to mimic thus the structure of a conventional plot. My first chapter might be characterised as the *exposition*; I outlined the emerging rhetorical conflict between age-old paradigms of house and case at the turn of the twentieth century and delineated the rise of a portable culture in line with the waning influence of a sedentarist mode and metaphysics. My second chapter approached the *development* of a portable paradigm from the particular angle of gender, while pointing to some of the factors casting that paradigm in a more problematic light. My third chapter considered the *complications*, instigated by the First World War and subsequently aggravated, which came to imbue interwar renderings of portability. My fourth chapter directly addressed the *crisis* and *climax* of the Second World War in examining the fate, not just of fiction, but of the individual in the face of what is construed as an apocalyptic disaster. This is a crude and convenient outline. But it does usefully beg the question of postwar *dénouement*, and I will dwell for the remainder of the conclusion on the status of literary portability after the Second World War.

In surveying the state of mid-century fiction in Britain, Marina MacKay and Lyndsey Stonebridge highlight a 'distinctive aesthetic in which realisms emerge that are written self-consciously "after" modernism', in contrast to the more usual perception of this period's literary output as a 'conservative literature of retreat'.[8] The period, indeed, witnesses new outlines of former realist models through returns to the house of fiction of the *Brideshead Revisited* genre and, as MacKay and Stonebridge further testify, resurrections of the Edwardian family saga. It would appear those 'houses that are sure' that Auden envisaged with envy not long before come to reassert a literary pre-eminence during this period. Yet revisitations are fraught and bloodstained – most obviously, Brideshead has become a military base in Waugh's 1945 novel – while re-enactments of the Edwardian *belle époque* form deliberately unsparing and disenchanted visions.[9] If realism comes back into plain view in the middle of the century, it is a realism no longer vaunting the grandeur of its house, following the disruptions, intrusions and mobilisations of modernity, the decline of the empire and two world wars. '[T]he story we tell here', remark MacKay and Stonebridge, 'describes how the English literary "centre" ceased to understand itself as central', and it would seem that this involved not quite a return to the house of fiction as much as a reappraisal of its diminished status.[10]

By the same token, portable forms and frameworks are never quite the same from the Second World War onwards either. On one level, luggage begins to evolve more quickly towards the kind of homogeneity of backpack and suitcase that Fussell remarked upon, thereby losing some of its semiotic appeal. On another level, portable culture moves ever nearer to that apex of liquidity Bauman described, casting forward to a cosmopolitan, globalised future and, concomitantly, the impossibility of restoring the insularity of a domesticated past. Marcel Duchamp's series of artworks entitled *Bôite-en-valise*, initiated between 1935 and 1941, then developed throughout the 1940s and 1950s, illustrates this sense of a distinctly modernist portability as something bygone. The series consists of boxes containing more than sixty replicated miniatures of Duchamp's former artworks. Of the 300 or so boxes he constructed altogether, he created twenty deluxe editions, in the early 1940s, custom-packed in leather suitcases. Nodding to the renaissance cabinet of curiosities and to Joseph Cornell's boxed assemblages, Duchamp himself saw the *Bôite-en-valise* as a personal portable archive, as he explained to James Johnson Sweeney in a television interview in 1956:

It was a new form of expression for me. Instead of painting something the idea was to reproduce the paintings that I loved so much in miniature. I didn't know how to do it. I thought of a book, but I didn't like that idea. Then I thought of the idea of the box in which all my works would be mounted like a small museum, a portable museum, so to speak, and here it is in this valise.[11]

As portable museum or personal archive, this work of art is a conspicuous 'expression' of the exigencies of a period of dislocation. Duchamp moved from France to the United States, evading the Nazis through disguise, while he was working on his *Bôite-en-valise* – it was at this time that he conceived of the valise itself as a framing device – and, in fact, he carried his materials for the series in a large suitcase. It is thus a project borne of and self-consciously reflecting upon displacement. T. J. Demos, drawing on Theodor Adorno's recognition of the redundancy of the very idea of the house as this was uncomfortably coupled with the simultaneous sense of a need for somewhere to live at this time, makes the following point:

Duchamp's suitcase occupies just such a paradoxical position, revealing the impossible desires for a home in a period of homelessness, for objects when possessions have been lost, and for an independent existence in an era of institutional determination, fascist domination, and exile's desperation.[12]

Yet the *Bôite-en-valise* has also been likened to a 'travelling salesman's sample bag', an alignment I have highlighted before.[13] In its references to the artist and to the refugee, in its acute attention to exact individual detail in miniature, while gesturing at geopolitical displacement on a global scale, in its allusions both to the experimental culture of the avant-garde (particularly, Surrealism and Dadaism) and what Demos calls the 'institutional acculturation' of that experimental art on a commercial level, Duchamp's *Bôite-en-valise* is like a mid-century crystallisation of the multifaceted portable model I have been discussing in this book as a memorial *objet d'art*.[14]

I maintain, in drawing this book to a close, that modernism represents the apotheosis of such a portable model, or what I have described at various points, with a nod to Henry James, as the 'case of fiction'. This is not at all to suggest a declining preoccupation with portability in the postwar era or beyond. If anything, we are more shaped by a portable ethos today than ever before, as the recent phenomenon of 'digital nomadism' makes abundantly clear.[15] In this sense, my conclusion must not be seen as a *dénouement*, but as an opening out and registration of the enduring relevance of literary portability, alongside literary architecture but equally on its own terms. However, the portable culture of today would be better expressed by a smartphone than a suitcase. The latter object communicates a portable aesthetic that is mark-edly modernist. Indeed, in spotlighting the object of the case, both Greene and Duchamp, for example, adopt a backward-looking gaze. (Tellingly, Duchamp dropped the suitcase altogether in his postwar editions of the *Bôite-en-valise* series.) Modernist writing engages with portable culture in an emergent form, and it is in this transitional capacity that luggage so often comes to the fore in a way that is historically distinctive. In other words, if luggage articulates an anti-architectural embrace of this emergent culture, it is also true that the persistent appeal of a domestic ideology is nowhere more forcefully conveyed than in the conception of the case as a temporary, mobile dwelling place, as a home in transit, as the fortress of the modern nomad. The case embodied, and has come to be associated with, the shifting concerns of the modernist era, in transition between solid and liquid modernities, and it is for this reason that it offered such a readily adaptable paradigm, motif and metaphor for its writers.

NOTES

1. Graham Greene, *Travels With My Aunt* (1969; London: Vintage-Random, 1999), p. 67.
2. This is not, of course, to suggest that various key modernist symbols have not been discussed before – we need only think of the motorcar or the mirror, to cite a couple of examples offhand – but that no single defining symbolic form has been identified to replace the house of fiction.
3. Virginia Woolf, 'Modern Fiction' (1925), in *The Essays of Virginia Woolf*, vol. 4, ed. Andrew McNeillie (London: Hogarth Press, 1994), pp. 157, 158.
4. Ibid., pp. 158–9.
5. Ibid., p. 159.
6. Ibid., pp. 160–1.
7. Franz Kafka, 'The First Sorrow', in *Kafka's "The Metamorphosis" and Other Writings*, trans. Volkmar Sander and Daniel Thiesen, ed. Helmuth Kiesel (London: Continuum, 2002), pp. 123, 124.
8. Marina MacKay and Lyndsey Stonebridge, 'Introduction: British Fiction After Modernism', in *British Fiction After Modernism: The Novel at Mid-Century*, ed. Marina MacKay and Lyndsey Stonebridge (Basingstoke: Palgrave-Macmillan, 2007), p. 7.
9. Ibid., p. 8.
10. Ibid., p. 10.
11. Interview reproduced as '"Regions which are not ruled by time and space . . . "', in Marcel Duchamp, *The Essential Writings of Marcel Duchamp*, ed. Michael Sanouillet and Elmer Peterson (London: Thames and Hudson, 1975), p. 136.
12. T. J. Demos, 'Duchamp's *Bôite-en-valise*: Between Institutional Acculturation and Geopolitical Displacement', *Grey Room*, 8, Summer 2002, p. 10. Demos makes some interesting comparisons between Benjamin's lost briefcase and Duchamp's valise throughout this article.
13. James Housefield, 'The Case of Marcel Duchamp: The Artist as Traveller and Geographer', in *Geographies of Modernism: Literatures, Cultures, Spaces*, ed. Peter Brooker and Andrew Thacker (London: Routledge, 2005), p. 108.
14. Demos, 'Duchamp's *Bôite-en-valise*', p. 13.
15. The term 'digital nomadism' was first introduced by Tsugio Makimoto and David

Manners in a book on the subject in 1997, *Digital Nomad*. It has since become something of a buzzword to denote the practice of working remotely, independent of any fixed location and facilitated by technology. Special forms of accommodation, from co-living spaces to subscription-based global housing networks, are also evolving to cater for mobile forms of professional practice. See Tsugio Makimoto and David Manners, *Digital Nomad* (Chichester and New York: Wiley, 1997).

BIBLIOGRAPHY

Allen, Grant, *The Woman Who Did* (1895; Oxford: Oxford University Press, 1995).

Appadurai, Arjun, 'Introduction: Commodities and the Politics of Value', in *The Social Life of Things: Commodities in Cultural Perspective*, ed. Arjun Appadurai (1996; Cambridge: Cambridge University Press, 2011), pp. 3–63.

Ardis, Ann, *New Women, New Novels: Feminism and Early Modernism* (New Brunswick, NJ: Rutgers University Press, 1990).

Arendt, Hannah, *The Jewish Writings*, ed. Jerome Kohn and Ron H. Feldman (New York: Schocken Books, 2007).

Aristarkhova, Irina, *Hospitality of the Matrix: Philosophy, Biomedicine, and Culture* (New York: Columbia University Press, 2012).

Armstrong, Nancy, *Desire and Domestic Fiction: A Political History of the Novel* (1987; Oxford: Oxford University Press, 1989).

Armstrong, Tim, *Modernism, Technology, and the Body: A Cultural Study* (Cambridge: Cambridge University Press, 1998).

Arnold, Matthew, *Selected Poems of Matthew Arnold* (London: Macmillan and Co., 1882).

Ashton, Helen, *Bricks and Mortar* (1932; London: Persephone, 2004).

Auden, W. H., *Collected Poems*, ed. Edward Mendelson (1976; London: Faber, 1991).

Auerbach, Erich, *Mimesis: The Representation of Reality in Western Literature*, trans. Willard R. Trask (Princeton: Princeton University Press, 2003).

Austen, Jane, *Mansfield Park*, ed. Tony Tanner (1814; Harmondsworth: Penguin, 1985).

Bachelard, Gaston, *The Poetics of Space*, trans. Maria Jolas (1958; New York: Orion, 1964).

Bailkin, Jordanna, *The Culture of Property: The Crisis of Liberalism in Modern Britain* (Chicago: University of Chicago Press, 2004).

Baring, Maurice, *Have You Anything to Declare? A Notebook With Commentaries* (1936; London: Heinemann, 1951).

Basu, Paul and Simon Coleman, 'Introduction: Migrant Worlds, Material Cultures', *Mobilities*, 3.3, 2008, pp. 313–30.

Bauman, Zygmunt, *Liquid Modernity* (Cambridge: Polity, 2012).

Beerbohm, Max, 'A Defence of Cosmetics', *The Yellow Book: An Illustrated Quarterly*, 1, April 1894, pp. 65–82.

—— *Yet Again* (1909; London: Heinemann, 1928).

Bénéjam, Valérie, 'Passports, Ports, and Portraits: Joyce's Harbouring of Irish Identity', *Genetic Joyce Studies* 5, Spring 2005, <http://www.geneticjoycestudies.org/GJS5/GJS5Benejam.htm> (last accessed 28 January 2016).

Benjamin, Walter, *Illuminations: Essays and Reflections*, trans. Harry Zorn, ed. Hannah Arendt (1968; London: Pimlico, 1999).

Bennett, Andrew and Nicholas Royle, *Elizabeth Bowen and the Dissolution of the Novel: Still Lives* (Basingstoke: Macmillan, 1995).

Berman, Marshall, *All That Is Solid Melts into Air: The Experience of Modernity* (New York: Simon and Schuster, 1982).

Bianchi, Emanuela, 'Receptacle/*Chōra*: Figuring the Errant Feminine in Plato's *Timaeus*', *Hypatia*, 21.4, Fall 2006, pp. 124–46.

The Bible: Authorized King James Version, ed. Robert Carroll and Stephen Prickett (1611; Oxford: Oxford University Press, 1998).

Bissell, David, 'Conceptualising Differently-Mobile Passengers: Geographies of Everyday Encumbrance in the Railway Station', *Social and Cultural Geography*, 10.2, 2009, pp. 173–95.

Bjorhovde, Gerd, *Rebellious Structures: Women Writers and the Crisis of the Novel 1880–1900* (Oslo: Norwegian University Press, 1987).

Bluemel, Kristin, *Experimenting on the Borders of Modernism: Dorothy Richardson's Pilgrimage* (Athens: University of Georgia Press, 1997).

Bly, Nelly [*sic*], *Around the World in Seventy-Two Days* (1890; Rockville, MD: Wildside, 2009).

Bolton, Jonathan, 'Mid-Term Autobiography and the Second World War', *Journal of Modern Literature*, 30.1, Fall 2006, pp. 155–72.

Boone, Joseph Allen, *Tradition Counter Tradition: Love and the Form of Fiction* (Chicago: University of Chicago Press, 1987).

Bowen, Elizabeth, *Afterthought: Pieces About Writing* (London: Longmans, 1962).

—— *Bowen's Court* (1942; New York: The Ecco Press, 1979).

—— *Collected Impressions* (1950; London: Longmans, 1951).

—— *The Death of the Heart* (1938; London: Vintage-Random, 1998).

—— *Eva Trout or Changing Scenes* (1968; Harmondsworth: Penguin, 1987).

—— *Friends and Relations* (1931; London: Penguin, 1946).

—— *The Heat of the Day* (1949; London: Jonathan Cape, 1982).

—— *The Hotel* (1927; Harmondsworth: Penguin, 1984).

—— *The House in Paris* (1935; London: Vintage-Random, 1988).

—— *The Last September* (1929; London: Vintage-Random, 1998).

—— *People, Places, Things*, ed. Allan Hepburn (Edinburgh: Edinburgh University Press, 2008).

—— *Pictures and Conversations* (London: Allen Lane, 1975).

—— *To the North* (1932; Harmondsworth: Penguin, 1986).

Bowlby, Rachel, *Carried Away: The Invention of Modern Shopping* (London: Faber, 2000).

—— *Just Looking: Consumer Culture in Dreiser, Gissing and Zola* (New York: Methuen, 1985).

—— *Still Crazy After All These Years: Women, Writing and Psychoanalysis* (London: Routledge, 1992).

Boyd, Brian, *Vladimir Nabokov: The Russian Years* (Princeton: Princeton University Press, 1990).

Bradbury, Malcolm, 'The Cities of Modernism', in *Modernism: A Guide to European Literature 1890–1930*, ed. Malcolm Bradbury and James McFarlane (1976; Harmondsworth: Penguin, 1991), pp. 96–104.

Bradbury, Malcolm and James McFarlane, 'The Name and Nature of Modernism', in *Modernism: A Guide to European Literature 1890–1930*, ed. Malcolm Bradbury and James McFarlane (1976; Harmondsworth: Penguin, 1991), pp. 19–55.

Bradbury, Nicola, 'Henry James and Britain', in *A Companion to Henry James*, ed. Greg W. Zacharias (Chichester: Wiley-Blackwell, 2008), pp. 400–15.

Briganti, Chiara and Kathy Mezei, *Domestic Modernism, the Interwar Novel and E. H. Young* (Aldershot, Hampshire: Ashgate, 2006).

—— 'Reading the House: A Literary Perspective', *Signs*, 27.3, Spring 2002, pp. 837–46.

'British Railways', advertisement, *The Times*, 8 October 1941, p. 3.

Broch, Hermann, *The Death of Virgil*, trans. Jean Starr Untermeyer (1945; Oxford: Oxford University Press, 1983).

Broe, Mary Lynn and Angela Ingram (eds), *Women's Writing in Exile* (Chapel Hill: University of North Carolina Press, 1989).

Bronfen, Elisabeth, *Dorothy Richardson's Art of Memory: Space, Identity, Text*, trans. Victoria Appelbe (Manchester: Manchester University Press, 1999).

Brown, Bill, 'Thing Theory', *Critical Inquiry*, 28.1, Autumn 2001, pp. 1–22.

—— 'The Secret Life of Things (Virginia Woolf and the Matter of Modernism)', *Modernism/Modernity*, 6.2, April 1999, pp. 1–28.

Bunyan, John, *The Pilgrim's Progress* (1678; Oxford: Oxford University Press, 2003).

Burgan, Mary, *Illness, Gender and Writing: The Case of Katherine Mansfield* (Baltimore: Johns Hopkins University Press, 1994).

Butler, Judith, *Precarious Life: The Powers of Mourning and Violence* (London and New York: Verso, 2006).

'By Way of Introduction', *The Bag, Portmanteau and Umbrella Trader and Fancy Leather Goods and Athletic Trades Review*, 1.1, June 1907, pp. 3–4.

Byron, Robert, *The Road to Oxiana* (1937; London: Penguin, 2007).

Callisthenes, 'The Impedimenta of Travel', *The Times*, 29 December 1923, p. 6.

Caplan, Ralph, 'Design for Travel(ers)', in *Bon Voyage: Designs for Travel*, ed. Nancy Aakre (New York: Cooper-Hewitt Museum and The Smithsonian Institution's National Museum of Design, 1986), pp. 95–127.

Carswell, Catherine, *Open the Door!* (1920; Edinburgh: Canongate, 1996).

Carter, Angela, *The Bloody Chamber* (Harmondsworth: Penguin, 1979).

Carter, Ian, 'The Lady in the Trunk: Railways, Gender and Crime Fiction', *The Journal of Transport History*, 23.1, March 2002, pp. 46–59.

'Central Criminal Court, July 28', *The Times*, 29 July 1905, p. 4.

Chalk, Bridget T., *Modernism and Mobility: The Passport and Cosmopolitan Experience* (New York: Palgrave Macmillan, 2014).

Chapman, Mary, *Making Noise, Making News: Suffrage Print Culture and U.S. Modernism* (Oxford and New York: Oxford University Press, 2014).

Chesterton, G. K., *G. K. Chesterton at the Daily News: Literature, Liberalism and Revolution, 1901–1913*, ed. Julia Stapleton (London: Pickering & Chatto, 2012).

Childs, Peter, *Modernism and the Post-Colonial: Literature and Empire 1885–1930* (London: Continuum, 2007).

Coates, John, *Social Discontinuity in the Novels of Elizabeth Bowen: The Conservative Quest* (Lewiston, NY: The Edwin Mellen Press, 1998).

Cohen, Deborah, *Household Gods: The British and Their Possessions* (New Haven, CT: Yale University Press, 2006).

Connolly, Cyril, *Enemies of Promise* (1938; London: André Deutsch, 1996).

—— *The Rock Pool* (1936; Oxford: Oxford University Press, 1981).

'Continental Notes: Contrasts with the English Trade by Our Special Correspondent', *The Bag Portmanteau and Umbrella Trader and Fancy Leather Goods and Athletic Trades Review*, 2.21, February 1909, p. 18.

Cooper, John Xiros, *Modernism and the Culture of Market Society* (Cambridge: Cambridge University Press, 2004).

Corcoran, Neil, *Elizabeth Bowen: The Enforced Return* (Oxford: Oxford University Press, 2004).

Cowley, Malcolm, *Exile's Return: A Literary Odyssey of the 1920s* (1934; New York: Viking, 1956).

Cox, Caroline, *Bags: An Illustrated History* (London: Aurum, 2007).

Cresswell, Tim, *On the Move: Mobility in the Modern Western World* (New York: Routledge, 2006).

Cunningham, Gail, *The New Woman and the Victorian Novel* (London: Macmillan, 1978).

Cunningham, Valentine, *British Writers of the Thirties* (Oxford: Oxford University Press, 1988).

Dangerfield, George, *The Strange Death of Liberal England* (1935; New York: Capricorn, 1961).

D'Arcy, Ella, 'The Pleasure–Pilgrim', *The Yellow Book: An Illustrated Quarterly* 5, April 1895, pp. 34–67.

Day-Lewis, Cecil, *A Hope for Poetry* (1934; Oxford: Basil Blackwell, 1936).

De Waal, Edmund, *The Hare With Amber Eyes: A Hidden Heritance* (2010; London: Vintage, 2011).

'The Deadly Hand-bag', *The Bag Portmanteau and Umbrella Trader and Fancy Leather Goods and Athletic Trades Review*, 11.453, July 1917, p. 25.

DeKoven, Marianne, 'Modernism and Gender', *The Cambridge Companion to Modernism*, ed. Michael Levenson (Cambridge: Cambridge University Press, 1999), pp. 174–93.

—— 'Gendered Doubleness and the "Origins" of Modernist Form', *Tulsa Studies in Women's Literature*, 8.1, Spring 1989, pp. 19–42.

Demos, T. J., 'Duchamp's *Bôite-en-valise*: Between Institutional Acculturation and Geopolitical Displacement', *Grey Room*, 8, Summer 2002, pp. 6–37.

Derrida, Jacques, *Of Hospitality: Anne Dufourmantelle Invites Jacques Derrida to Respond*, trans. Rachel Bowlby (Stanford: Stanford University Press, 2000).

Dickens, Charles, *Bleak House* (1852–3; London: Vintage-Random, 2008).

—— *The Christmas Stories*, ed. Ruth Glancy (London: Everyman-Dent, 1996).

—— 'A Preliminary Word', *Household Words*, 1, 30 March 1850, pp. 1–2.

Dickens, Charles, with Charles Allston Collins, Arthur Locker, John Oxenford and Julia Cecilia Stretton, *Somebody's Luggage*, ed. Melissa Valiska Gregory and Melisa Klimaszewski (1862; London: Hesperus, 2006).

Dolin, Tim, *Mistress of the House: Women of Property in the Victorian Novel* (Aldershot: Ashgate, 1997).

'Donna Quixote', *Punch* 106, 28 April 1894, p. 195.

Duchamp, Marcel, *The Essential Writings of Marcel Duchamp*, ed. Michael Sanouillet and Elmer Peterson (London: Thames and Hudson, 1975).

Duckworth, Alistair M., *Howards End: E. M. Forster's House of Fiction* (New York: Twayne, 1992).

Dunbar, Pamela, *Radical Mansfield: Double Discourse in Katherine Mansfield's Short Stories* (Basingstoke: Macmillan, 1997).

DuPlessis, Rachel Blau, *Writing Beyond the Ending: Narrative Strategies of Twentieth-Century Women Writers* (Bloomington: Indiana University Press, 1985).

Durrell, Lawrence, *The Black Book* (1938. New York: Dutton, 1963).

Eagleton, Terry, *Exiles and Émigrés* (London: Chatto and Windus, 1970).

Edel, Leon, 'Dorothy Richardson, 1882–1957', *Modern Fiction Studies* 4, Winter 1958, pp. 165–8.

Edelstein, Linda and Pat Morse, *Antique Trunks: Identification and Price Guide* (Iola, WI: Krause, 2003).

'Editorial', *The Bag, Portmanteau and Umbrella Trader and Fancy Leather Goods and Athletic Trades Review*, 2.24, April 1909, p. 3.

'Editorial', *Transport and Travel Monthly (Formerly The Railway and Travel Monthly)*, 20, April 1920, p. 215.

Edson, Laurie, *Reading Relationally: Postmodern Perspectives on Literature and Art* (Ann Arbor: University of Michigan Press, 2000).

Egerton, George, *Keynotes; Discords* (1893–4; London: Virago, 1983).

Eliot, T. S., *The Waste Land*, in *The Norton Anthology of Poetry*, ed. Margaret Ferguson, Mary Jo Salter and Jon Stallworthy (New York: Norton, 1996), pp. 1236–48.

Ellmann, Maud, *Elizabeth Bowen: The Shadow Across the Page* (Edinburgh: Edinburgh University Press, 2003).

Ellmann, Richard, *James Joyce* (New York, Oxford and Toronto: Oxford University Press, 1982).

—— *A Long the Riverrun: Selected Essays* (Harmondsworth: Penguin, 1989).

Esty, Jed, *A Shrinking Island: Modernism and National Culture in England* (Princeton: Princeton University Press, 2004).

Felski, Rita, *The Gender of Modernity* (Cambridge, MA: Harvard University Press, 1995).

Fernihough, Anne, 'Introduction', in *The Cambridge Companion to D. H. Lawrence*, ed. Anne Fernihough (Cambridge: Cambridge University Press, 2001), pp. 1–12.

Finney, Gail, 'Ibsen and Feminism', in *The Cambridge Companion to Ibsen*, ed. James McFarlane (Cambridge: Cambridge University Press, 1994), pp. 89–105.

Fischer, Sandra K., 'Isabel Archer and the Enclosed Chamber: A Phenomenological Reading', *The Henry James Review*, 7.2–3, Winter–Spring 1986, pp. 48–58.

Fisher, Elizabeth, *Woman's Creation: Sexual Evolution and the Shaping of Society* (New York: McGraw Hill, 1979).

Fittko, Lisa, 'The Story of Old Benjamin', in *The Arcades Project*, by Walter Benjamin, trans. Howard Eiland and Kevin McLaughlin, prepared on the basis of the German volume, ed. by Rolf Tiedemann (Cambridge, MA and London: Belknap-Harvard, 1999), pp. 946–54.

Ford, Ford Madox, *The Good Soldier* (1915; Manchester: Carcanet Press, 1996).

Forster, E. M., *Albergo Empedocle and Other Writings by E. M. Forster*, ed. George H. Thomson (New York: Liveright, 1971).

—— *The Feminine Note in Literature: A Hitherto Unpublished Manuscript*, ed. George Piggford (London: Cecil Woolf, 2001).

—— *Howards End* (1910; New York: Signet-Penguin, 1992).

—— *A Room with a View* (1908; Harmondsworth: Penguin, 1978).

—— *Two Cheers for Democracy* (London: Edward Arnold, 1951).

Frank, Ellen Eve, *Literary Architecture: Essays Towards a Tradition: Walter Pater, Gerard Manley Hopkins, Marcel Proust, Henry James* (Berkeley: University of California Press, 1979).

Freedgood, Elaine, *The Ideas in Things: Fugitive Meaning in the Victorian Novel* (Chicago: University of Chicago Press, 2006).

Freud, Sigmund, *Beyond the Pleasure Principle and Other Writings*, trans. John Reddick, ed. Adam Phillips (1920; London: Penguin, 2003).

—— *The Interpretation of Dreams*, trans. James Strachey, ed. James Strachey, assisted by Alan Tyson (1900; London: Penguin, 1991).

—— *Fragment of an Analysis of a Case of Hysteria ('Dora')* in *Case Histories 1: 'Dora' and 'Little Hans'*, trans. Alix and James Strachey, ed. James Strachey, assisted by Angela Richards and Alan Tyson (London: Penguin, 1977), pp. 29–164.

Fussell, Paul, *Abroad: British Literary Traveling Between the Wars* (New York: Oxford University Press, 1980).

—— 'Bourgeois Travel: Techniques and Artifacts', in *Bon Voyage: Designs for Travel*, ed. Nancy Aakre (New York: Cooper-Hewitt Museum and The Smithsonian Institution's National Museum of Design, 1986), pp. 55–94.

Galsworthy, John, *The Country House* (1907; London: Penguin, 1943).

—— *The Man of Property* (1906; London: Heinemann, 1953).

Gay, Peter, *The Bourgeois Experience: Victoria to Freud*, vol. 1 (New York: Oxford University Press, 1984).

Ghilchik, D. I., cartoon, *Punch*, 171, 29 September 1926, p. 362.

Gibson, Andrew, *Reading Narrative Discourse: Studies in the Novel from Cervantes to Beckett* (New York: St Martin's Press, 1990).

Gibson, Mary Ellis, 'Illegitimate Order: Cosmopolitanism and Liberalism in Forster's *Howards End*', *English Literature in Transition*, 28.2, 1985, pp. 106–23.

Ginsburg, Mirra, 'Introduction', in *We*, by Yevgeny Zamyatin, trans. Mirra Ginsburg (1924; New York: EOS-HarperCollins, 1999), pp. v–xx.

Gissing, George, *Human Odds and Ends: Stories and Sketches* (1898; New York and London: Garland, 1977).

Glendinning, Victoria, *Elizabeth Bowen: Portrait of a Writer* (1977; London: Phoenix, 1993).

Glikin, Gloria, 'Dorothy M. Richardson: The Personal "Pilgrimage"', *PMLA*, 78.5, December 1963, pp. 586–600.

'Going Home: (Three Variations on a Holiday Theme.)', *Punch*, 180, 14 January 1931, p. 52.

Goldman, Jane, 'Forster and Women', in *The Cambridge Companion to E. M. Forster*, ed. David Bradshaw (Cambridge: Cambridge University Press, 2007), pp. 120–37.

Grand, Sarah, 'The Undefinable', in *A New Woman Reader: Fiction, Articles, Drama of the 1890s*, ed. Carolyn Christensen Nelson (Peterborough, ON: Broadview Press, 2001), pp. 35–51.

Grant, Charlotte, 'Reading the House of Fiction: From Object to Interior 1720–1920', *Home Cultures*, 2.3, 2005, pp. 233–50.

Grave, Charles, 'Diplomatic Exchanges (Unofficial)', cartoon, *Punch*, 191, 9 September 1936, p. 283.

Graves, Robert and Alan Hodge, *The Long Week-End: A Social History of Great Britain 1918–1939* (1940; London: Faber, 1950).

Green, Henry, *Pack My Bag* (1940; London: Hogarth Press, 1952).

—— *Party Going* (1939; London: Vintage-Random, 2000).

—— *Surviving: The Uncollected Writings of Henry Green*, ed. Matthew Yorke (London: Harvill-HarperCollins, 1993).

Green, V. M., 'Smiling at the Porter', *LMS Railway Magazine*, 2.9, September 1925, p. 279.

Greene, Graham, *The Lawless Roads* (1939; London: Vintage-Random, 2002).

—— *The Lost Childhood and Other Essays* (London: Eyre and Spottiswoode, 1951).

—— *The Ministry of Fear* (1943; London: Heinemann and Bodley Head, 1973).

—— *The Power and the Glory* (1940; Harmondsworth: Penguin, 1983).

—— *Travels With My Aunt* (1969; London: Vintage-Random, 1999).

Gulshan, Helenka, *Vintage Luggage* (London: Phillip Wilson, 1998).

Guthrie, Anstey, 'Bombs for Women!' *Punch*, 135, 8 July 1908, p. 26.

Hamilton, Cicely, *Marriage as a Trade* (1909; Detroit: Singing Tree Press, 1971).

Hannam, Kevin, Mimi Sheller and John Urry, 'Editorial: Mobilities, Immobilities and Moorings', *Mobilities*, 1.1, 2006, pp. 1–22.

Hapgood, Lynne, 'Transforming the Victorian', in *Outside Modernism: In Pursuit of the English Novel 1900–1930*, ed. Lynne Hapgood and Nancy Paxton (Basingstoke: Macmillan, 2000), pp. 22–39.

'The Happy Traveller', *The Times*, 28 December 1940, p. 5.

Harper, Judith E., *Susan B. Anthony: A Biographical Companion* (Santa Barbara: ABC-CLIO, 1998).

Hart, Clive, 'The Structure and Technique of *Party Going*', *Yearbook of English Studies* 1, 1971, pp. 185–99.

Harvey, W. J., '*Bleak House*: The Double Narrative', in *Dickens: Bleak House – A Casebook*, ed. A. E. Dyson (Basingstoke: Macmillan, 1977), pp. 224–34.

Haslam, Watkin, 'Transport in the English Novel', *LMS Railway Magazine*, 7.4, April 1930, pp. 84–5.

Heffermehl, Karin Bruzelius, 'The Status of Women in Norway', *The American Journal of Comparative Law* 20.4, Autumn 1972, pp. 630–46.

Heidegger, Martin, *Poetry, Language, Thought*, trans. Albert Hofstadter (1971; New York: Perennial-Harper, 2001).

Hemingway, Ernest, *A Moveable Feast* (1964; New York: Scribner's, 2009).

Hentea, Marius, 'A Guilty Self-Portrait: Henry Green's *Pack My Bag*', *The Cambridge Quarterly*, 40.1, 2011, pp. 36–52.

Hildebidle, John, *Five Irish Writers: The Errand of Keeping Alive* (Cambridge, MA: Harvard University Press, 1989).

Hitchcock, Peter, 'Passing: Henry Green and Working-Class Identity', *Modern Fiction Studies*, 40.1, Spring 1994, pp. 1–31.

Holcombe, Lee, *Wives and Property: Reform of the Married Women's Property Law in Nineteenth-Century England* (Toronto and Buffalo: University of Toronto Press, 1983).

Holt, William, *I Haven't Unpacked: An Autobiography* (1939; London: The Book Club, 1942).

Hotchner, A. E., 'Don't Touch "A Moveable Feast"', *The New York Times*, 19 July 2009, <http://www.nytimes.com/2009/07/20/opinion/20hotchner.html?_r=1> (last accessed 27 January 2016).

Housefield, James, 'The Case of Marcel Duchamp: The Artist as Traveller and Geographer', in *Geographies of Modernism: Literatures, Cultures, Spaces*, ed. Peter Brooker and Andrew Thacker (London: Routledge, 2005), pp. 99–111.

Hueffer, Ford Madox, *The Critical Attitude* (London: Duckworth, 1911).

Huxley, Aldous, *Crome Yellow* (1921; London: Vintage-Random, 2004).

—— *Point Counter Point* (1928; London: Chatto and Windus, 1934).

Hynes, Samuel, *The Auden Generation: Literature and Politics in England in the 1930s* (London: Faber, 1979).

Ibsen, Henrik, *Four Major Plays: A Doll's House, Ghosts, Hedda Gabler, The Master Builder*, trans. James McFarlane and Jens Arup, with an introduction by James McFarlane (Oxford and New York: Oxford University Press, 1998).

Isherwood, Christopher, *Goodbye to Berlin* (1939; London: Minerva Press, 1989).

—— *Lions and Shadows: An Education in the Twenties* (1938; London: Methuen, 1979).

—— *Mr Norris Changes Trains* (1935; London: Hogarth Press, 1969).

James, Henry, *The Critical Muse: Selected Literary Criticism*, ed. Roger Gard (Harmondsworth: Penguin, 1987).

—— *The Portrait of a Lady* (1881; London: Penguin, 1997).

—— *The Letters of Henry James*, vol. 2, ed. Leon Edel (Cambridge, MA: Belknap-Harvard University Press, 1975).

John, Angela V., 'Men Manners, and Militancy: Literary Men and Women's Suffrage', in *The Men's Share?: Masculinities, Male Support and Women's Suffrage in Britain, 1890–1920*, ed. Claire Eustance and Angela V. John (London: Routledge, 1997), pp. 88–109.

Joyce, James, *Letters of James Joyce*, vol. 1, ed. Stuart Gilbert (New York: Viking Press, 1957).

—— *Ulysses*, ed. Jeri Johnson (Oxford: Oxford University Press, 1998).

Jung, Carl, *Memories, Dreams, Reflections*, trans. Richard and Clara Winston, ed. Aniela Jaffé (1963; London: Flamingo, 1990).

Kafka, Franz, *Kafka's 'The Metamorphosis' and Other Writings*, trans. Volkmar Sander and Daniel Thiesen, ed. Helmuth Kiesel (London: Continuum, 2002).

Kaplan, Caren, *Questions of Travel: Postmodern Discourses of Displacement* (Durham, NC: Duke University Press, 1996).

Kaplan, Sydney Janet, *Feminine Consciousness in the Modern British Novel* (Urbana: University of Illinois Press, 1975).

Keats, John, *The Letters of John Keats 1814–1821*, vol. 2, ed. Hyder Edward Rollins (Cambridge: Cambridge University Press, 1958).

Kenney Jr, Edwin J., *Elizabeth Bowen* (Lewisburg: Bucknell University Press, 1975).

Kermode, Frank, *The Genesis of Secrecy: On the Interpretation of Narrative* (Cambridge, MA: Harvard University Press, 1980).

Kress, Jill M., *The Figure of Consciousness: William James, Henry James and Edith Wharton* (New York: Routledge, 2002).

Kristeva, Julia, 'Revolution in Poetic Language', in *The Kristeva Reader*, ed. Toril Moi (New York: Columbia University Press, 1986), pp. 89–136.

'The Lady Guide and the Tory Tourist', cartoon, *Fun*, 49.1249, 17 April 1889, p. 167.

Lakoff, George and Mark Johnson, *Metaphors We Live By* (Chicago: University of Chicago Press, 1980).

Langland, Elizabeth, 'Gesturing Towards an Open Space: Gender, Form and Language in *Howards End*', in *E. M. Forster*, ed. Jeremy Tambling (London: Palgrave-Macmillan, 1995), pp. 81–99.

Lapierre, Alexandra, 'Foreword' in *Women Travelers: A Century of Trailblazing Adventures*, by Christel Mouchard, trans. Deke Dusinberre (Paris: Flammarion, 2007), pp. 4–5.

Lawrence, D. H., *Lady Chatterley's Lover* (1928; Harmondsworth: Penguin, 1994).

—— *Selected Essays* (Harmondsworth: Penguin, 1950).

—— *Women in Love* (1920; Harmondsworth: Penguin, 1979).

Lawrence, Karen, '"Twenty pockets aren't enough for their lies": Pocketed Objects as Props for Bloom's Masculinity in *Ulysses*', in *Masculinities in Joyce: Postcolonial Constructions*, ed. Christine van Boheemen-Saaf and Colleen Lamos (Amsterdam, Netherlands and Atlanta: Rodopi, 2001), pp. 163–76.

Le Guin, Ursula K., *Dancing at the Edge of the World: Thoughts on Words, Women, Places* (New York: Grove Press, 1989).

Ledger, Sally, *The New Woman: Fiction and Feminism at the Fin De Siècle* (Manchester: Manchester University Press, 1997).

Lee, Hermione, *Virginia Woolf* (London: Vintage-Random, 1997).

Léonforte, Pierre, '100 Legendary Trunks', in *Louis Vuitton: 100 Legendary Trunks*, by Pierre Léonforte, Éric Pujalet-Plaà with the collaboration of Florence Lesché and Marie Wurry, trans. Bruce Waille (New York: Abrams, 2010), pp. 21–386.

Levenson, Michael, *Modernism and the Fate of Individuality: Character and Novelistic Form from Conrad to Woolf* (Cambridge: Cambridge University Press, 1991).

Levin, Harry, *Refractions: Essays in Comparative Literature* (New York: Oxford University Press, 1966).

Levine, Karen, *Hana's Suitcase: A True Story* (London: Evans, 2003).

Lewis, Wyndham, 'Manifesto – 1', *BLAST*, 1, 20 June 1914, pp. 11–28.

Light, Alison, *Forever England: Femininity, Literature and Conservatism Between the Wars* (London: Routledge, 1991).

Lowe, Emily, *Unprotected Females in Norway; Or, The Pleasantest Way of Travelling There, Passing Through Denmark and Sweden* (London and New York: G. Routledge & Co., 1857).

Lukàcs, Georg, *The Theory of the Novel: A Historical-Philosophical Essay on the Forms of Great Epic Literature*, trans. Anna Bostock (1916; London: Merlin, 2006).

Lukacs, John, 'The Bourgeois Interior: Why the Most Maligned Characteristic of the Modern Age May Yet Be Seen as its Most Precious Asset', *American Scholar*, 39.4, Autumn 1970, pp. 616–30.

'Lux', advertisement, *The Times*, 18 August 1927, p. 9.

Macaulay, Rose, *Dangerous Ages* (London: W. Collins, 1921).

—— '[During the Second World War]', ERM 8[15 (1)], Papers of Rose Macaulay, The Wren Library, Trinity College, University of Cambridge.

—— 'Miss Anstruther's Letters', in *London Calling*, ed. Storm Jameson (New York: Harper and Brothers, 1942), pp. 299–308.

—— '[Miss Anstruther's Letters, Corrected Proof]', ERM 5[4 (1–10)], Papers of Rose Macaulay, The Wren Library, Trinity College, University of Cambridge.

Machlan, Elizabeth Boyle, '"There are plenty of houses": Architecture and Genre in *The Portrait of a Lady*', *Studies in the Novel*, 37.4, Winter 2005, pp. 394–411.

MacKay, Marina, '"Is your journey really necessary?": Going Nowhere in Late Modernist London', *PMLA*, 124.5, October 2009, pp. 1600–13.

—— *Modernism and World War II* (Cambridge: Cambridge University Press, 2007).

MacKay, Marina and Lyndsey Stonebridge, 'Introduction: British Fiction After Modernism', in *British Fiction After Modernism: The Novel at Mid-Century*, ed. Marina MacKay and Lyndsey Stonebridge (Basingstoke: Palgrave-Macmillan, 2007), pp. 1–16.

McLaughlin, Kevin, 'Losing One's Place: Displacement and Domesticity in Dickens's *Bleak House*', *MLN*, 108.5, December 1993, pp. 875–90.

Maines, Rachel P., *The Technology of Orgasm: 'Hysteria', the Vibrator, and Women's Sexual Satisfaction* (Baltimore: Johns Hopkins University Press, 1999).

Makimoto, Tsugio and David Manners, *Digital Nomad* (Chichester and New York: Wiley, 1997).

Mann, Erika and Klaus, *Escape to Life* (Boston: Houghton Mifflin Company, 1939).

Mansfield, Katherine, *Collected Stories of Katherine Mansfield* (1945; London: Constable, 1980).

—— *The Journal of Katherine Mansfield*, ed. John Middleton Murry (1927; London: Constable, 1954).

—— *Novels and Novelists*, ed. John Middleton Murry (London: Constable and Company Limited, 1930).

Mao, Douglas, *Solid Objects: Modernism and the Test of Production* (Princeton: Princeton University Press, 1998).

'Mark Cross', advertisement, *The Times*, 27 March 1924, p. 11.

Marrus, Michael R., *The Unwanted: European Refugees from the First World War Through the Cold War* (Philadelphia: Temple University Press, 2002).

Medalie, David, *E. M. Forster's Modernism* (Basingstoke: Palgrave-Macmillan, 2002).

Mengham, Rod, *The Idiom of the Time: The Writings of Henry Green* (Cambridge: Cambridge University Press, 1982).

Mertus, Julie, Jasmina Tesanovic, Habiba Metikos and Rada Boric (eds), *The Suitcase: Refugee Voices from Bosnia and Croatia*, trans. Jelica Todosijevic (Berkeley: University of California Press, 1997).

Miller, Jane Eldridge, *Rebel Women: Feminism, Modernism and the Edwardian Novel* (London: Virago, 1994).

Miller, Tyrus, *Late Modernism: Politics, Fiction and the Arts Between the World Wars* (Berkeley: University of California Press, 1999).

Millett, Kate, *Sexual Politics* (London: Hart-Davis, 1971).

Mirrlees, Hope, *Paris: A Poem* (London: Hogarth Press, 1919).

'Montre-moi tes bagages et je te dirai qui tu es', advertisement, reprinted in *Louis Vuitton: 100 Legendary Trunks*, by Pierre Léonforte, Éric Pujalet-Plaà with the collaboration of Florence Lesché and Marie Wurry, trans. Bruce Waille (New York: Abrams, 2010), p. 364.

Moore, George, *Esther Waters* (1894; London: William Heinemann, 1932).

Moretti, Franco, *Signs Taken for Wonders*, trans. Susan Fischer, David Forgacs and David Miller (London: Verso, 1983).

Morrow, George, 'The Spread of Tango: Arrest of a Militant Suffragette', cartoon, *Punch*, 145, 26 November 1913, p. 458.

'M.P.A. Portable Sets', advertisement, *The Times*, 25 September 1926, p. 8.

Nabokov, Vladimir, *The Gift*, trans. Michael Scammell and Dmitri Nabokov (1938; London: Penguin, 2001).

—— *The Real Life of Sebastian Knight* (1941; London: Penguin, 1964).

Némirovsky, Irène, *Suite Française* (Paris: Denöel, 2004).

Northcote Parkinson, C., *Left Luggage: From Marx to Wilson* (London: John Murray, 1968).

Nunokawa, Jeff, *The Afterlife of Property: Domestic Security and the Victorian Novel* (Princeton: Princeton University Press, 1994).

Orwell, George, *Coming Up for Air* (1939; Harmondsworth: Penguin, 1976).

—— *The Collected Essays, Journalism and Letters of George Orwell*, vol.1, ed. Sonia Orwell and Ian Angus (London: Secker and Warburg, 1968).

Parkins, Wendy, *Mobility and Modernity in Women's Novels, 1850s–1930s: Women Moving Dangerously* (Basingstoke and New York: Palgrave Macmillan, 2009).

—— 'Moving Dangerously: Mobility and the Modern Woman', *Tulsa Studies in Women's Literature*, 20.1, Spring 2001, pp. 77–92.

Parks, Tim, 'Introduction', in *Party Going*, by Henry Green (1939; London: Vintage-Random, 2000), pp. v–xv.

Parrinder, Patrick, *Nation and Novel: The English Novel from its Origins to the Present* (Oxford: Oxford University Press, 2006).

Pater, Walter, *Appreciations: With an Essay on Style* (1889; London: Macmillan, 1907).

Peat, Alexandra, *Travel and Modernist Literature: Sacred and Ethical Journeys* (New York: Routledge, 2011).

Peripatetus, 'Current Trade Topics', *The Bag, Portmanteau and Umbrella Trader and Fancy Leather Goods and Athletic Trades Review*, 13.511, August 1919, p. 16.

—— 'London Letter', *The Bag, Portmanteau and Umbrella Trader and Fancy Leather Goods and Athletic Trades Review*, 4.89, July 1910, p. 8.

Perry, Ruth, *Novel Relations: The Transformation of Kinship in English Literature and Culture, 1748–1818* (Cambridge: Cambridge University Press, 2004).

Plotz, John, *Portable Property: Victorian Culture on the Move* (Princeton and Oxford: Princeton University Press, 2008).

Podnieks, Elizabeth, 'The Ultimate Astonisher: Dorothy Richardson's "Pilgrimage"', *Frontiers: A Journal of Women Studies* 14.3, 1994, pp. 67–94.

Pollock, Griselda, *Vision and Difference: Femininity, Feminism and Histories of Art* (London: Routledge, 1988).

Potter, Rachel, *Modernism and Democracy: Literary Culture, 1900–1930* (Oxford: Oxford University Press, 2006).

Pound, Ezra, *Personae: The Shorter Poems*, ed. Lea Baechler and A. Walton Litz (New York: New Directions, 1990).

'Pour Les Dames', *The Bag, Portmanteau and Umbrella Trader and Fancy Leather Goods and Athletic Trades Review*, 4.126, April 1911, p. 10.

Powys, John Cowper, *Dorothy Richardson* (1931; London: Villiers, 1974).

'A Preface', *The Century Guild Hobby Horse*, 3.13, January 1889, pp. 1–8.

Pujalet-Plaà, Éric, 'The Trunk in All its States', in *Louis Vuitton: 100 Legendary Trunks*, by Pierre Léonforte, Éric Pujalet-Plaà with the collaboration of Florence Lesché and Marie Wurry, trans. Bruce Waille (New York: Abrams, 2010), pp. 387–471.

Radford, Jean, *Dorothy Richardson* (Hemel Hempstead: Harvester Wheatsheaf, 1991).

—— 'Late Modernism and the Politics of History', in *Women Writers of the 1930s: Gender Politics and History*, ed. Maroula Joannou (Edinburgh: Edinburgh University Press, 1999), pp. 33–45.

Randall, Bryony, *Modernism, Daily Time and Everyday Life* (Cambridge: Cambridge University Press, 2007).

Raven-Hill, Leonard, 'St. George for Merrie Europe; Or, Chivalry Begins Abroad', cartoon, *Punch*, 188, 24 April 1935, p. 451.

'Reception of Refugees: An Invitation to Householders', *The Times*, 14 May 1940, p. 10.

Reddy, Michael J., 'The Conduit Metaphor', in *Metaphor and Thought*, ed. Andrew Ortony (1979; Cambridge: Cambridge University Press, 1998), pp. 164–201.

'Refugees from Poland', *The Times*, 16 October 1939, p. 10.

Rhys, Jean, *Good Morning, Midnight* (1939; London: Penguin, 1969).

—— *Smile Please: An Unfinished Autobiography* (Harmondsworth: Penguin, 1979).

—— *Voyage in the Dark* (1934; London: Penguin, 1969).

Richards, I. A., 'Metaphor', in *Philosophical Perspectives on Metaphor*, ed. Mark Johnson (Minneapolis: University of Minnesota Press, 1981), pp. 48–62.

Richardson, Dorothy, *Pilgrimage*, 4 vols (London: Dent and Cresset, 1938).

Richardson, Samuel, *Pamela; Or, Virtue Rewarded* (1740; London: Penguin, 1980).

Rokem, Freddie, 'Slapping Women: Ibsen's Nora, Strindberg's Julie, and Freud's Dora', in *Textual Bodies: Changing Boundaries of Literary Representation*, ed. Lori Hope Lefkovitz (New York: State University of New York Press, 1997), pp. 221–43.

Rosenberg, John, *Dorothy Richardson: The Genius They Forgot* (London: Duckworth, 1973).

Rosner, Victoria, *Modernism and the Architecture of Private Life* (New York: Columbia University Press, 2005).

Royle, Nicholas, *E. M. Forster* (Plymouth, Devon: Northcote House, 1999).

Ruskin, John, *The Seven Lamps of Architecture* (1849; London: George Allen, 1903).

Russell, John, *Henry Green: Nine Novels and an Unpacked Bag* (New Brunswick, NJ: Rutgers University Press, 1960).

Sabiston, Elizabeth Jane, *The Prison of Womanhood: Four Provincial Heroines in Nineteenth-Century Fiction* (Basingstoke: Macmillan, 1987).

Sackville-West, Vita, *The Edwardians* (1930; Leipzig: Tauchnitz, 1931).

Sarraute, Nathalie, *L'ère du soupçon: essais sur le roman* (Paris: Gallimard, 1956).

Scott, Bonnie Kime, *Refiguring Modernism*, 2 vols (Bloomington: Indiana University Press, 1995).

Selig, Robert L., '"The poet's portmanteau": A Flirtation That Dares not Speak Its Name', *The Gissing Journal*, 36.1, January 2000, pp. 30–4.

Sheller, Mimi and John Urry, 'The New Mobilities Paradigm', *Environment and Planning A* 38.2, February 2006, pp. 207–26.

Sherry, Norman (ed.), *Joseph Conrad: The Critical Heritage* (London and New York: Routledge, 1973).

Shiach, Morag, 'Periodizing Modernism', in *The Oxford Handbook of Modernisms*, ed. Peter Brooker, Andrzej Gąsiorek, Deborah Longworth and Andrew Thacker (Oxford: Oxford University Press, 2010), pp. 17–30.

Shklovsky, Viktor, *Zoo, or, Letters Not about Love*, trans. Richard Sheldon (Normal, IL: Dalkey Archive Press, 2001).

'The Shop-Wrecking Mania', *The Bag Portmanteau and Umbrella Trader and Fancy Leather Goods and Athletic Trades Review*, 5.175, March 1912, p. 4.

Sims, Peter, 'A Pocket Guide to "Ulysses"', *James Joyce Quarterly*, 26.2, Winter 1989, pp. 239–58.

Slocum, Sally, 'Woman the Gatherer: Male Bias in Anthropology', in *Toward an Anthropology of Women*, ed. Rayna R. Reiter (New York: Monthly Review Press, 1975), pp. 36–50.

Smith, Paul, '1924: Hemingway's Luggage and the Miraculous Year', in *The Cambridge Companion to Hemingway*, ed. Scott Donaldson (Cambridge: Cambridge University Press, 1999), pp. 36–54.

'Some L.M.S.R. Evacuation Statistics', *The Railway Gazette*, 71.17, 27 October 1939, p. 559.

Spurr, David, *Architecture and Modern Literature* (Ann Arbor: The University of Michigan Press, 2012).

Stallman, R. W., 'The Houses that James Built – *The Portrait of a Lady*', *The Texas Quarterly*, Winter 1958, pp. 176–96.

Stanton, Donna, 'Difference on Trial: A Critique of the Maternal Metaphor in Cixous, Irigaray, and Kristeva', in *The Poetics of Gender*, ed. Nancy K. Miller (New York: Columbia University Press, 1986), pp. 151–81.

Stevenson, Randall, 'Forster and Modernism', in *The Cambridge Companion to E. M. Forster*, ed. David Bradshaw (Cambridge: Cambridge University Press, 2007), pp. 209–22.

Stevenson, Robert Louis, *New Arabian Nights* (1882; London: Heinemann, 1927).

Stewart, Susan, *On Longing: Narratives of the Miniature, the Gigantic, the Souvenir, the Collection* (1984; Durham, NC: Duke University Press, 2003).

Stokes, Edward, *The Novels of Henry Green* (London: Hogarth Press, 1959).

Stone, Alison, 'Against Matricide: Rethinking Subjectivity and the Maternal Body', *Hypatia*, 27.1, Winter 2012, pp. 118–38.

Stonebridge, Lyndsey, 'Refugee Style: Hannah Arendt and the Perplexities of Rights', *Textual Practice*, 25.1, 2011, pp. 71–85.

'Supposed Murder and Suicide at Kensal-Rise', *The Times*, 25 March 1904, p. 9.

Tambling, Jeremy, '*Martin Chuzzlewit*: Dickens and Architecture', *English*, 48.192, Autumn 1999, pp. 147–68.

Tanner, Tony, *Adultery in the Novel: Contract and Transgression* (Baltimore: Johns Hopkins University Press, 1979).

—— 'Introduction', in *Mansfield Park*, by Jane Austen (1814; Harmondsworth: Penguin, 1985), pp. 7–36.

Thacker, Andrew, *Moving Through Modernity: Space and Geography in Modernism* (Manchester: Manchester University Press, 2003).

Torpey, John, *The Invention of the Passport: Surveillance, Citizenship and the State* (Cambridge: Cambridge University Press, 2000).

'Travelling Light', *The Times*, 27 December 1922, p. 11.

Treglown, Jeremy, *Romancing: The Life and Work of Henry Green* (London: Faber, 2000).

Tristram, Philippa, *Living Space in Fact and Fiction* (London: Routledge, 1989).

Trotter, David, *The English Novel in History 1895–1920* (London: Routledge, 1998).

—— *Literature in the First Media Age: Britain Between the Wars* (Cambridge, MA and London: Harvard University Press, 2013).

'Trunk Crime', *The Times*, 16 July 1934, p. 14.

'Trunk Crime No. 2', *The Times*, 18 July 1934, p. 14.

'Trunk Murder Charge', *The Times*, 30 June 1927, p. 5.

Tytell, John, *Ezra Pound: The Solitary Volcano* (New York: Anchor, 1987).

'Under the Dome', *The Dome: An Illustrated Magazine and Review of Literature, Music, Architecture and the Graphic Arts*, December 1898, pp. 94–6.

Veith, Ilza, *Hysteria: The History of a Disease* (Chicago: University of Chicago Press, 1965).

Verne, Jules, *Le tour du monde en quatre-vingts jours* (1873; Paris: Bookking International, 1994).

Vidler, Anthony, *The Architectural Uncanny: Essays in the Modern Unhomely* (Cambridge, MA: The MIT Press, 1992).

'Vita-Weat', advertisement, *The Times*, 6 October 1939, p. 11.

Watt, Donald, 'Introduction', in *The Critical Heritage: Aldous Huxley*, ed. Donald Watt (London: Routledge, 1975), pp. 1–36.

Waugh, Evelyn, *Brideshead Revisited* (1945; London: Penguin, 2000).

—— *A Handful of Dust* (1934; Harmondsworth: Penguin, 1951).

—— *Scoop: A Novel About Journalists* (1938; Harmondsworth: Penguin, 1957).

—— *Vile Bodies* (1930; Harmondsworth: Penguin, 1951).

West, Rebecca, *Black Lamb and Grey Falcon: The Record of a Journey Through Yugoslavia in 1937*, vol. 2 (1941; London: Macmillan, 1942).

—— *The Young Rebecca: Writings of Rebecca West 1911–1917*, ed. Jane Marcus (Bloomington: Indiana University Press, 1982).

Wharton, Edith, *The Uncollected Critical Writings*, ed. Frederick Wegener (Princeton: Princeton University Press, 1996).

White, Allon, *The Uses of Obscurity: The Fiction of Early Modernism* (London: Routledge and Kegan Paul, 1981).

Wilde, Alan, 'Surfacings: Reflections on the Epistemology of Late Modernism', *boundary 2*, 8.2, Winter 1980, pp. 209–27.

Wilde, Oscar, *The Collected Works of Oscar Wilde* (Ware: Wordsworth, 1998).

Wilson, Leigh, '"She in her 'armour' and he in his coat of nerves": May Sinclair and the Rewriting of Chivalry', in *Feminist Forerunners: New Womanism and Feminism in the Early Twentieth Century*, ed. Ann Heilman (London: Pandora, 2003), pp. 179–88.

Wipf-Miller, Carol A., 'Fictions of "going over": Henry Green and the New Realism', *Twentieth Century Literature* 44.2 (Summer 1998), pp. 135–54.

Woolf, Virginia, *The Diary of Virginia Woolf*, vol. 1, ed. Anne Olivier Bell (London: Hogarth Press, 1977).
—— *The Essays of Virginia Woolf*, vol. 4, ed. Andrew McNeillie (London: Hogarth Press, 1994).
—— *Jacob's Room* (1922; London: Penguin, 1992).
—— *The Moment and Other Essays* (1947; San Diego: Harcourt Brace Jovanovich, 1974).
—— *Mrs Dalloway* (1925; London: Vintage-Random, 2004).
—— *Orlando: A Biography* (1928; London: Hogarth Press, 1964).
—— *A Room of One's Own* (1929; London: Hogarth Press, 1959).
—— *The Voyage Out* (1915; Harmondsworth: Penguin, 1992).
—— *A Woman's Essays*, ed. Rachel Bowlby (Harmondsworth: Penguin, 1992).
Wynne, Deborah, *Women and Personal Property in the Victorian Novel* (Farnham: Ashgate, 2010).
Yorke, Sebastian, 'A Memoir', in *Surviving: The Uncollected Writings of Henry Green*, by Henry Green, ed. Matthew Yorke (London: Harvill-HarperCollins, 1993), pp. 286–302.
Young, Francis Brett, *Mr Lucton's Freedom* (1940; London: The Book Club, 1941).
'Your Parcels and Letters Depend on the Lines Behind the Lines', poster, Imperial War Museum Online Collection, <http://www.iwm.org.uk/collections/item/object/32539> (last accessed 27 April 2016).
Zamyatin, Yevgeny, *We*, trans. Mirra Ginsburg (1924; New York: EOS-HarperCollins, 1999).
Zweig, Stefan, *The Post Office Girl*, trans. Joel Rotenberg (1982; London: Sort Of Books, 2009).
—— *The World of Yesterday: An Autobiography* (1942; London: Cassell, 1943).
Zweig, Stefan and Lotte Zweig, *Stefan and Lotte Zweig's South American Letters: New York, Argentina and Brazil, 1940–42*, ed. Darién J. Davis and Oliver Marshall (New York and London: Continuum, 2010).

INDEX